D1217390

America's Wonderlands

INSIDE FRONT COVER: "VALLEY OF THE YOSEMITE" BY ALBERT BIERSTADT.
COURTESY, MUSEUM OF FINE ARTS, BOSTON. M. & M. KAROLIK COLLECTION.

A VOLUME IN THE NATIONAL GEOGRAPHIC *WORLD IN COLOR* LIBRARY

524 ILLUSTRATIONS, 465 IN FULL COLOR

CONTRIBUTORS: *Daniel B. Beard, William Belknap, Jr., James P. Blair, David S. Boyer, Jack Breed, Andrew H. Brown, Lewis F. Clark, Robert T. Cochran, Jr., Dean Conger, Frank and John Craighead, Willard R. Culver, Walter Meayers Edwards, Ralph Gray, Gilbert Grosvenor, Melville Bell Grosvenor, Ernest Gruening, Val Hart, E. "Tex" Helm, Otis Imboden, Paul Jensen, John M. Kauffmann, Nathaniel T. Kenney, Eugene Kingman, Bates Littlehales, Justin Locke, George W. Long, Bart McDowell, Carl F. Miller, W. Robert Moore, Adolph Murie, Thomas Nebbia, Edwards Park, Winfield Parks, Kathleen Revis, J. Baylor Roberts, Louis Schellbach, Merle Severy, Bob and Ira Spring, B. Anthony Stewart, Mason Sutherland, Frederick G. Vosburgh, Bradford Washburn, Don Watson, Paul A. Zahl, and others.*
Wildlife paintings by Walter A. Weber; decorative maps by Irvin E. Alleman.

MOUNTAIN GOAT
IN GLACIER NATIONAL PARK
BY WILFORD L. MILLER

America's

THE SCENIC NATIONAL PARKS

PREPARED BY THE

FOREWORD BY

INTRODUCTION BY

THE NATIONAL

RHODODENDRON BY PAUL JENSEN

NEW
ENLARGED
EDITION

Wonderlands

AND MONUMENTS OF THE UNITED STATES

National Geographic Book Service, MERLE SEVERY, CHIEF

Melville Bell Grosvenor, PRESIDENT AND EDITOR, NATIONAL GEOGRAPHIC SOCIETY

George B. Hartzog, Jr., DIRECTOR, NATIONAL PARK SERVICE

Conrad L. Wirth, FORMER DIRECTOR, NATIONAL PARK SERVICE

GEOGRAPHIC SOCIETY, WASHINGTON, D. C.

U. S. AIR FORCE AND (BELOW) B. ANTHONY STEWART, NATIONAL GEOGRAPHIC PHOTOGRAPHER

Jackson Lake mirrors rivers of snow on the mountains in Grand Teton National Park, Wyoming. At Katmai National Monument in Alaska, The Society's President and Editor (below) hoists a trout from Lake Grosvenor, named for his father.

STAFF FOR ENLARGED EDITION
Merle Severy, editor; *Edwards Park, Seymour L. Fishbein,* associate editors; *Ross Bennett,* project editor; *Anne Dirkes Kobor,* picture editor; *Ann Martin,* assistant; *Berry L. Reece, Jr., David F. Robinson,* editorial staff; *Jocelyn C. White,* assistant; *Joseph Baumer, Charles Hyman,* design; *James P. Kelly,* production; *Robert W. Lanni, Paula C. Simmons, Werner L. Weber,* assistants; *Raymond B. Benzinger, William W. Smith,* engravings; *Joe M. Barlett,* printing.

Composed by National Geographic's Phototypographic Division, *Herman J. A. C. Arens,* Director; *Robert C. Ellis, Jr.,* Manager. Printed and bound by R. R. Donnelley and Sons Co., Chicago.

First edition: 400,000 copies
New enlarged edition, first printing 250,000 copies
Library of Congress Catalog Card No. 66-17745

Foreword

"BRING ME MEN TO MATCH MY MOUNTAINS!" These words of poet Sam Walter Foss ring in my ears as I leaf the pages of this book. Only through the efforts of courageous men of vision have America's wonderlands been preserved for all to enjoy. Without men like John Muir, Stephen T. Mather, Horace M. Albright, and John D. Rockefeller, Jr., without conservation-minded patriots in Congress and the White House, our national parks could never have been created. Men like Conrad L. Wirth and George B. Hartzog, Jr., carry on the crusade for an unspoiled America.

Fortunate we are, too, in our national park rangers. They spare these precious parklands from becoming shopworn and trampled by millions. And with what patience they keep us visitors from feeding ourselves to the bears!

This unique book, the most complete and lavishly illustrated volume in its field, is made possible by vast resources of text and color plates produced by the non-profit National Geographic Society and its famed Magazine. Hence its moderate cost. To cover all facets of the National Park System would give none its due. Therefore we concentrated on outstanding scenic and archeological areas. The historic parks are included in a companion volume, *America's Historylands.*

The new enlarged edition of *America's Wonderlands,* necessitated by the tremendous response of members and the establishment of additional park areas, is the loving creation of skilled editor Merle Severy and his associates in the

Present-day pueblo dweller visits Mug House, which may have sheltered his distant ancestors. National Geographic research grants helped restore this and other Wetherill Mesa cliff dwellings in Colorado's Mesa Verde National Park.

WILLIAM BELKNAP, JR.

National Geographic's Book Service. Park superintendents, naturalists, historians, archeologists checked every page to ensure authenticity.

These pages remind me how my father, Gilbert Grosvenor, fired my enthusiasm for these scenic sanctuaries when I was a boy. I recall Stephen Mather, the first Director of the Park Service, with whom my father, as President of the National Geographic Society, worked so closely to save our Nation's wilderness domain. In half a century of cooperation with the Park Service, our Society has contributed in extraordinary ways: the discovery of the Valley of Ten Thousand Smokes; the first expedition to explore Carlsbad Caverns; the donation to the American people of a large tract of big trees in Sequoia's Giant Forest; the gift of the scientific trove, Russell Cave; the sponsorship of an ecological survey of California's giant coast redwoods; the unearthing of Pueblo Bonito, and the recent excavations at Wetherill Mesa.

During these same years *National Geographic* has published more than 100 articles portraying the glories of our national park lands.

For me the book has stirred warm memories: the Utah and Mount Holyoke girls who waited on our table at Grand Teton and Yellowstone; the Arkansas football star who carried our luggage at Yosemite. As I met fellow tourists enjoying our heritage, it struck me again and again—there's something about these parks that brings out the finest in people.

The Society proudly presents *America's Wonderlands,* so that all may know our national parks and how well the men dedicated to them serve our Nation. These parks "strengthen bodies, refresh minds, uplift the spirits . . . enrich leisure." Come, use, and enjoy them.

Melville Bell Grosvenor

INTRODUCTION

THE YEARS AHEAD

By GEORGE B. HARTZOG, JR.
Director, U.S. National Park Service

THERE WAS A TIME when visitors flocked *away* from a national park. It happened in the 1870's, when Indians chased guests and officials alike out of Yellowstone!

Since then it's been a happier story. Visitors in ever-growing numbers flock to the national parks: some 50 million in 1955, more than 110 million in 1965. And my forecasters tell me to expect 185 million in 1975!

Now, the law of the land tells the Park Service to preserve America's park resources and make them available for the millions today. To this I say a fervent "Amen." But how do we preserve the wondrous solitudes of the parks while welcoming more and more people who seek inspiration there? And what do we do when one guest wants to admire the placid mirror of a mountain lake, another wants to cast for trout in its cool depths, and a third wants to enjoy it on a pair of water skis? Such are the challenges that face your National Park System as we prepare to welcome our rising millions of guests.

Conrad Wirth, my able predecessor, fore-

World's third tallest tree, named the National Geographic Society Tree, soars 364.3 feet into the California mist; dead limb writhes above the camera. The Arcata Lumber Company has preserved this majestic coast redwood and its peers in the Arco Grove of the Giants; the Park Service hopes to include them in a new redwoods national park.

GEORGE F. MOBLEY, NATIONAL GEOGRAPHIC PHOTOGRAPHER

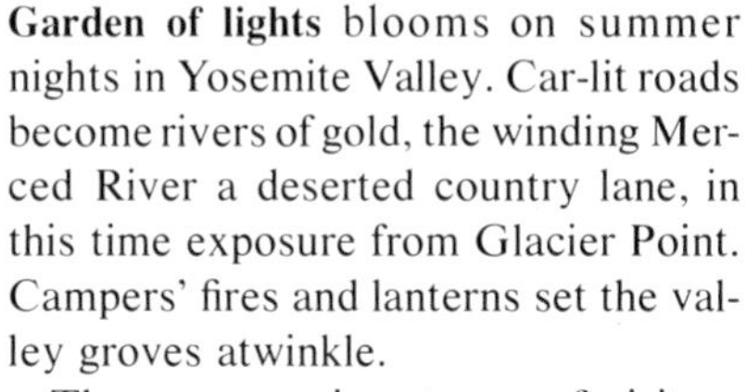

Garden of lights blooms on summer nights in Yosemite Valley. Car-lit roads become rivers of gold, the winding Merced River a deserted country lane, in this time exposure from Glacier Point. Campers' fires and lanterns set the valley groves atwinkle.

The ever-growing stream of visitors attracted to America's natural treasures challenges Parks Director Hartzog (above). He seeks expanded facilities to let more people enjoy existing parks, new kinds of parks to offer variety.

saw many of these challenges. The ten-year Mission 66 program which he launched in 1956 added new sites, modernized facilities, and started the park system well along the road to the future. Now we plan to build on that solid foundation with a broad new program we call Parkscape—USA.

Parkscape seeks to make the beauty of our land and the history of our Nation a richer and more meaningful part of the daily life of every American. We'll strive for a park system with greater variety, one which will protect many more of the landmarks of our country's heritage.

We need to improve the environment and expand recreational opportunities for the three out of every four Americans who live in cities. These people need

JONATHAN BLAIR AND (LEFT) EMORY KRISTOF, NATIONAL GEOGRAPHIC PHOTOGRAPHER

to get out of the "concrete jungles" and enjoy the true outdoors. Parkscape puts new emphasis on recreation parks close to urban centers. One dramatic example is the newly authorized Delaware Water Gap National Recreation Area near both New York and Philadelphia; some 30 million Americans live within 100 miles of the varied outdoor activities and scenic beauty this new unit will provide.

In many of these parks, most of them new ones, you'll be able to enjoy the full range of outdoor sport—boating, fishing, water- and snow-skiing, swimming and snorkeling. And these units will offer an additional bonus: they'll help relieve the pressure on the classic nature parks. Sports enthusiasts will be happier. So will the outdoorsmen who like their nature uncrowded.

We've made an encouraging start on another kind of park, the national scenic riverways. Americans love their rivers and are turning to them more and more to fish, boat, or just enjoy the old delight of watching flowing water. Canoes, johnboats, even outboards in some places, will take you through lively stretches and around quiet bends, past unspoiled river banks.

Our Nation commemorates historic battles and birthplaces; how about the landmarks of such important movements as our industrial revolution, advances in medicine, progress in the arts? These too are part of America's great heritage —and part of Parkscape's planning for the future. And the appalling speed of the steel and concrete surge across our land means we had best get all the parks we need—including more of the scenic parks—before it is too late.

We're looking, for example, at pristine wilderness areas in Alaska which have scarcely been explored; at Hawaii, where waterfalls lace green cliffs and surf crashes on coral sands; at prairie grasslands, where buffalo might roam as they did before hunters nearly wiped them out; at California's magnificent coast redwoods, where a national park has long been an urgent need; at the splendid sweep of wild alpine country in Washington's North Cascades; at the beautiful, history-rich Guadalupe Mountains of Texas. These, and more, may be on your "must-see" list when you plan your vacations in the years ahead.

Aquatic ranger scrubs a sign in Buck Island Reef National Monument in the Virgin Islands. Its scenery lies in an emerald lagoon; visitors "hike" its trails in trunks and flippers. The Park Service plans similar underwater parks.

JERRY GREENBERG

CONTENTS

BALD EAGLE BY IKE VERN

PAGE

Foreword 5

Introduction 8 The Years Ahead

17 The National Parks

PART ONE 65 *The Rocky Mountains*

67 Yellowstone
93 Grand Teton National Park
111 Glacier National Park
139 Rocky Mountain National Park
148 Devils Tower
148 Theodore Roosevelt Memorial Park
151 Mount Rushmore
154 Wind Cave
155 Jewel Cave
156 Badlands

PART TWO 159 *The Great Plateau*

161 Grand Canyon
182 Lake Mead
185 Zion National Park
199 Bryce Canyon
208 Cedar Breaks
208 Capitol Reef
211 Rainbow Bridge
217 Natural Bridges
217 Arches National Monument
221 Canyonlands
230 Black Canyon of the Gunnison
230 Colorado National Monument
233 Dinosaur National Monument
241 Lehman Caves
241 Timpanogos Cave
241 Craters of the Moon

PART THREE 243 *The Southwest*

245 Carlsbad Caverns
261 Big Bend
265 White Sands
275 Saguaro National Monument
275 Organ Pipe Cactus
275 Chiricahua
277 Petrified Forest
282 El Morro National Monument
284 Great Sand Dunes
285 Capulin Mountain
287 Ancient Indian Cultures
288 Chaco Canyon
297 Mesa Verde
312 Hovenweep
313 Aztec Ruins
314 Bandelier National Monument
316 Navajo National Monument
320 Canyon de Chelly
327 Sunset Crater
329 Walnut Canyon
330 Wupatki National Monument
333 Montezuma Castle and Tuzigoot
334 Casa Grande Ruins
335 Tonto and Gila Cliff Dwellings

PART FOUR 337 *The Golden West*

339 Yosemite
352 Point Reyes
355 Muir Woods
356 Devils Postpile
356 Pinnacles National Monument
359 Sequoia and Kings Canyon
370 Death Valley
375 Joshua Tree National Monument

PART FIVE 377 *The Pacific Northwest*

379 Olympic National Park
396 Mount Rainier
408 Crater Lake
414 Oregon Caves
414 Lava Beds National Monument
415 Lassen Volcanic National Park

PART SIX 419 *The East*
420 Everglades
450 Great Smoky Mountains
462 Blue Ridge Parkway
466 Shenandoah
471 Cape Hatteras
476 Fire Island
476 Padre Island
476 Assateague Island
479 Cape Cod
484 Acadia National Park
490 Mammoth Cave
495 Russell Cave
504 Pipestone
505 Effigy Mounds
505 Ocmulgee National Monument
505 Mound City Group
506 Isle Royale National Park

PART SEVEN 509 *Alaska, Hawaii, and the Virgin Islands*
511 Mount McKinley
524 Katmai National Monument
534 Glacier Bay
537 Hawaii Volcanoes and Haleakala National Parks
546 Virgin Islands National Park

Travel Tips 550 How to Make the Most of Your National Parks Vacation

Index 551

GRIZZLY BEAR
IN MOUNT McKINLEY NATIONAL PARK
BY WARREN F. STEENBERGH

INTRODUCTION

THE NATIONAL PARKS

Our heritage of beauty and history

By CONRAD L. WIRTH
Former Director, U.S. National Park Service

IN SPRING, snow melt makes torrents of Rocky Mountain streams, and the elk move from Jackson Hole to the high meadows of Yellowstone. When this season arrived during my years as Director of the National Park Service, I often went missing from my usual haunts in Washington, D. C.

"No, sir, he's out of town," my secretary would tell the telephone. "Inspection trip, you know. Oh, no, sir, I'm sure he didn't take any fishing tackle with him. . . ."

ELK IN YELLOWSTONE PARK BY ANDREW H. BROWN, NATIONAL GEOGRAPHIC STAFF.

BRUCE DALE AND (OPPOSITE) WALTER MEAYERS EDWARDS, NATIONAL GEOGRAPHIC STAFF

Former Parks Director Wirth visits a park he helped create—Cape Cod National Seashore. A National Geographic Society Trustee, he remains active on many fronts to conserve the nation's scenic beauty.

Seriously, managing your National Park System entirely from a desk in Washington would have been unthinkable, and no director has ever attempted it. My trips were strictly business, even those that included a little fishing. I am sure that George Hartzog, my successor and a fine administrator, is doing the same as the six directors who preceded him in the 50 years of the Park Service.

As a matter of fact, I'd be happy to have you along on one of my swings. Let's begin at Grand Canyon National Park in Arizona (see National Parks map in pocket at back of book). That's where I started when I first went to work for the Park Service in 1931.

"Before you get settled behind your desk," said Horace Albright, then Director of National Parks, "you'd better find out what a park looks like. Here's a ticket to Grand Canyon."

The chief ranger met me at the train. With a scornful look at my eastern clothes, he ordered me aboard a mule parked nearby, mounted another one himself, and led the way to a thrilling experience. We went right over the rim of the canyon, down the Bright Angel Trail. No matter how hard I tried to make my mule walk close to the inside of the zigzagging path, he always stayed on the edge of a sheer precipice.

Somehow we made it to the bottom. We crossed the Colorado River, brown with silt, and rode halfway up to the North Rim, then came back down for a night at Phantom Ranch. As I recall it—and believe me, I recall it—the chief impression of the park that day was on the seat of my inadequate trousers.

"When we head back tomorrow," I announced as I ate my dinner standing up, "I'm going to carry the mule!"

Tomorrow, of course, was a brighter day. We rode back as thousands of tourists have done, and from the comfort of headquarters I looked back on a memorable experience.

The greatest benefit I got from the trip was a greater awareness of what was mine

Giddy drop awes riders as stolid mules plod Bright Angel Trail below Grand Canyon's South Rim.

Hairpin curve (overleaf) presents a vista of the canyon's stratified walls. Like pages in a book, they reveal earth's history. This mightiest of gorges, still being cut by the Colorado River, bares rocks 1½ billion years old.

OVERLEAF: JUSTIN LOCKE

as an American. I had felt a little like a pioneer, aware of dangers the settlers faced as they subdued a wild land. What they struggled to build I must help preserve.

More than likely your first visit to a national park was quite different. But the important thing is for you to receive a full dividend from your experience, as I did, not only through lungs filled with clean air and eyes soothed by natural beauty, but in spirits enriched perhaps beyond immediate understanding.

I myself don't know how to describe this ability of the parks to lift up the soul. One of the best writers on the parks, Freeman Tilden, refers to an ancient undefined Greek concept of a "fifth essence," beyond fire, air, earth, and water. "Any thoughtful person," he wrote, "may find and meditate upon this Fifth Essence in his own backyard. Not a woodland brook, not a mountain, not a field of grass rippling in the breeze does not proclaim the existence of it. But a consummate expression of this ultimate wealth of the human spirit . . . is to be found in the National Park System. . . . Many a man has come to find merely serenity or scenic pictures—and has unexpectedly found a renewal and affirmation of himself."

Grand Canyon not only proclaims this "fifth essence" but takes us far back into ages past as well; Tilden called it "that overpowering Ladder of Time." Better than any other place on earth, it tells the world's story during the last billion and a half years or so. At the bottom of its gorge are rocks in which scientists have never found any evidence of primal life. Higher in the walls they have found some of the oldest known traces of life, in the form of fossil plants and marine animals.

Lower rock levels of Zion Canyon in Utah's Zion National Park are about the same age as those that once topped Grand Canyon but long ago eroded away. Nearby Bryce Canyon and Cedar Breaks bring the story still closer to human times. Thus the four parks interlock in telling the story of the earth itself. Together, I think they make up one of the most important museums in the world.

ONE TIME somebody asked me: "What kind of people visit the national parks?" "What kind don't?" I parried, thinking of the millions of visits each year. Mill hands and office clerks. Tycoons and poor folk. Lawyers, doctors, and thieves. Some are fond of flowers, some like snow and ice. Some prefer snakes, though most are amazed that the Park Service protects even rattlers. Bears are liked by all—except the hundred or so people who get mauled or bitten each year for ignoring warnings about them.

The parks mean different things to different people. For instance, in Glacier National Park one day I saw a middle-aged couple packing their car.

"Good morning to you," I said. "How do you like the park?"

"Best of the ten we've seen this vacation," the man replied. "But mister, please don't keep me from my packing. We have only three more days of vacation and three parks still to see." While he bustled around, I found out from his wife that they had arrived in Glacier the night before. "We drove by one of those glaciers,"

Fireman's holiday: a summer lookout rappels down a cliff in Mount Rainier Park. Crowned by 40 square miles of glaciers, Washington's 14,410-foot peak rises beyond flowered, forested Paradise Valley.

RUTH KIRK

she said, "and we saw Indians on the hotel lawn. This is a wonderful place."

Too rushed to get much out of the parks? Maybe. But these two were having the time of their lives. I defend their right to see Glacier any way they want.

Still, I feel the parks repay close acquaintance. I met two boys at the ranger patrol cabin on the Southeast Arm of Yellowstone Lake one summer. They had the barest amount of worn-out camping gear. Untrimmed hair and bushy beards gave them the look of old-time mountain men.

"How long have you fellows been out?" I asked.

"Two months," said one. "And what a time we've had! A cow moose kept us treed all one night. We can tell you, I bet, where the biggest cutthroat trout in the world live. We've gained 15 pounds apiece on beans, bacon, sourdough biscuits, and fish." They had a canoe, and they were planning to paddle back to their car.

B. ANTHONY STEWART, NATIONAL GEOGRAPHIC PHOTOGRAPHER

Rain or shine, visitors savor Mount Rainier's varied wonders. Some hike a misty trail (left); others rent plastic-seated trousers for sledless "tin pants" tobogganing (below). Tunnel in a summer snowbank leads to the inn (lower); many sightseers never glimpse Rainier's oft-shrouded crest.

LILA M. BISHOP. LOWER: BARRY C. BISHOP, NATIONAL GEOGRAPHIC STAFF

I took a look at the thing. It was more patches than canoe.

"Maybe you could take these fellows over in the patrol boat," I told the ranger. "If you do, find out for me where they caught those trout."

I don't know who talked longest and loudest about their trip, the Glacier pair or the two boys. But I have faith in the ability of the parks to spray some of Mr. Tilden's "fifth essence" on every visitor.

Sooner or later each park guest meets

a ranger. His full title is United States Park Ranger and he is one of the key men in the Park Service. He is the visitor's friend. He shows the guest how to reach the interesting places, warns him against feeding the bears, finds him when he is lost, and deals firmly with him when he violates the regulations, which are few and reasonable.

A ranger is a man's man. He likes animals and flowers, lakes and mountains. He can spend all day on a horse and half the night on a square-dance floor. He comes in two styles: the year-round career man, and the seasonal ranger who works only during rush tourist periods. Either kind talks facts and listens well.

Don't try to bluff a ranger. I made that mistake once. We were in the high country of Kings Canyon National Park, seeing if dude horses were damaging the meadows. We camped by a stream brimming with snow melt. Cold winds whistled through the stunted pines at timber line. I looked around at my companions stretched wearily on the ground after a hard day in the saddle, and I thought I had them pretty well sized up.

"Personally," I said, "I could go

Ice-sculptured peaks mount a blue jewel: St. Mary Lake

Indians believed that the Wind Maker, their underwater god, lived in St. Mary and spoke to them when his waters were ruffled. Glacier National Park's Montana skyline includes Little Chief (far left), Citadel, Gunsight, Fusillade, Reynolds, Going-to-the-Sun, and Goat.

RAY ATKESON

for a nice bath in that pool down there. But of course you fellows are too tired, and I don't want to go alone, so I guess I'll have to do without."

To my horror, the ranger in our party rose and started peeling off his shirt. The icy water nearly killed me. As I said, don't try to bluff a ranger.

When the time arrives, a ranger becomes a hero—quietly, as befits a man who feels he is only doing a job he is getting paid for. Now and then a ranger pulls a struggling swimmer from the surf at one of our national seashores. Other rangers regularly risk their lives to save climbers in trouble on the heights of the Tetons and other ranges. Being trapped in the wilderness by blizzards is routine for Yellowstone ski patrols. The patrol ranger's wife, meanwhile, may be snowbound herself in their isolated cabin home. She, too, is a hero.

Many of our first rangers were simple outdoorsmen without much formal education. Some, like Billy Nelson of Yosemite, would be called "characters" today. He had King Albert of the Belgians out on a pack trip. Billy was cooking under the giant sequoias of the Mariposa Grove. "Hey, King," he suddenly shouted over the crackle of the campfire, "shoot me that side of bacon, will you?" Members of the royal party and the Yosemite superintendent blanched. But the King cheerily threw Billy the bacon. From then on it was "King" and "Billy" in conversation between the two men.

Present-day rangers are college men and have more polish, but are just as good in the wilds as their predecessors were. When they graduate from one of the ranger schools after three months of training, they know Park Service regulations and objectives, how to look after a horse, how to fight forest fires and find lost people, and how diplomatically to keep visitors from picking flowers. They also learn the history of the National Park System.

THE IDEA came to fruition at a campfire in Yellowstone on the night of September 19, 1870. While the flames danced under the starry sky, a group of men discussed what should be done with this astounding country they had been exploring for nearly five weeks. They argued about staking personal claims, but Cornelius Hedges, a judge in Montana Territory, advanced the idea that Yellowstone's unique beauty ought to belong to all the people as a national park.

The others were persuaded and promised to urge the proposal as vigorously as they could. They kept their word: Two years later Congress established Yellowstone as the world's first national park. Each Congress and administration since then has strengthened the concept born at that Yellowstone campfire.

Curious visitors started coming to the first national park right away. Yellowstone became a huge success, and Congress created more parks. Sequoia, Yosemite, and Mount Rainier came into the new system of "pleasuring grounds," as they were first known, before the turn of the century. The Antiquities Act of 1906 gave Presidents the power to make national monuments of historically and

Rivers, gorges, and falls show at a glance on a relief map of California's 760,951-acre Yosemite Park. Granite-walled Yosemite Valley cuts horizontally at center. Red lines are roads; yellow ones, trails.

J. BAYLOR ROBERTS, NATIONAL GEOGRAPHIC STAFF

scientifically interesting places by simple proclamation. This important law, conceived to protect the Indian ruins of the Southwest from souvenir hunters, has preserved scores of fascinating sites.

Before 1916 the Department of the Interior ran the parks as a part-time chore. Borax tycoon Stephen T. Mather complained about this setup to his friend, Secretary of the Interior Franklin K. Lane. Replied Lane: "If you don't like the way the parks are being run, come . . . and run them yourself." Mather accepted.

One of the first men he met in Washington was Gilbert Grosvenor, then Editor, later President and Chairman of the Board of Trustees of the National Geographic Society. In 1915, Dr. Grosvenor went on a camping trip Mather arranged in California's Sierra Nevada for some influential people he hoped would help sell his park ideas. Mather and Grosvenor, scorning tents, spread blankets on the forest floor beneath a giant tree and talked probably half the night about the Park Service. One result of this trip was a contribution by The Society to help the Park Service acquire this magnificent grove of ancient sequoias. Dr. Grosvenor also gave enthusiastic support to Mather's plan for a specialized Park Service, helped write the legislation that established it as a bureau of the Department of the Interior in 1916, and guided the National Geographic Society to a friendship with the parks that is as firm today as it was in the beginning.

In 1958, The Society gave the American people Russell Cave in Alabama. Here the Smithsonian Institution excavated Indian homesites 9,000 years old. Russell Cave is one of the few properties in the Park System that memorialize North American man in the long period between his arrival here from Asia, more

GILBERT GROSVENOR

General Sherman: Sequoia's giant among giants

When California's Giant Forest was threatened by lumbering in 1915, Stephen Mather, then Assistant to the Secretary of the Interior, invited a group of eminent Americans to visit the grove. One of these was Gilbert Grosvenor, Editor of the *National Geographic*, who made this dramatic picture as 20 men, fingertip to fingertip, encircled General Sherman's 102-foot waist.

A picnic among the big trees saw Mr. Mather at head of table with Dr. Grosvenor on his left. The Society and some of its members later contributed $100,000 to preserve 2,239 acres of *Sequoia gigantea*.

"Within these plantations of God, a decorum and sanctity reign":

JOHN M. KAUFFMANN

Emerson's words sound a blessing for dinner amid Giant Forest in Sequoia National Park.

WALTER MEAYERS EDWARDS AND (OPPOSITE) PAUL A. ZAHL, NATIONAL GEOGRAPHIC STAFF

Students at Grand Canyon's Albright Training Center learn to run fictitious "Avalanche Peaks National Park." Schools here and in West Virginia equip rangers for key roles ahead.

than 30,000 years ago, and the time he built villages in the Southwest, about the beginning of the Christian Era.

In 1933, a whole host of national monuments, military parks, memorials, and cemeteries came under Park Service care. Two years later Congress authorized the establishment of national historic sites; today we have more than a score of them. Also in the thirties the Park Service took in the park system of Washington, D. C., which today contains more than 750 pieces of property. The White House is on the books, too. The Park Service doesn't tell the First Lady how to run her household, of course, but it keeps the gardens neat and the lawns mowed.

Today the National Park Service looks after about 27 million acres of land in about 220 units scattered throughout the United States, Puerto Rico, and the Virgin Islands. Yellowstone was the first park; new units are being added each year. Katmai National Monument, with 2,697,590 acres, is the largest; the House Where Lincoln Died, covering a twentieth of an acre in Washington, D. C., the smallest. About a third are primarily scenic. Though only 32 bear the official

Homemade snowscooter with an airplane propeller meets National Geographic naturalist Paul A. Zahl at the start of a research trip deep into Yellowstone National Park's snow-smothered wilderness.

title "national park," the word "park" is often used to cover others as well.

In 1956, five years after I became Parks Director, we launched the biggest improvement program the parks had ever had—Mission 66. To understand the need for this ten-year project, let's go to Yosemite, where Billy Nelson flouted protocol, and recall a time I stood by the road.

"More than 7,000 cars, carrying maybe 25,000 people, are in the valley today," the superintendent told me. "The tent people are overflowing the campgrounds. Every hotel room and cabin is taken. Fishermen stand shoulder to shoulder in the streams. Traffic crawls bumper to bumper on the road up to Glacier Point. Connie, they are mashing the valley flat—God bless 'em!"

There was our problem. Creating the Park Service, Congress bade it "conserve the scenery and the natural and historic objects and the wildlife therein and . . . provide for the enjoyment of the same." But how do you "conserve" the natural things with 25,000 people milling about on 4,500 acres? You could fence the people out, but what happens to the "enjoyment"? From the beginning the Park Service has protected the fragile and irreplaceable, but at the same time it has built roads, trails, hotels, campgrounds, and visitor centers so the people can come and enjoy the wonders protected for them.

For some years it had been obvious that the use-versus-preservation conflict was not being resolved. In 1925 the parks drew 2,054,000 visits. Three decades later a system equipped for 21 million visits a year was handling more than twice that many. Facilities were out-of-date and run-down, roads were in bad shape, trails, employee morale, even scenic beauty were deteriorating.

Mission 66 saved them. Its aim was to produce a model park system by 1966;

Yosemite's granite fantasy: Half Dome turns a stony shoulder as the Merced

River surges over Nevada and Vernal Falls, then tumbles into the valley. Hikers pause at Glacier Point.

ANSEL ADAMS

J. BAYLOR ROBERTS, NATIONAL GEOGRAPHIC STAFF

hence its name. In its ten years the program spent about a billion dollars. For a system whose postwar budgets had been averaging $27 million a year and whose facilities had seen little capital investment in 15 years, this was big money.

What have the American people gotten for these dollars? Whole new parks, for one thing. About 50 areas were added to the park system during the course of Mission 66. Among them are Canyonlands National Park in Utah, a quarter-million-acre fantasyland of wild canyons and weird rock formations; Cape Cod National Seashore in Massachusetts, a 42-mile stretch of sand and sea; a host of historical landmarks, recreational areas, natural wonders—the list goes on. Many of these you'll visit in chapters that follow.

BUT YOU'LL SEE the imprint of Mission 66 in the older parks, too. The Stevens Canyon Road in Mount Rainier National Park had been abuilding since 1931; half of each year's small appropriation had to be spent repairing the previous winter's damage. Mission 66 completed the road. In Yosemite, a long section of the old Tioga Road was rerouted and improved to let more visitors enjoy the lovely High Sierra country, and at the same time to relieve the crush in the valley. We kept parts of the old road "as is," providing pine-roofed motor trails to out-of-the-way glades and campgrounds.

The Blue Ridge Parkway, designed to wind along the highlands of Virginia and North Carolina, was begun in 1933; under Mission 66 the 469-mile parkway took a giant step toward completion. Roads to Hermit's Rest and Desert View in Grand Canyon, the Grand Loop Road opening a window into Yellowstone's wil-

Sugary dunes, weird arches, cryptic doodles add variety's spice to the grandeur of western parks

Soft as snow, fine as sugar, gypsum dunes at New Mexico's White Sands National Monument (opposite) make perfect teen-age romping grounds.

Indian petroglyphs on Newspaper Rock (below) might recount news of eight centuries ago—if we could decode them. Myriad symbols challenge youngsters in Petrified Forest, Arizona. Father prefers a paper he can read.

Double-slotted Druid Arch greets Secretary of the Interior and Mrs. Stewart L. Udall (right) after a hot, grueling climb in Utah's canyon country. Bates E. Wilson, first white man to approach Druid on foot, guides the hikers. During this 1961 inspection, Secretary Udall found "a complex of natural wonders unequaled anywhere." Three years later, 257,640 acres became Canyonlands National Park.

EDWARDS PARK AND (ABOVE) OTIS IMBODEN, NATIONAL GEOGRAPHIC STAFF

The Big Room at New Mexico's Carlsbad: stalactites festoon the ceiling; stalagmites ride like icebergs in

E. "TEX" HELM

colored sea. Visitors a fifth of a mile back appear ant-size in world's largest known underground chamber.

tain as closely as possible nature's balance.

I think back to Bradley Patterson, a White House aide who helped us put together the Cabinet presentation that launched the Mission 66 program. To our "thank you" letter came his moving reply:

"If there was a pinch of added enthusiasm, and a few extra hours on my part, let it be in remembrance of some of those days which have enriched my life beyond measure.

"From my bank account will never come an inheritance for my children, but let there be bequeathed to them, and to their children to come, Lake Solitude, Camp Muir on Rainier, a swim in Lake Tenaya, a stroll in Crescent Meadow, a campfire at Elizabeth Lake. With these safely in trust for them, Midas could not give them more."

A hoary marmot surveys his domain in Mount McKinley Park.

Of all the parks, the influence of man has been felt the least in those of Alaska. Mount McKinley National Park contains the highest mountain on the North American continent, and offers a varied assortment of wild creatures living together successfully under the stern laws of nature.

Some of these animals need wilderness for survival. The Barren Ground caribou, which inhabits no other park, lives here. So does the grizzly bear; the Alaska moose, largest of its kind; the timber wolf; and the Dall sheep, kin to the Rocky Mountain bighorn.

The country at Alaska's Katmai National Monument is so wild that, until Park Service explorers went in recently, the most reliable information on the area came from quarter-century-old records of seven National Geographic Society expeditions. Here even such cataclysmic events as volcanic explosions can take place unheard and unseen. A mountain erupts. Smoke and ash drift over settled parts of Alaska. A military plane then goes in to see what happened, but by the time it arrives the volcano may already have started to simmer down.

Comfortable camps have been built on some of the area's blue lakes in recent years. Fishermen and sightseers come in uneventfully by seaplane, the only way they can get there without walking. One inspection flight I made was unusual in that it almost ended in disaster.

Five of us made a full load for the aircraft. We flew first into the Valley of Ten

Mount McKinley's snowfields glow with sunset gold at noon. In central Alaska the December sun barely skims the horizon at midday. A cloud halo caps the 20,320-foot peak, loftiest in North America.

ERNEST GRUENING AND (ABOVE) WARREN F. STEENBERGH

Thousand Smokes. Earth's inner fires were banked; only a relatively few steamy plumes rose from the desolate wilderness below us. Climbing in tight circles, we topped Mount Katmai and looked down into the green lake that never freezes, even in the toughest winters, because of the volcanic heat rising from deep within the slumbering mountain.

We started away. Suddenly the seats dropped from under us. Our cameras and loose gear banged about in the cabin as though weightless. Later the pilot told us we had struck a violent downdraft and dropped like a stone for 2,000 feet.

"I leveled off just above some of the wickedest terrain I ever saw," he said.

On the way back to King Salmon Airport, I thought of the endless variety of the National Park System. Here in Katmai, had we crashed, only a prowling fox

WINFIELD PARKS, NATIONAL GEOGRAPHIC PHOTOGRAPHER

Chill waters of Katmai National Monument offer some of the world's finest fishing. Here anglers hook salmon in Brooks River. Smoke-scented Alaskan air hones hikers' appetites (above) in this largest of park units.

or bear might ever have found us. Inside the Statue of Liberty—yes, that's a national monument too—I could not even have tripped and fallen; somebody would have caught me before I hit!

Where Katmai's volcanoes are wild things, Hawaii's are fairly well domesticated. Kilauea and Mauna Loa, the two most active ones, are in Hawaii Volcanoes National Park on the "big island" of Hawaii. Haleakala, "house of the sun," is a dormant giant in Haleakala National Park on Maui. Volcanologists have been studying them all for many years and most of the time know when they are about to get dangerous, enabling people to escape their fiery lava flows.

Islanders call Halemaumau, the main vent of Kilauea, the "drive-in volcano." A highway runs almost to the rim of the steaming pit. The visitor drives his car onto a handy parking lot, then walks a few yards to the brink of eternity. Between him and eternity, however, stands a stout wire fence.

Let's head eastward now, first for a brief stop at one of my favorite parks: Mesa Verde National Park in the southwest corner of Colorado. Archeologists tell us the ruins at Mesa Verde date from early in the Christian Era, when primitive Indians wandered in, saw a land then verdant and suitable for farming, and settled down for more than ten centuries.

The first settlers lived in simple pit houses with crude roofs, but their descendants built great

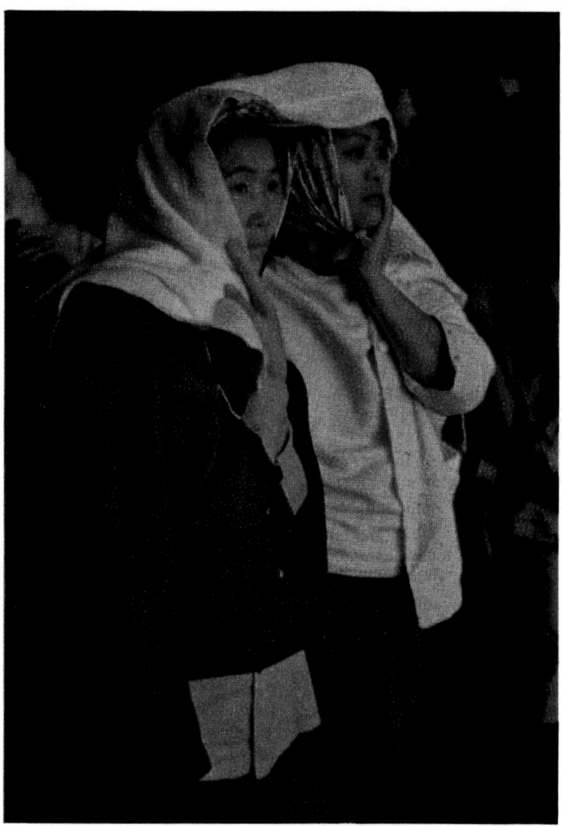

ROBERT B. GOODMAN, BLACK STAR

Devil's caldron of liquid fire baptizes a volcano reborn; awed sightseers stand mute in its rosy glow. Kilauea Iki crater, on the island of Hawaii, broke a silence of 91 years in 1959, belched steam and incandescent lava from a dozen fountains, and turned its somber pit into a raging inferno.

Active vents stud Hawaii Volcanoes National Park; warning tremors precede most eruptions. Dormant Haleakala dozes in its own park on Maui.

Big Bend visitors scan the Chisos Mountains, roof of Texas, from the South Rim; sawtooth ridges

masonry and adobe pueblos. They made beautiful pottery and feather-cloth garments and wove colored designs into cotton cloth. And they fashioned jewelry from local turquoise. Their decline began in the 13th century. A long drought spurred the Indians to move; nobody much saw the mesa again until the 1880's, when cowboys found it and spread the news.

I love these ruins. I stand on Park Point, highest spot in Mesa Verde, and I know

THOMAS NEBBIA, NATIONAL GEOGRAPHIC PHOTOGRAPHER

hide the Rio Grande's ragged U-turn that gives the national park its name. Mexico lies beyond.

I stand where bronze warriors once kept lookout for raiding nomadic enemies. I see the cliff dwellings stuck like swallows' nests to the yellow sandstone. I can imagine Indian women grinding corn, and I can see fat children playing on the patios hundreds of feet above the canyon floor. And in the visitor center, I see the story of their lives in the finest display of its kind I know.

To the south and east lies Carlsbad Caverns in New Mexico, our biggest

A mantle of snow quiets the vibrant colors of Utah's Bryce Canyon.

WILLIAM BELKNAP, JR.

Vhipped cream clouds, hovering low, creep into each rocky crevice and alcove.

FREDERICK KENT TRUSLOW

Five-foot spread of antlers crowns one of the world's most dangerous animals, a bull moose in rutting season. This bull in Isle Royale National Park drove wildlife photographer Fred Truslow into a lean-to with nothing but screen between them. Only by freezing motionless did Truslow escape unscathed.

A burgeoning moose herd overbrowsed the Michigan island in the 1930's; hundreds starved. New browse grew; so did the herd. Then wolves crossed the winter ice from Canada; their predation checks moose numbers. Biologists now study this living laboratory, where nature struck a stern balance.

underground wonder; in fact, it is one of the world's largest caves. The things visitors see defy description: the Big Room, a mile and a quarter around and 232 feet high in places; the King's Palace and Queen's Chamber with gleaming stone draperies and curtains; tremendous stalagmites such as the Giant Dome.

Water made Carlsbad by dissolving limestone—actually an ancient barrier reef. Unless water flows in still unplumbed depths, Carlsbad has stopped growing. Mammoth Cave in Kentucky, on the other hand, has underground rivers we know about; we can be sure it is still undergoing some change.

ALL OF THE EARLY PARKS came out of tracts of land already owned by the Federal Government. And all were in the West, for the simple reason that the East never had any substantial amount of public domain.

When the time came to create eastern parks, private owners held the land from which national parks could be made. When Congress declined to buy any with taxpayers' money, private philanthropy stepped in. Substantial folk from Boston and New York gave their summer-home property on Maine's Mount Desert Island, and Acadia National Park joined the people's estate. John D. Rockefeller, Jr., donated the properties necessary to round out the Federal holdings at Acadia. A Rockefeller family gift of $5,000,000 to match state and other contributions helped establish Great Smoky Mountains National Park in Tennessee and North Carolina, one of the most visited of all national parks.

We owe Linville Falls on the Blue Ridge Parkway to Mr. Rockefeller, and he contributed thousands of acres in Jackson Hole for Grand Teton National Park. His son Laurance, a National Geographic Trustee, gave us one of our newest national parks, Virgin Islands, a tropical playground dedicated in 1956. The Rockefeller family's magnificent gifts have made it the greatest single private benefactor of the National Park System.

Shenandoah, second national park in the East, came as the welcome gift of Virginia. It was quite a chore rounding up the land, for on it lived hundreds of proud mountaineers who built their own log cabins and could shoot a squirrel in the eye from as far away as they could see him. One owner wouldn't sell. No native mountaineer was he, but former President Herbert Hoover.

"Take it as a gift," he said, and deeded over his Camp Rapidan, where he fished and rested during vacations from the White House.

In the fall the hardwood forest along Shenandoah's famous Skyline Drive blazes with the reds and yellows of changing leaves. The park staff that must handle traffic has no trouble believing that a third of the country's population lives within a day's journey by automobile.

Former Senator Harry Flood Byrd, Sr., of Virginia, when governor, played an important part in the drive to acquire land for Shenandoah. A real parks enthusiast, he has donated money over the years for building overnight shelters—"Byrd's Nests," as they have been aptly nicknamed—along the Appalachian Trail where it winds through Shenandoah on its way from New England to Georgia.

He and I once hiked in Glacier. We came to a sign: "4 Miles to Pinnacle Wall." We walked for two hours, then came to another: "3½ Miles to Pinnacle Wall."

Boys and breakers frolic where Blackbeard the pirate once roamed; here at Cape Hatteras National Seashore stairways to nowhere (opposite, above) shade picnickers, let Atlantic breezes through. Carefree children find Cape Cod's 150-foot bluffs (right) a superb sandbox.

Puzzled, the senator flopped down beside the trail. "How in the world do you measure distances here?" he panted.

"We have a bicycle wheel on a stick, with a meter hooked to it," replied Park Superintendent Jack Emmert. "Ours is right old, and I guess there's some slack in the gears."

"Go get a new one," said the senator. "I'll personally see to it there's an extra $1.50 in the next Park Service appropriation for it." I guess he delivered. The sign was fixed by the next time I visited Glacier.

Foundations established by Mrs. Ailsa Mellon Bruce and Paul Mellon donated half the purchase price of the 28,500-acre Cape Hatteras National Seashore on the Outer Banks of North Carolina, the first seashore in the system. North Carolina gave the other half, which means that each of its citizens played a part in this generous act.

We have Texas to thank for Big Bend National Park, 708,221 acres of glorious desert-mountain scenery on the Mexican border. Big Bend is one of five living desert museums in the park system; the others are Death Valley National Monument;

EMORY KRISTOF, (BELOW) DEAN CONGER, AND (LEFT) WINFIELD PARKS, NATIONAL GEOGRAPHIC PHOTOGRAPHERS

Joshua Tree National Monument in California; Saguaro National Monument near Tucson, home of a magnificent stand of saguaro cactus; and Organ Pipe Cactus National Monument, part of the great Mexican desert that spills into Arizona.

Everglades National Park, gift from Florida, is a subtropical wonderland, a place of mystery. Strange hammocks, islands of rank vegetation, stud its flat expanses of waving marsh grass. I can imagine thin smokes rising from these hammocks—campfire smokes of the Seminole Indians who once roamed this region. Never defeated by the United States although thousands of soldiers hunted them, the brightly clad Seminoles no longer live inside park boundaries, but

ROBERT F. SISSON AND (BELOW) JAMES P. BLAIR, NATIONAL GEOGRAPHIC PHOTOGRAPHERS

Giant saguaro cacti, backlighted by the setting sun, spike a hillside in Saguaro National Monument; feathery paloverde trees shade the titans' feet. This park in two parts brackets Tucson, Arizona; visitors sample scenery ranging from desert to conifer-studded mountain forest.

Wildlife abounds. Sassy roadrunner (right) hunts snakes, lizards, and insects on the desert floor. It can sprint up to 15 miles an hour, flies only when it must. This one outran the photographer for two hours.

FREDERICK KENT TRUSLOW. JAMES P. BLAIR (BELOW) AND EMORY KRISTOF (OPPOSITE), NATIONAL GEOGRAPHIC PHOTOGRAPHERS

Square-ended johnboats ply the Current River in Missouri (opposite); here 137 miles of free-flowing streams form Ozark National Scenic Riverways.

Everglades visitors thread jungle trails (right) and spot exotic birds like the wood ibis (above).

visitors may glimpse them as they come and go.

Not all gifts are on the Everglades scale. The National Park Trust Fund has welcomed donations as small as two dollars. Anyone wishing to donate should write the Parks Director for details. I should add that since Mission 66 the Congress has been generous in appropriating funds to buy new park areas.

Everglades is a nature park and so are the others you'll visit in this book—even the Indian ruins, for the Indian lived close to nature and rarely upset its balance. The landmarks of American history comprise a fascinating subject in themselves and are dealt with in the companion to this volume, *America's Historylands.*

Other things about the National Park Service

Clouds caress the highlands of Great Smoky Mountains National Park as dawn

might surprise you. It is the country's largest maker of museum exhibits; it uses the product in visitor centers. It stocks zoos with surplus elk and bears which have taken to associating too closely with people. It does this free. It cooperates with scientific organizations in excavating archeological sites threatened by new dams or highways. It helps other Federal agencies plan recreational use for their lands; Lake Mead, in Arizona and Nevada, is an example of this.

The national parks exist to strengthen bodies, refresh minds, uplift the spirits. They enrich leisure, and I believe that the way Americans use their ever-increasing leisure time will determine, more even than how we work, what kind of Nation

THOMAS NEBBIA, NATIONAL GEOGRAPHIC PHOTOGRAPHER

breaks over North Carolina; early risers in Tennessee greet the sunrise atop Mount Le Conte.

this will be fifty or a hundred years from now. Stephen Mather sums it up best. "Who will gainsay," he wrote, "that the parks contain the highest potentialities of national pride, national contentment, and national health? A visit inspires love of country; begets contentment; engenders pride of possession; contains the antidote for national restlessness.

"A visit to a park teaches love of nature, of trees and flowers, the rippling brooks, the crystal lakes, the snow-clad mountain peaks, the wildlife encountered everywhere amid native surroundings. He is a better citizen with a keener appreciation of . . . living here who has toured the national parks."

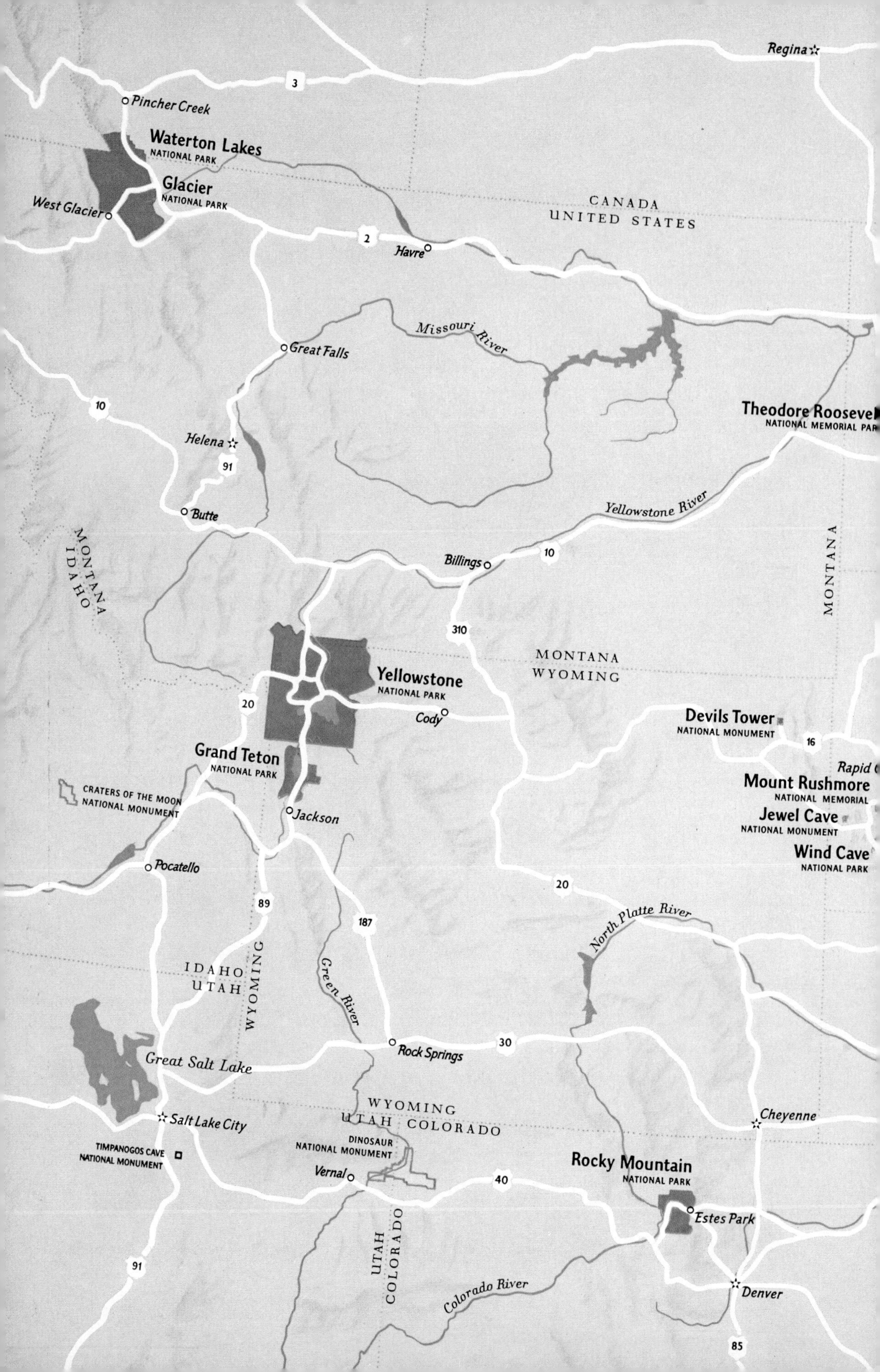

Regina
3
Pincher Creek
Waterton Lakes
NATIONAL PARK
Glacier
NATIONAL PARK
West Glacier
CANADA
UNITED STATES
2
Havre
Missouri River
Great Falls
10
Theodore Roosevelt
NATIONAL MEMORIAL PARK
Helena
91
Butte
Yellowstone River
MONTANA
IDAHO
Billings
10
MONTANA
310
MONTANA
WYOMING
Yellowstone
NATIONAL PARK
20
Cody
Devils Tower
NATIONAL MONUMENT
16
Grand Teton
NATIONAL PARK
Rapid
Mount Rushmore
NATIONAL MEMORIAL
CRATERS OF THE MOON
NATIONAL MONUMENT
Jackson
Jewel Cave
NATIONAL MONUMENT
Wind Cave
NATIONAL PARK
Pocatello
20
89
187
North Platte River
IDAHO
UTAH
WYOMING
Green River
Rock Springs
30
Great Salt Lake
WYOMING
UTAH COLORADO
Cheyenne
Salt Lake City
DINOSAUR
NATIONAL MONUMENT
TIMPANOGOS CAVE
NATIONAL MONUMENT
Rocky Mountain
NATIONAL PARK
Vernal
40
Estes Park
UTAH
COLORADO
91
Colorado River
Denver
85

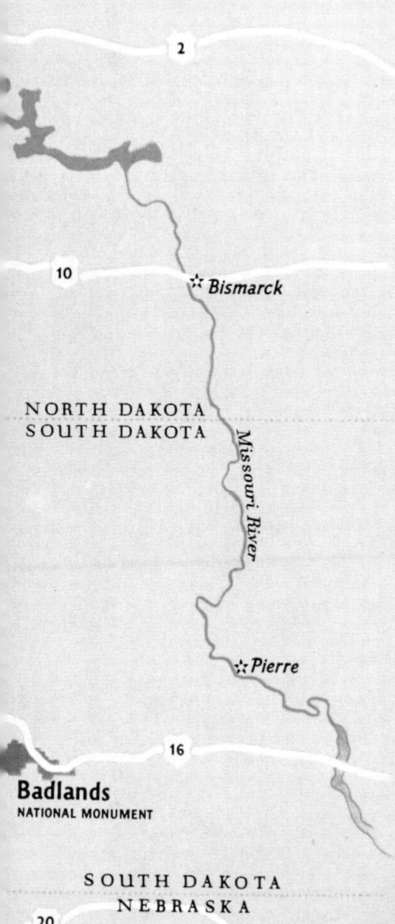

PART ONE

THE ROCKY MOUNTAINS

SCOUTS and mountain men, treading these craggy highlands, called them the Stony Mountains. Today they are the Rockies, and no longer need the feet be bruised by travel through them. What was once a grim barrier to all but the most adventurous is now a rampart of another sort, preserving precious areas of wilderness.

And what a wilderness! Torn by ancient volcanoes, sculptured by glaciers and rushing rivers, sheared by stupendous earth-fault, the Rockies are indeed a marvel to the eye. But this savage marvel has a gentle aspect, too. Beneath the crystalline peaks lie sparkling lakes, meadows strewn with wildflowers, and forests threaded by tumbling streams—a natural balance of land and water and sturdy vegetation, of prey and predator in undisturbed exchange.

A museum, a haven, a place to test the muscle, to study the way of natural things; all these the parks of the Rockies are. But they are more: a place where a man can regenerate his spirit, and see with quiet clarity the size and meaning of his world.

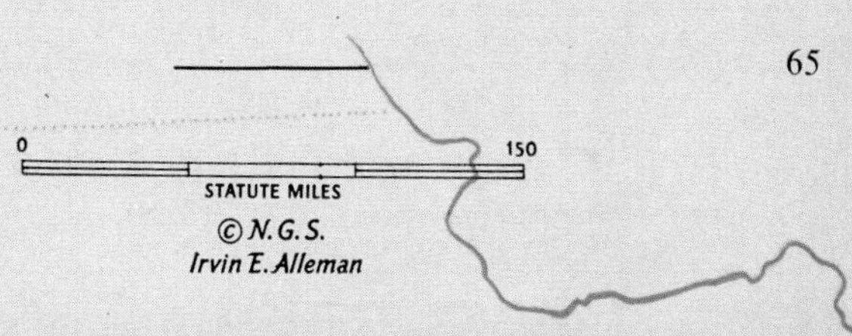

KENNETH FINK

Perky weasel wears coat of summer brown; for winter's snows he dons pure white.

YELLOWSTONE

By FREDERICK G. VOSBURGH, Associate Editor, National Geographic

MEN CAME OUT OF THE WEST with wild, incredible tales. High in the Rockies, they said, was a land where the earth boiled under your feet, where spouts of hot water as tall as a flagpole came roaring out of the trembling ground, and whole valleys steamed with sulphurous fumes as if the lid over Hell itself had been shot full of holes.

"Out thar in the Yellowstone," Jim Bridger related, "thar's a river that flows so fast it gets hot on the bottom."

Boiling springs bubbled by an icy lake, and a man could catch and cook a trout without moving a step or taking the fish off the line. There were mountains of glass and mountains of sulphur and mountains that spoke with growling voices. A galloping river leaped over a cliff and landed in a gorge a thousand feet deep all lined with yellow stone. Down a terraced mountainside ran the waters of immense hot springs, scalding at first and cooling as they flowed, so a man could take a bath of any temperature he chose.

Thus ran the tales of the mountain men, long-haired, leather-garbed scouts and trappers such as John Colter, Joe Meek, and Bridger, who ranged westward from St. Louis early in the 19th century.

Today two million visitors to Yellowstone National Park every year see for themselves that many of the old-timers' yarns were the truth and that there are more wonders in Yellowstone than even Jim Bridger knew.

You can wade in the river that "gets hot on the bottom"—the Firehole River

Queen of geysers, Old Faithful performs on the average every 67 minutes. Named by General Washburn in 1870, she has never been known to miss a cue.

WALTER MEAYERS EDWARDS, NATIONAL GEOGRAPHIC STAFF

 Grand Canyon of the Yellowstone: hurtling down 308-foot-high Lower Falls, the river foams

past Inspiration Point (inset).

RAY MANLEY. INSET: MERLE SEVERY, NATIONAL GEOGRAPHIC STAFF

near Old Faithful. But the heat comes from hot springs in the bed, not from friction of water on rock.

At Fishing Cone beside Yellowstone Lake you could catch and cook a fish without moving out of your tracks—if the rangers would let you. Park rules forbid fishing at this spot or putting anything into the hot pools.

Glass mountains? There's Obsidian Cliff, of black volcanic glass. There's Sulphur Mountain; and Roaring Mountain, named for the steam vents near its top. And in the awed accounts of the early trappers the present-day visitor recognizes such familiar yet marvelous features as Old Faithful and the great geyser basins, Mammoth Hot Springs, and that colorful, unbelievable canyon "where falls the Yellowstone."

Like most visitors to the park, my family and I were eager to watch Old Faithful in eruption and see a bear.

"Bears?" said the ranger at South Entrance. "They'll be holding you up before you have driven very far in the park."

He was right. Near Old Faithful a black bear and her cub held up traffic.

"Do not feed the bears," the rangers warn. Yet some heedless visitors feed and even fondle these dangerous wild animals, and every summer scores of persons are bitten or clawed. A few bears get so bold and destructive that they must be trapped and trucked to exile in a far corner of the park.

Past more of the furry official greeters we rolled at last to Old Faithful where the queen of Yellowstone rises regularly in draperies of steam.

In only three places in all the world can you see the never-forgotten sight

Minerva Hot Spring startled the eyes of mountain men

Little did they suspect that here at Mammoth Hot Springs "a mountain was turning itself inside out." Welling up from the cavernous depths of Terrace Mountain, lime in solution forms draped balconies of travertine like this.

Visitors peer into the trumpet-shaped throat of famed Morning Glory Pool in Upper Geyser Basin. Though its depths still shimmer blue-green, its lip has reddened since the violent Montana earthquake of 1959 dropped its average temperature 10°—to about 158° F.—permitting rust-hued algae to spread from the shallows down into the bowl.

ANDREW H. BROWN AND (BELOW) DEAN CONGER, NATIONAL GEOGRAPHIC STAFF

A rocky diving board adds zest to a dip in the Firehole River.

Rendezvous at Yancey's Hole. A jostling ride across sagebrush flats from Roosevelt Lodge brings stage passengers to the spot where John Yancey's hotel once stood. Here they pile out, rub backsides unused to wooden wheels, and listen to tales about this way-stop for riders of yesteryear.

Modern wayfarers mindful of park rules keep windows up when a begging bruin approaches (below). Despite their name, American black bears display a variety of colors—black, brown, cinnamon red, even platinum blonde.

ANDREW H. BROWN AND (OPPOSITE) DEAN CONGER, NATIONAL GEOGRAPHIC STAFF

of tons of hot water shooting out of the earth, propelled by the awesome explosive force of nature's hidden fires. One is Iceland, whence came the word "geyser," from an Icelandic verb meaning to gush. Another is New Zealand. But the biggest geysers and the largest number are here in Yellowstone.

Deep under this ground—perhaps a mile down, the geologists tell us—seethe superhot magmas left from the days when belching volcanoes were building up these mountains. Cold ground waters, trickling downward, strike rising vapors of indescribable heat. They boil, flash into steam. If the explosion takes place in a tube of rock hard enough to stand the strain, the cooler water above is driven out in a geyser eruption.

Such manifestations of nature's power are found throughout much of the park —ten thousand or more hot pools, geysers, and patches of boiling mud. Most of the big "hot water volcanoes" are here in Upper Geyser Basin. Giant, Giantess, Beehive, and Grand Geyser all erupt higher than Old Faithful, but you may have to wait days to see them. More gracious is the queen. Though she may nap from 33 to 96 minutes between blows, her variations follow a predictable pattern.

"Next eruption of Old Faithful about 6:40," read a sign at the visitor center. Near a low gray cone of geyserite a ranger-naturalist was speaking:

"Old Faithful plays as regularly and as high as it did when discovered.... Height varies from 115 to 150 feet and once a 180-foot eruption was measured.

Steaming pillar of Old Faithful casts a cool shadow over Old Faithful Inn, "world's largest log cabin." Early risers watch as 10,000 gallons of water roar 150 feet into the air in the four-minute spectacle.

UNION PACIFIC RAILROAD COLORPHOTO

Intervals between eruptions average 67 minutes.... The source of heat—"

But what was that? From beneath the earth came a rumbling sound, as if a giant were preparing to speak. From the top of the cone welled a little water. Higher it rose, fell back, then triumphantly tons upon tons of steaming water surged toward the darkening sky. From hundreds of throats came an exclamation, a gasp. Great billows of steam rolled off on the breeze.

Higher, yet higher, leaped the column, a hundred feet, a hundred and fifty, still higher, while billowing steam rose far above, a pillar between earth and sky.

Four minutes, and the spouting flood had spent its power. Old Faithful's high plumed head sank lower, and slowly she withdrew to her home in the earth, like a genie into its box. Again people spoke; the spell was broken.

Another favorite is Riverside. Filling the air with sulphurous fumes, Riverside's slanting stream, like a huge fire hose, pours into the Firehole River.

"Doesn't that hot smelly water kill the fish?" asked a visitor.

"Not at all," said the ranger. "You'll find plenty of trout here. The river temperature rises about six degrees as it flows through this area, but that isn't enough to hurt the fish. And bad as it smells, geyser water is pure; it tastes about like water boiled in your teakettle. In fact, geyser drainage is good for fishing. It helps produce a supply of food, and the fish grow all year round."

At Gibbon Geyser Basin, believe it or not, are steam-heated bear dens! Wise bruins have found that vapor-warmed rocks make a snug hideaway. Steam-heated birds' nests are another Yellowstone oddity, several species making their homes within reach of the warm drifting vapor from geyser basins.

NEW GEYSERS ARE RARE, but long-dormant craters sometimes burst into life. Steamboat Geyser simmered for 50 years, then in 1961 blasted steam 1,000 feet into the air. Steamboat's deafening eruptions, though unpredictable, are the most violent in the park.

Geysers of the fountain type—as opposed to the nozzle type such as Steamboat and Old Faithful—are often glassy pools until almost the instant of eruption. A good example is Grand Geyser. One minute it is a placid mirror; the next the water is blasting into the air as if propelled by dynamite.

One of the best known pools is Morning Glory, around which a superstition centers. Somehow the idea has spread over the country that tossing a penny into Morning Glory brings good luck. Bad luck is much more likely, for the tosser may be fined for defacing the pool.

Periodically, a ranger cleans out Morning Glory with a kitchen spoon on the end of a pole. "The superintendent sends the money to Washington," he said, "and the U. S. Treasury logs it in as an increase in national wealth."

One of the strangest things about these hot pools and geysers is the effect

Old Faithful Inn's sturdy timbers ring with the laughter and song of trail-weary sightseers. A snapping fire chases the evening chill from the cavernous lobby, famous for its five tiers of balconies.

TED SPIEGEL. PAGES 78-79: JAMES P. BLAIR, NATIONAL GEOGRAPHIC PHOTOGRAPHER

GHOST IN MISTY VAPORS, *Will Gray trails his family through steaming vents and hot springs of Norris Geyser Basin at Yellowstone National Park.*

STONY MINERALS *coat grass and moss (magnified 7½ times) beside a scalding pool.*

that ordinary soap has upon them. Like small boys they can't seem to stand it. Many of the pools are in delicate hair-trigger balance, so that a slight change in pressure will turn them into geysers.

A dramatic example is Chinaman Spring, a few steps from Old Faithful Geyser. A Chinese laundryman at the hotel many years ago thought it a shame to let all this hot water go to waste. He put up a tent over the pool, tossed in the clothes, added soap, and was rubbing his hands in satisfaction when suddenly up roared the pool—tent, laundry, laundryman and all.

"Soaping" today, of course, is strictly forbidden.

The vicinity of these hot pools is no place for the absent-minded. Anybody who walked into one would parboil in a trice. In Skeleton Spring are skeletons of two boiled bison which have been there since the early days of the park.

AT OLD FAITHFUL, as everywhere in Yellowstone, wild animals are constantly appearing. A big elk bound for the river strolled past a crowd at Grand Geyser. Under the porch at the lodge lived golden-mantled marmots, grandfatherly little dignitaries who showed no fear of visitors. During an eruption of Old Faithful a black cub ambled by—and promptly stole the show.

At night at a campfire session I looked at the strangely assorted people singing "Home on the Range"—tenderfeet on their first trip west, schoolteachers, businessmen, doctors, clerks, lawyers, engineers.

Oh, give me a home where the buffalo roam,
Where the deer and the antelope play. . . .
Where the graceful white swan goes gliding along
Like a maid in a heavenly dream.

"That's a good song to be singing here," said the ranger, "for Yellowstone is one place in the world where all of those creatures are still to be found, even the rare trumpeter swan. Up near the Gardiner entrance plenty of 'antelope play,' and on Mirror Plateau hundreds of 'buffalo roam.' "

Old Faithful Inn, dear to countless honeymooners, was hacked from forests in 1903 to become one of the world's largest wooden buildings. No guest will forget its sprawling, gingerbread charm, its 92-foot-high entrance hall, ringed by five tiers of rustic balconies.

Many rooms face the geyser, offering a midnight view of Old Faithful unfolding her stately dance by the light of the moon. Her performance gains glory when nothing moves on the chalky geyser mounds but the prima donna herself.

Fifty-four miles away, another huge hostelry, Canyon Hotel, long stood as a landmark beside the Grand Canyon of the Yellowstone. It has been replaced by modern Canyon Village offering hundreds of cottages, a visitor center, shops, and a streamlined lodge decorated with murals. Carefully planned to avoid marring its setting, the village lies well back from the canyon rim, screened by pines.

Wary pronghorns stand hillside sentinel. North America's fastest mammal, *Antilocapra americana* can sprint 50 miles an hour. His bobbing white rump flashes danger to the herd. Both male and female have hollow, branched horns, which they shed every fall.

PAUL A. ZAHL, NATIONAL GEOGRAPHIC STAFF

GEORGE D. MARLER. BELOW: WALTER A. WEBER, NATIONAL GEOGRAPHIC STAFF ARTIST. OPPOSITE: NATIONAL PARK SERVICE

If Colter had ever told in St. Louis that a mountain out in the Yellowstone was turning itself inside out, he would have been laughed out of town. Yet that is exactly what is happening at Mammoth Hot Springs. From limestone beds hundreds of feet down in Terrace Mountain, hot springs are bringing up lime in solution and depositing it on the outside in the form of travertine (calcium carbonate). This light porous rock builds up fast—six inches to a foot a year—compared to a mere thirty-second of an inch for the hard geyserite of the geyser basins. Huge terraces have been formed on the mountainside—and one can imagine caverns, correspondingly huge, deep in the earth below.

On one of these terraces stands the little town of Mammoth Hot Springs, the park headquarters. Soil was hauled in by horse and spread over the rock when this was Fort Yellowstone.

In winter, animals replace tourists at Yellowstone's geysers and hot springs.

Park denizens gather at warm spots like country folks around a pot-bellied stove. Buffalo (left) find snow-free forage on a steam-heated range. Hardy bighorn sheep (right), driven from mountain heights by snow, seek shrubby browse at lower levels.

Lordly Shiras moose (below) jealously guards his harem during the fall mating season. This light-hued race was named for George Shiras 3d, for 31 years a National Geographic Trustee.

Nature's dining room: lodgepole pines whisper luncheon music beside the gentle Yellowstone,

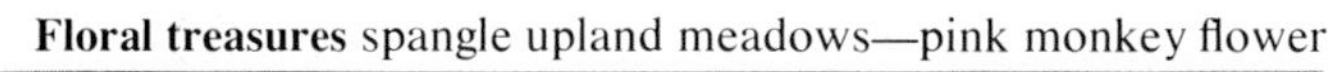

Floral treasures spangle upland meadows—pink monkey flower

ANDREW H. BROWN, NATIONAL GEOGRAPHIC STAFF

above its thundering falls (page 89).

Down the face of the mountain we wound to Mammoth, past Jupiter Terrace and the other formations standing like pulpits above the town. Over them ran steaming hot water, and many wore mantles of vivid algae. Far down at the base of the lowest terrace emerges Hot River, the subterranean stream that drains this eccentric mountain.

Climbing the terraces, we found in one pool an egg someone had left to boil. Farther on, a new spring had broken out in the middle of the path.

"They change course overnight," said the ranger-naturalist.

"Why aren't there any geysers here? Because the rock is soft. The water just boils up and flows away. There's no hard, siliceous sinter here to form breeches and barrels for water cannon like Old Faithful."

Jim Bridger, in his best romancing mood, used to tell that out in the Yellowstone there were not only "peetrified" trees but on their branches perched "peetrified birds a-singing peetrified songs."

No "peetrified" birds or stone songs have been found, but the truth is almost as strange. Science knows, for example, that there are not one but a dozen petrified forests piled one on top of another. Giant trees were smoth-

wild aster

wild geranium

KENNETH FINK

Anglers gang up on cutthroat trout at outlet of Yellowstone Lake. Snow lingers on Mount Sheridan

Fish braving the headwaters of the Yellowstone River face triple jeopardy: boatmen dangle tempting bait; shore-based sportsmen wade deep to cast their lures; others throng Fishing Bridge (where picture was taken). Boats may be rented, but many vacationers bring their own atop cars or trailers.

Below: A happy angler displays her catch of brown trout from Shoshone Lake. Isolated Shoshone is accessible by trail or by small boat dragged up the swift outlet stream. No fishing license is required in the park.

Lower right: A sight-seeing cavalcade led by a bus from Yellowstone's famous yellow fleet threads the Hoodoos, stark blocks of ancient travertine that tumbled from Terrace Mountain, three miles south of Mammoth Hot Springs.

ANDREW H. BROWN, NATIONAL GEOGRAPHIC STAFF

ered by ashes and lava spewed out by thundering volcanoes, and on the debris new forests grew, until there were a dozen of them, like layers in a cake. Now the Lamar River has cut the cake for the wondering eye to see.

But of all the wonders of wonderland, none hit this beholder with a stronger impact than the Grand Canyon of the Yellowstone.

AWED INDIANS untold years ago peered into a golden gorge where a river leaped like a plume of smoke from the top of a high cliff. They called it the river of the yellow stone. Restrained and simple, the name is perfect, but it fails to prepare you for the tremendous sight that inspired it.

Yellow it is, this breathtaking gorge, and myriad blending shades as well, from ocher to orange and deep, rich red. "Land of sand and ruin and gold. . . ." Somehow the line from Swinburne kept running through my mind. But this was rock and ruin and gold—ruin wrought by a river on solid rock with the aid of hot water and steam.

Ospreys usually look down on man. Here the tables are turned as the big fish hawks soar below in the gorge and nest in plain sight on pinnacles of rock. Many visitors mistake them for eagles.

If you descend into the canyon, and if you are lucky, you may see the little water ouzel, or dipper, dive into the Yellowstone's foam-flecked torrents to "fly under water" in quest of aquatic food.

Outside of Alaska most of the Nation's surviving grizzly bears find sanctuary in Yellowstone. Near the canyon, at Trout Creek dump, they feast on table scraps. As we watched from a safe distance, a mother grizzly sniffed suspiciously before leading off her three butterball cubs.

"Know how to tell a grizzly from a black bear?" asked the ranger. "Let the bear chase you up a tree. If it comes up after you, it's not a grizzly."

Past Mud Volcano and Dragons Mouth Spring, with its flickering tongue of hot water and steam, we drove upriver from Canyon to Yellowstone Lake. On Fishing Bridge anglers almost elbow to elbow were casting for cutthroats, the gorgeous native Yellowstone, or Montana black-spotted, trout.

One of the highest big lakes in the world, Yellowstone today drains to the Atlantic via the Yellowstone River, the Missouri, Mississippi, and Gulf of Mexico. But centuries ago glacier ice blocked the outlet and the lake drained to the Pacific through the Snake and the Columbia. That explains the presence of Yellowstone's cutthroat trout, a distinct species, but related to Pacific coast cutthroats.

Which of all the marvels of Yellowstone, I wondered, makes the greatest impression? I asked this question at each of the five gates where cars pour in and out of the park.

"What hit me hardest?" said an easterner. "Old Faithful, of course."

A giant unchained, Lower Falls on the Yellowstone dwarfs visitors who walk its brink. During June run-off, 60,000 gallons a second thunder through this huge spout, carved in a rib of volcanic rock.

ANDREW H. BROWN, NATIONAL GEOGRAPHIC STAFF

"Bears!" yelled another.

"That wonderful canyon!" a woman exclaimed.

"The unparalleled thermal activity," said a serious-minded student.

But I think the best reaction to Yellowstone is that of old White Hawk, a Bannock Indian. At Old Faithful someone once asked White Hawk whether it was true that Indians used to shun the geyser areas, believing them the abode of evil spirits.

The old chief shook his head and gazed with practical eye at the plumes of hot water, the gemlike seething pools.

"Ugh," said he. "Good place cookum meat."

The new look in park architecture

ANDREW H. BROWN AND (ABOVE) J. BAYLOR ROBERTS, NATIONAL GEOGRAPHIC STAF

Snug in a cabin, the Browns, from sweltering Washington, D. C., rise and dress for an active day. Heavy blankets ward off mile-and-a-half-high chill.

Canyon Village Lodge houses dining room, cafeteria, lounge, and shops for 500 motel units.

YELLOWSTONE NATIONAL PARK *Northwestern Wyoming. Area 3,472 sq. mi.*

Features: World's most spectacular thermal area, with more than 10,000 geysers, hot springs, pools, steam jets, mud volcanoes. Largest mountain lake in North America (elev. 7,731 ft.). Grand Canyon of the Yellowstone. Upper, Lower, and Tower Falls. Obsidian Cliff; standing petrified trees. Black and grizzly bears, moose, deer, elk, pronghorn, bighorn, coyote, bison; some 240 species of birds.

Activities: Visitor centers. Grand Loop Road (142 mi.) connects major features. Sightseeing bus trips; 1,000 mi. of hiking and riding trails. Campfire programs, guided walks, exhibits. Trout fishing, boating, wilderness camping, wildlife photography.

Season: Park open May 1–Oct. 31; most facilities June 1–Sept. 15.

Weather: Warm, sparkling days, cool evenings (average elev. 7,500 ft.).

What to bring: Hiking shoes and rough-it clothing; woolens for evening. Raincoat, camera and light meter, binoculars.

How to get there: Major highways converge on Yellowstone's five entrances (see map at back of book). Consult touring services on routes and snow conditions in high passes during May, June, September, and October. Park buses connect with trains and buses. Write Yellowstone Park Co., Yellowstone Park, for schedules. Northwest, Western, Frontier, and United Airlines serve nearby cities; surface connections to park.

Accommodations: Make reservations early; opening and closing dates for each place vary; write Yellowstone Park Co. for list. Hotels: Old Faithful (Inn), Lake, Mammoth Hot Springs. Lodges: Old Faithful, Lake, Canyon, Roosevelt. Campers' cabins: Old Faithful, West Thumb, Fishing Bridge, Canyon. 16 camp and trailer grounds: first come, first served.

Services: Main centers provide restaurants, stores, garages; car rentals at Old Faithful, Canyon, Mammoth. Hospital at Lake; clinic at Mammoth; physician at Old Faithful Inn. Religious services in park; interdenominational chapel at Mammoth.

Park regulations: Campfires outside campgrounds by permit only. No feeding or molesting animals or defacing natural features. Daily maximum five fish, no fishing license required. Ask for fishing regulations. Boat permits required; no boat over 40 ft., no sailboats because of squalls. Pets allowed on leash, but not in boats or on trails.

For further information write Superintendent, Yellowstone National Park, Wyoming

A **mule deer** searches her snowbound home for a cold dinner of serviceberry and bitter brush.

GRAND TETON

NATIONAL PARK

By FRANK and JOHN CRAIGHEAD

FRENCH-CANADIAN TRAPPERS more than a hundred years ago gave the Tetons their name. Gazing in awe at that spectacular granite skyline, they dubbed three towering summits the "Trois Tetons," for their fancied resemblance to a woman's breasts.

Later explorers thought "Tetons" a misnomer. "He indeed must have been long a dweller amid these solitudes who could trace in these cold and barren peaks any resemblance to the gentle bosom of a woman," wrote Nathaniel P. Langford on his expedition to nearby Yellowstone in 1870.

But we have no desire to enter an old argument. To us and to all who visit Grand Teton National Park today, the special appeal of the Tetons lies in the way they rise so precipitously from the lake-studded floor of the Jackson Hole valley, the tallest peak clawing the sky at nearly 14,000 feet.

Our own first glimpse of this game-rich valley in the Wyoming Rockies, back in 1934, fired us with its promise as an outdoor laboratory for wildlife research. From Togwotee Pass on the east we let our eyes sweep the snow-flecked crests of the Teton Range. At its base shimmered broad Jackson Lake, through which flows the upper Snake River. Repeated visits to the Jackson Hole country won us completely to its sagebrush flats and timbered slopes.

From wartime service in warm oceans and hot tropical forests, we returned to Jackson Hole and canyon roads of snow, to a dazzling whiteness scarcely

Trail riders jog along a ledge in Cascade Canyon, past Mount Teewinot (left) and cloud-crowned Grand Teton. Two hundred miles of park trails beckon horseman and hiker to hidden cataracts, lush meadows, tranquil moose ponds.

DAVID S. BOYER, NATIONAL GEOGRAPHIC STAFF, AND (ABOVE) FRANK AND JOHN CRAIGHEAD

Bare of foothills, Wyoming's magnificent Tetons explode in craggy abruptness from the gentle

FRANK AND JOHN CRAIGHEAD

floor of Jackson Hole. Into this sheltered "hole," or valley, came Indians to stalk elk, and mountain men to trap beaver. Homesteaders and cattlemen followed, guided by three snowy peaks on the horizon: South, Middle, and Grand Teton. Snake River cuts the bank at far right.

toned down by forest green, to nightly subfreezing temperatures. During the following weeks the spring sun slugged it out with snow flurries that roared down the canyons of the Tetons and tried to spread over the valley. As if by magic a hot sun burned the snow blanket until the fence tops showed, then the tips of the sagebrush. The porous glacial soil absorbed the melt and slowly released it to the Snake River. Almost overnight in early May, spring came to the valley, and winter slowly receded up the mountains.

Buttercups turned the first bare ground to a glistening gold. Shaggy, ill-tempered moose dragged out of the Snake River willow bottoms, waded into the unfrozen beaver ponds, and daily grew warier as they gained strength and flesh from the slimy green algae. Grouse drummed in courtship day and night. A lonesome saw-whet owl called monotonously for a mate. There were swirls of feeding trout, and then the aspens turning green and the willows red.

From the sagebrush of the valley and the blue waters of Jenny Lake we followed a trail over the glacial moraines cloaked in lodgepole pine and climbed Cascade Canyon into the subalpine zone of fir and spruce. Above timber line on the Skyline Trail towered a tremendous stratified limestone wall contrasting

From giant puffballs, enough to feed ten men, to tiny pine-nut morsels, the wilderness food locker

Mountain men found food for the plucking in the Rockies. One lost explorer survived 37 days on little else but thistle roots!

Puffball mushrooms, like the girl holds above, pop out of meadows in spring or fall. Peeled, sliced, and fried in butter, they lend a banquet touch to elk steak or trout.

Onionlike camass bulbs (right) taste like potatoes when baked or boiled. They helped save Lewis and Clark explorers on Idaho's Lolo Trail. (The death camass, a similar bulb, is poisonous.)

And for dessert: pine nuts and golden currants.

FRANK AND JOHN CRAIGHEAD

Baby scales 35 ounces. When grown, this great horned owl may gulp seven field mice in one meal. Banding birds reveals range and life span.

with the Pre-Cambrian granite of the Teton peaks. And above the cliffs and peaks, birds of prey soared and wheeled while scanning the meadows below.

We felt like staying forever up in the rock gardens above the valley. But the Tetons can be moody as well as magnificent. During one of our summer climbs storms that had been milling around all day fused at last in one rumbling mass

provides a ready menu full of zest and life.

Resinous cones of the whitebark pine yield pine nuts.

Golden currants ripen in late summer and fall.

of clouds and searing flashes. Thunder broke directly overhead. The air was charged, crackling. Electricity stood our hair on end, made the skin tingle. Lightning struck close by, leaving a strong ozone smell in its wake.

A band of elk crossed our path, headed down. Rain and hail flailed us as we crawled into timber-line lean-tos, natural shelters where mountain sheep and elk bed down beneath the matted roofing of gnarled and ageless firs.

Mumbling, the storm moved on, tagged by the sun reflected in a million water crystals adhering to the flowers. The next morning light snow covered the peaks. Clouds drifted low over the alpine gardens, letting the sun through here and there, but never for long. The mood of the mountains had changed.

The elk in summer move to the high country of the Teton National Forest and the timbered and grassy vales of the Yellowstone plateau. There they fatten, raise their calves, and frolic amid the cool alpine meadows.

On clear September days, when aspens glitter golden on the hills, it is a tingling

thrill to hear a bull elk bugling. Frequently we glimpse him on a hilltop in proud pose, his many-pointed rack silhouetted against the sky. This is the season of the rut, and the bull elk is in his splendid prime.

With the first heavy snows in late October or early November, a herd estimated at 10,000 to 14,000 drifts down to winter in the lower Jackson Hole valley. During these weeks rifle fire echoes among the hills and on the flats. Legal hunting is encouraged. Wildlife research shows that even now, despite this annual check, the herd has multiplied beyond the capacity of its winter range.

MANY OF OUR sharpest memories of life in Jackson Hole focus on adventures with its mammals and birds. We always have had pets around our cabins: ground squirrels, chipmunks, magpies, ravens, horned owls, prairie falcons, even white-footed mice. Kali, a female coyote, we raised from a pup. She played with the children, chewed up shoes, came at our call, and acted like a well-behaved dog.

When winter whitens Jackson Hole, elk, or wapiti, get hay handouts at the National Elk Refuge next to the park. Largest bulls may weigh half a ton, stand as high as horses. Antlers fall off in late winter.

JAMES R. SIMON AND (LEFT) FRANK AND JOHN CRAIGHEAD

Sky-piercing peaks challenge the climber's skill. Novices flock to summer school; some graduate by scaling "The Grand"

Towering over all, the rugged spire of 13,766-foot Grand Teton (right) surrendered to man in the 19th century. Since then mountaineers have blazed a score of routes to the top. Today the Teton Range is a mecca for climbers; thousands swarm up its major peaks each year. The Craigheads, who have climbed them all, warn: "The Tetons are tempting but treacherous, not to be tackled lightly. You must not climb them alone."

At Jenny Lake, the Exum School of Mountaineering readies novices every summer for a try at the bristling granite ramparts. On gentle slopes the tenderfoot tries his first rappel (below). Learning the tougher free rappel (left), he swings from an overhang in a nylon harness; to control descent, he tightens or slackens pressure on the slender lifeline. Quick learners join guided parties on the two-day trip up "The Grand" after only one day of school.

The Tetons began forming 15 million years ago when earth forces thrust up a block 7,000 feet above Jackson Hole. Erosion sculptured the mass until, millions of years later, mountains emerged. Blunt at first, the peaks grew sharp as they wore down to their Pre-Cambrian cores.

DAVID S. BOYER AND (OPPOSITE) DEAN CONGER, NATIONAL GEOGRAPHIC STAFF

Wilderness wonderland unfolds along Snake River for First Lady

All smiles, Mrs. Lyndon Johnson and Secretary of the Interior Stewart Udall bask in "beauty, peace, and serenity" while rafting down the Snake in 1964. Mrs. Johnson was often first in the party to spy elk, moose, mule deer, bald eagles, and Canada geese. "She has rancher's eyes," noted an aide. Said guide Brent Eastman: "The best game spotter I've ever seen."

The same scenic splendors delight 6,000 park visitors each year. Boarding the inflated rubber rafts near Jackson Lake Lodge, they float between forested banks teeming with wildlife. As the Snake meanders into open country, the breath-taking Tetons fill the western sky (left). Now the river quickens; the raft, guided fore and aft by giant paddles, whips around sandbars and skims white water to complete the 25-mile ride near park headquarters at Moose.

THOMAS NEBBIA AND (OPPOSITE) RALPH GRAY, NATIONAL GEOGRAPHIC STAFF

And like a good dog she assumed responsibilities. One day John heard Kali barking excitedly. Between barks she was trying to pull something out of the irrigation ditch. Instantly John ran, for he saw that his year-old son Derek had crawled into the ditch. The coyote's warning probably saved the baby from drowning. Kali later ate four of our laying hens; we merely reprimanded her.

Since our first visits, Jackson Hole has been invaded by paved roads, motels, service stations, and a swelling tide of tourist traffic, but the glorious semi-wilderness back country happily remains intact. Some areas within the park are as wild as when John Colter, mountain man and trapper, set foot here in 1807.

After the trappers and hunters of last century took heavy toll of its animals, Jackson Hole relapsed into neglect. The westward trek of settlers washed around it to the Pacific, for the Hole was not farming or industrial country. Untapped by rails, the valley knew only limited lumbering. Much of Jackson Hole, therefore, still holds elk, moose, deer, and bighorn sheep. Beaver boldly cut aspen and cottonwood for their dams. Game birds abound, and rising trout ripple the lakes and streams.

Years before we found our way to Jackson Hole, the recreational value of the area and its potential as an "unfenced zoo" had been recognized. In 1897 Teton

A character out of the Old West entertains a park visitor with tales of gunslingers and border fights. Rustlers and posses are gone but dude ranches and lodges carry on Jackson Hole's boot-and-saddle ways.

National Forest was created. In 1912 Congress set aside land in the valley for a National Elk Refuge, and in 1929 established Grand Teton National Park. Wyoming's Game and Fish Commission has aided Federal programs to preserve the Jackson Hole country for the enjoyment of Americans forever.

Congress in 1950 tripled the park's area by including lands formerly in Jackson Hole National Monument and private holdings; 30,000 of these acres were presented to the American people by John D. Rockefeller, Jr.

"Conservation today means far more than just preserving our natural resources," said his son, Laurance S. Rockefeller, a National Geographic Trustee, at the dedication of Jackson Lake Lodge. "It means their wise use and protection so that more and more people may enjoy and benefit by them."

Colter Bay was developed as a model for park accommodations sought under the Park Service's Mission 66 program. Campgrounds, trailer sites, and scores of cabins nestle among tall evergreens. The community includes a visitor center, general store, service station, cafeteria and grill, showers, laundromat, a beach, and a marina where you can rent boats or launch your own.

When you arrive in the park, we suggest you first drive up Signal Mountain for its commanding view of the valley and range. Later you may wish to exchange the driver's seat for the saddle. Whether you elect to take a short horseback ride,

Elk Island cookout topped by a western ballad ends a perfect day. Moonlight cruises carry visitors across Jackson Lake to the island. Shoreside corrals offer breakfast rides and steak supper outings.

LOWELL J. GEORGIA. ABOVE: J. BAYLOR ROBERTS, NATIONAL GEOGRAPHIC STAFF

join an overnight pack trip, or strike out afoot, you have 200 miles of varied trails from which to choose. A favorite is Cascade Canyon Trail, winding between crags to Lake Solitude, an 18-mile round trip. And ever beckoning the skilled climber are those cliff-hung towers of naked rock—Grand, Middle, and South Teton, Teewinot, Owen, Moran. Each craggy summit offers its special challenge.

Float trips down the Snake, whispering in its gravelly bed, are a delightful way to see the park. You can join an organized trip or launch your own rubber raft. The fast-flowing river stays open even through winter's coldest weather, and we have pioneered winter rafting on it to study big game and Canada geese. It was one of these trips that showed us a rare woodland drama. We tied our raft to the bank and snowshoed up a side canyon. High above us on an open slope we saw a band of mule deer, lunging forward, belly-deep in snow. They would stop, rest, plunge ahead some more. Panting with exhaustion, they reached a hard-packed snow cornice that overhung a cliff.

Hardly had they paused when a golden eagle swooped down and attacked; it struck the deer with its wings, raked their backs with its talons. Evidently the

bird was trying to panic its prey into lunging over the cliff to death on the rocks below. But the deer held together, fended off attack by rising on their hind legs and flailing at the eagle with their forefeet. The air-ground combat continued until the eagle soared off to find an easier meal.

Even when snow crunches underfoot in Jackson Hole everybody plays outdoors. Valley folk have a choice of skiing, cutter racing, ice fishing and snowplane trips. Then on summer nights, from the windows of our cabins, we look across sagebrush flats at a thousand-eyed dragon writhing along beneath the Teton ramparts —the procession of automobiles carrying visitors to this enchanted landscape.

JAMES P. BLAIR, NATIONAL GEOGRAPHIC PHOTOGRAPHER

A storybook village in a frozen valley, Jackson, Wyoming, enchants winter visitors. Snowshoers gaze down on the southern gateway to the park from the crest of a ski run on Snow King Mountain.

Whatever the season, hoofs clatter through the mile-high resort town. Around Washington's Birthday, sleigh drivers and their quick-stepping steeds vie for the annual cutter-racing championship (below). In summer, young dudes catch the stage for a leisurely rumble past old western storefronts (above).

JAMES R. SIMON AND (ABOVE) JOSEF MUENCH

WILLARD R. CULVER

Jackson Lake Lodge looks on splendor. Built by John D. Rockefeller, Jr., the $6,000,000 lodge can accommodate 1,100 guests in its 300 rooms. King-size window in the lounge brings the Tetons indoors.

Recently we drove to park headquarters, near Moose, to see Grand Teton's superintendent.

"Use of the park is skyrocketing," he said. "We now have two and a half million visitors each year. That's more than 10 times as many as we had 15 years ago. We're now the second most visited national park."

People en masse could destroy the fragile balance of wild creatures and wild land. But, to their everlasting credit, Americans are responding to the basic idea of their national parks. The cooperation of visitors and the efforts of the Park Service and other conservation agencies ensure that Grand Teton National Park will be available to future millions in all its untouched grandeur.

Thus does the park fulfill its promise as a place of rare and rich resources where city-weary families may re-create body and spirit.

GRAND TETON NATIONAL PARK *Northwestern Wyoming. Area 484 sq. mi.*

Features: Teton Range, one of world's boldest, most majestic mountain fronts, rising 7,000 feet above game-rich Jackson Hole.
Activities: Visitor centers at Moose, Jenny Lake, Colter Bay. Scenic drives, 200 miles of hiking and bridle trails. Pack trips. Climbing instruction at Jenny Lake. Boating, trout fishing; float trips down Snake River. Scenic flights, chair lift at Jackson.

Season: Road through park open year round; most activities June 15–Labor Day.
Weather: Warm, sunny days, cool evenings (elevation at lodges 6,500 ft.).
What to bring: Hiking shoes, rough-it clothing, shorts; woolens for evening. Sun lotion, camera and light meter, binoculars.
How to get there: Major highways intersect in park. See map at back of book. Wyo. 22 over Teton Pass steep, not for trailers. Air service to Jackson. For rail or bus write Grand Teton Lodge Co., Moran, Wyo.
Accommodations: Lodges at Jackson Lake, Jenny Lake; cabins at Colter Bay; write Grand Teton Lodge Co. Signal Mt. Lodge, Leek's Lodge; address, Moran, Wyo. Write park for dude ranch list. Camp and trailer grounds: first come, first served.
Services: Stores, garages; car rentals at Jackson or Jackson Lake Lodge. Nurse at Lodge, hospital in Jackson. Church services in park.
Park regulations: Camping in specified areas only. Climbers must register at Jenny Lake Ranger Station; no solo climbing. Boat permit; Wyo. fishing license. Pets on leash.

For further information write Superintendent, Grand Teton National Park, Moose, Wyoming

Glacier and its Canadian twin, Waterton Lakes Park,
form the world's first border-straddling park,
symbol of friendship between neighboring nations

GLACIER NATIONAL PARK

By GEORGE W. LONG, former Assistant Editor, National Geographic
Photographs by KATHLEEN REVIS

BEFORE US loomed a colossal wall of snow-topped mountains, rising thousands of feet straight from the Montana prairies. Towering, upswept peaks marched south in shining array from Canada. Clouds wreathed the tallest pinnacles; purple shadows, creeping across stony faces, lent mystery and allure.

As we sped westward, a gap in the mountain barrier swung open and we began the climb to Marias Pass, lowest cut across the northern U. S. Rockies and southern boundary of Glacier National Park.

We arrived in West Glacier refugees from a record eastern heat wave. The bracing mountain air reminded us of a crisp October day back home, and at Lake McDonald Lodge a welcome fire crackled in the huge lobby fireplace. It was a different world, and next morning I felt frisky as a colt when I met the superintendent at park headquarters.

"Take it easy," he said. "You'll have to do plenty of hiking and riding to know Glacier. We try to

DOUGLAS WHITESIDE

Hikers tread a catwalk on Glacier's Garden Wall. Below them tiny cars crawl along spectacular Going-to-the-Sun Road to Logan Pass, under the eaves of distant Reynolds Mountain. Mule deer (right) sports velvet antlers in July.

preserve the park's wild beauty; so there are only 70 miles of park roads compared with more than 1,000 of trails. My advice is to get out on the trails—but go easy. You've got a million acres to see."

First, to get an over-all picture of this alpine wonderland, I flew with the fire patrol in a single-motored plane. Like one of Glacier's golden eagles, we soared over lonely crags, skimmed 10,000-foot peaks, and glided over sapphire lakes.

Josephine Lake mirrors Mount Gould, banded by ancient black

We threaded valleys green with pine forests and scudded past skyland wastes torn and scarred by the elements. We swooped into huge rock amphitheaters for close looks at some of the park's several dozen glaciers.

I was impressed by the park's size. Compared with Montana, from which it is carved, it looks deceptively small on a map. Actually Glacier is a third again as big as Rhode Island. And how few the signs of human activity in this

lava 100 feet deep. The Salamander, an ice formation, suns itself on the flank of Garden Wall.

Glacier National Park: ice-carved citadel of beauty on the Continental Divide

Awe-struck Indians from the plains of Montana looked on these mountains as rocky bones pinned to the sky. Here massed against the horizon, jagged Garden Wall seemed the world's backbone; neighboring peaks fanned out like ribs. The highland proved too rugged for homesteaders, too poor for miners. Its greatest wealth lay in scenery. In 1910, 1,583 square miles became Glacier National Park, now fourth largest in the Nation after Yellowstone, Mount McKinley, and Everglades.

Soon the Great Northern Railway built Many Glacier Hotel (right), the park's biggest. Later, an annex rose beneath Allen Mountain (left). From this site, deep in the park, trails spread into the high country like arteries from the heart. Some visitors ride horses to Iceberg Lake. Others shoulder packs and strike out for Granite Park Chalet or a starlit campsite. Less active souls stroll easy walkways or boat on Swiftcurrent Lake (center).

GEORGE W. LONG

Bronzed Blackfoot displays regalia his forebears donned in wartime and for victory celebrations. Eagle feathers form his bonnet; ermine tails frame his face. Trappings glow with beading in bold patterns, a trademark of the fierce tribes that once dominated the Glacier region.

Today more than 5,000 Blackfeet farm and raise livestock on a reservation, nearly as big as Delaware, adjoining the park on the east. During the summer these next-door neighbors occasionally perform traditional tribal dances at Glacier Park Lodge. A museum in Browning, 12 miles east of East Glacier Park, recalls the past life and customs of the Indians of the Great Plains.

gigantic preserve! Smoke hung over half a dozen far-flung campgrounds; a speedboat buzzed on Lake McDonald. Cars and buses crawled along magnificent Going-to-the-Sun Road, which cuts across the rugged heart of glacierland; at Logan Pass, its 6,664-foot crest, sightseers waved gaily at us.

One day my family and I drove over this road-builders' miracle, one of the most spectacular 50-mile stretches in the New World. Not until 1933, when Going-to-the-Sun was completed, did a highway cross Glacier. A few years earlier a road had been blasted across Marias Pass. Before that, a motorist who wanted to cross the park had to ship his car over the pass by rail or detour some 500 miles by way of Great Falls and Missoula.

Tunneling, the road climbed high above tree-clad McDonald Valley. Near its one switchback, Ed Beatty, then chief park naturalist and our guide, pointed to rosettes etched in the rock. They looked like cross sections of cabbages.

"Fossil algae," Beatty explained. "Colonies of single-celled plants that lived half a billion years ago. This is among the oldest sedimentary rock in the world—exposed when the mountains were lifted and pushed eastward. In Grand Canyon you have to go a mile deep to see rock this old."

Steadily we climbed toward timber line. Shimmering cascades dropped thousands of feet from high snow fields. For miles the jagged Garden Wall stretched above us; great chasms yawned below. Joining a tourist group at Logan Pass, on the Continental Divide, we gazed on mountains carved like Matterhorns, pyramids, Mayan temples—even a savage gorilla's head. Masses of wildflowers carpeted broad meadows nearby, aptly called the Hanging Gardens.

"More than 700,000 visitors come to Glacier every summer," a ranger told us. "Over 98 percent come by car, and most just drive through on this road.

A legendary Indian walked to the sun above this spot

Going-to-the-Sun Mountain and the roadway at its foot perpetuate the myth of Napi, Old Man of the Blackfeet, who created the rocks and forests, the animals, birds, and fishes. He molded a clay man and woman and gave them life. He taught them to hunt and to farm.

His mission ended, Napi set out for his home in the sun. He climbed the noble mountain and disappeared amid swirling snows and lightning flashes. When the sun burst forth, the Indians saw his profile engraved in rock and filled with snow. Napi's face may still be seen on the far side of the 9,604-foot peak, here looming above Logan Pass.

Alpine blossoms adorn glacierland's lofty meadows. Gentians (lower right) add blue to the wildflower mosaic. The hardy glacier lily will chase receding snow to the mountaintops.

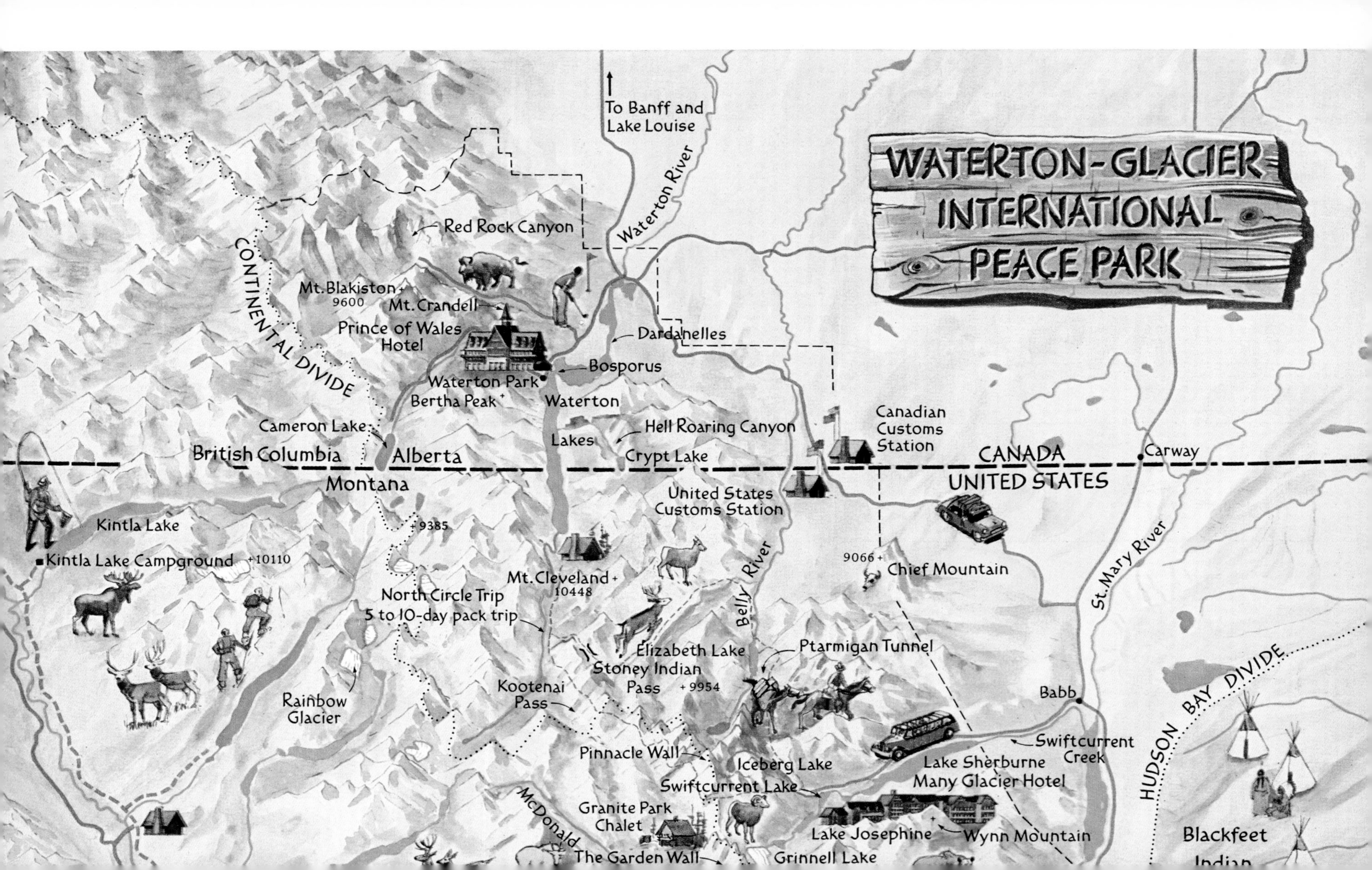
WATERTON-GLACIER INTERNATIONAL PEACE PARK
To Banff and Lake Louise
Waterton River
Red Rock Canyon
CONTINENTAL DIVIDE
Mt. Blakiston 9600
Mt. Crandell
Prince of Wales Hotel
Dardanelles
Bosporus
Waterton Park
Bertha Peak
Waterton
Lakes
Hell Roaring Canyon
Crypt Lake
Cameron Lake
Canadian Customs Station
British Columbia
Alberta
CANADA
Carway
UNITED STATES
Montana
United States Customs Station
Kintla Lake
Kintla Lake Campground
10110
9385
9066
Chief Mountain
St. Mary River
Belly River
Mt. Cleveland 10448
North Circle Trip
5 to 10-day pack trip
Elizabeth Lake
Ptarmigan Tunnel
Stoney Indian Pass
9954
Kootenai Pass
Rainbow Glacier
Babb
HUDSON BAY DIVIDE
Swiftcurrent Creek
Pinnacle Wall
Iceberg Lake
Lake Sherburne
Many Glacier Hotel
Swiftcurrent Lake
Granite Park Chalet
McDonald
Lake Josephine
Wynn Mountain
The Garden Wall
Grinnell Lake
Blackfeet

Going-to-the-Sun Road
Pass
Hanging Gardens
Goat Mt.
St. Mary Lake
Postcard Point
Blackfeet Highway
Mt. Cannon
Avalanche Creek Campground
Baring Falls
9157 Reynolds Mt.
Red Eagle Mt.
9552 Mahtotopa Mt.
Fusillade Mt.
Little Chief Mt.
Mt. Brown
Sperry Chalet
Sperry Glacier
9034 Citadel Mt.
Cut Bank Creek
Lake McDonald Lodge
Gunsight Pass & Lake
Sprague Creek Campground
Lake Ellen Wilson
Jackson Glacier
To Browning & Museum of the Plains Indian
Flathead River
Lake McDonald
CONTINENTAL DIVIDE
Triple Divide Peak 8011
Kiowa
Apgar
Glacier National Park Headquarters
Mt. Stimson 10165
Flathead
Trick Falls
West Glacier
Two Medicine Lake
Glacier Park Lodge
National
East Glacier Park
Whitefish
Coram
Columbia Falls
Hungry Horse
Hungry Horse Dam
Forest
8700
Marias Pass 5215
Hungry Horse Reservoir
Flathead River
Essex
Great Northern Railway
0 5 10
STATUTE MILES
© National Geographic Map
Drawn by Irvin E. Alleman
I. Alleman

DONALD S. MATTESON

Sure-footed nanny and her kid sidle up to a ledge above Gunsight Lake. Here in summer the mother sheds. Some 800 mountain goats, with soft-centered nonskid hoofs, make Glacier Park their home.

Fortunately not all are as hurried as one man who rushed up to me, glanced at his watch, and said, 'I've got just two hours. What can I see?' "

On our way back from St. Mary Lake we stopped for a look at distant Jackson Glacier, once part of Blackfoot Glacier, one of the largest ice masses in the U. S. Rockies. Blackfoot shrank into several small glaciers.

"For awhile we were afraid we'd lose all our glaciers," Beatty said. "Several of the biggest disappeared, and others shrank as much as 75 percent. But since 1950 they've held their own. During recent years the park's average temperature has dropped several degrees, and the amount of rain and snow has nearly doubled. We think the world may be entering a colder, wetter cycle."

When our drive was over, my younger daughter complained, "No bears."

"They're all up in the hills eating berries," Beatty told her. "There's a big crop this year, which helps solve our bear problem. Sometimes they get too friendly and injure people without trying. Perhaps you've noticed the roadside jingle: 'Highway bears are often rude. They eat fingers as well as food.' "

In the evenings I had noticed a light hanging far above the hotel like a star. Mount Brown fire lookout, I was told. Eager to go up, I arranged to ride with

Not-so-sure-footed girl inches along a rocky thumb overlooking Lake Ellen Wilson. Trout in this deep-blue cup on the lip of the Continental Divide offer fishermen some of the finest sport in the park.

the lookout inspector on his next trip.

Miss Kathleen Revis, who made these splendid color photographs for the National Geographic Society, went along to take pictures of mountain goats. Her tirelessness on the park's trails had surprised even the rangers.

The lookout trail, with 33 switchbacks, climbs 3,500 feet in four steep miles. Up this zigzag path mules haul the watchers' water and supplies. When I spoke of it to Jay Lytle, an old-time wrangler, he shook his head.

"Son," he chuckled, "that trail's a horse-killer on the way up and a dude-killer on the way down." But Jay, I found, had stretched the truth a mite.

Married couples, mostly college students, man the lookout towers. Honeymooning Jack and Nyla Hobbs of Chanute, Kansas, were the Mount Brown team. Their tower windows faced a sea of wild, snowcapped peaks. Mountain goats frolicked at close range.

"They're friskiest at night," Nyla smiled. "At first they kept us awake for hours, racing up and down the steps and butting the tower."

Mount Brown was my first saddle trip in the park. That evening as I tenderly lowered myself into a soft lobby chair, I recalled Irvin Cobb's quip after he took a Glacier horseback trip.

"Call that thing a saddle?" snorted the humorist. "It's a chafing dish!"

But you can have a jostling in the park without getting aboard a horse. Even motorists get their teeth rattled on Glacier's oldest road—to Kintla Lake in the remote northwest corner, an area kept almost as virgin wilderness. Big lakes lure fishermen, while frontier conditions test hardy campers and hikers.

As we drove through pine forests and skirted lush meadows, ranger Harold Estey told of winter ski patrols here, when snow drifts up to 30 feet deep.

"Great country for game," he said. "A regular zoo. We see big herds of deer, elk, moose—even wolves and mountain lions. Ever hear about the moose that

July snowfields lure shirt-sleeved hikers. Party above tramps a slope in sight of Mount Cannon. Rompers at right slither toward Grinnell Lake, whitened by rock powder ground beneath a glacier.

Naturalist's rope holds Boy Scouts from a crevasse's icy jaws on Grinnell Glacier,

a frigid tide still on the move.

Creeping about 35 feet a year, Grinnell gathers a rocky harvest. Stone imbedded in the glacier's bottom acts as a massive rasp. When the frozen river meets uneven bedrock, stresses open yawning fissures.

BETH VIEREGGE

Wildflowers blanket rock-strewn Fifty Mountain Camp near Kootenai Pass. During the short summer, Glacier's highlands display gardens with nearly every vista. Here arnica mixes its yellow with the red of monkey flowers. Close-up above shows the latter's resemblance to a monkey's mouth. Two petals form the upper lip, three the lower.

battled a bulldozer on this road? Thought it was a rival, I guess. He shook his antlers, pawed the ground, and charged head on into the 'dozer—not once, but three times. Finally staggered off. That driver sure was glad to see him go."

At Kintla Lake women were cooking lunch over open fires. Men chopped wood, hauled water, or unlimbered fishing tackle while children played. One camper strummed a guitar. We liked the easy, welcome-stranger atmosphere.

"Surprising number of people get up here," the ranger said. "We logged 2,000 camper-days last month, and many campers return year after year."

One morning I joined a group on chilly Logan Pass for a hike along the Garden Wall. The spectacular trail is strung above timber line between Going-to-the-Sun Road and the Wall's jagged, narrow top. As we neared Granite Park Chalet the ranger-naturalist pointed to a steep path angling upward.

"In several summers here I've never climbed the Garden Wall," he said.

Hoary marmot abandons caution for a friendly handout. Unable to outrun natural foes—bear, coyote, and golden eagle—the marmot family posts a lookout. Sentry's whistle sends his fellows scurrying.

Gabled roof of the continent: clouds swirl beneath isolated Granite Park Chalet,

"It's a real stiff climb—1,500 feet up in only nine-tenths of a mile—but I hear the view up there is terrific. Any volunteers?"

To my surprise, 16 out of 24 did volunteer. We started up, while the others pushed on toward the chalet. After a hundred yards, my knees rebelled, then thought better of it. Loose shale and a rollicking wind made footing difficult. A magnificent Rocky Mountain bighorn ram bounded effortlessly ahead of us.

Finally we reached the top—9,000 feet. Before us stretched the fabulous Many Glacier region. Grinnell Glacier lay in a vast rocky cradle. Snow fields draped peaks and slopes like colossal sheets put out to dry. Beyond lakes spar-

goal of hikers on Garden Wall Trail. Snow fields patch the slopes of 9,004-foot Heavens Peak.

kling like scattered bits of jade we could make out the distant prairies, faint and flat. It was a full minute before anyone could speak.

I must confess to a feeling of conquest when I reached the hotel that evening. I had hiked 16 miles since morning, climbed more than 2,000 feet, and stood atop the Garden Wall! I came to earth with something of a thud when I overheard two waitresses, college girls, talking while serving dinner.

"How was your day off?" one asked the other.

"Oh, wonderful. Hiked to Canada. Thirty-two miles—up over Stoney Indian Pass to Waterton. Simply marvelous."

Waterton Lake forms a path through the heart of the International Peace Park

Canada's 204-square-mile Waterton Lakes National Park begins where Glacier National Park leaves off. In 1932 the two parks were dedicated as Waterton-Glacier International Peace Park, marking a long era of good will. A 20-foot swath through forest identified the boundary; people pass freely from one side to the other.

Both parks preserve glacier-carved scenery, but, oddly enough, all remaining glaciers lie south of the border.

Here Canada looks down 7 miles of mountain-walled water into the United States. The Canadian government operates Waterton Park townsite (right) but permits private homes and stores.

Motor launch *International* leaves town on a morning run to the United States end of the lake. Hikers below await its arrival near Waterton Ranger Station in Glacier Park.

GETTING back into condition, I reveled in our almost daily hikes. I relished the picnic lunches on lofty meadows deep with flowers and the ice-cold mountain water. On the high trails there is a curious sense of being walled off from the world's turmoil. Life's pace is scaled down to a placid two miles an hour. Night brings delicious fatigue and deep, untroubled sleep.

Moving to Many Glacier, we explored the Swiftcurrent Lake region I had seen from the Garden Wall. Here, several ancient glaciers had joined forces and bulldozed their way to the plains, leaving unbelievably beautiful valleys that reached into this mountain land like the imprint of a colossal hand.

One name you hear frequently in this part of the park is Grinnell. It labels a glacier, mountain, waterfall, point, lake, and the reddish rock that colors so many formations. And little wonder. George Bird Grinnell—explorer, naturalist, and author—roamed here in the 1880's and '90's, when it was a frontier,

"Giddap" is your open-sesame to the Canadian wilderness

The riding party organizes at Prince of Wales Hotel, a 250-guest lodge that looks like a Hänsel-and-Gretel cottage in the distance (above). At the Bosporus, a strait joining two of the three Waterton Lakes, wranglers swim the mounts (left); riders cross by boat. On the trail, horses file through rocks and stunted evergreens in sight of Bertha Peak and Mount Crandell. At journey's end, riders climb to Crypt Lake (next page).

Mountains hide Crypt Lake, a jewel cut by glaciers

To reach this Shangri-La the visitor must crawl through a 50-foot tunnel and traverse a sheer ledge into the amphitheater, or cirque, gouged by ice from crumbling sedimentary rock. The lovely tarn, whose flowered slopes lie in Canada and shadowed cliffs in the United States, drains through a cavern into Hell Roaring Canyon.

and discovered the glacier that bears his name. A tireless fighter for conservation, he urged vigorously that Glacier be made a national park. So, too, did the *National Geographic* in an article vividly describing the mountain fastness.

One morning, with some 50 hikers, we climbed the steep flank of Mount Grinnell to Grinnell Glacier. This huge ice lake covers an area equal to about 35 city blocks and measures 400 feet deep in places. Relentlessly it grinds forward, its melting front feeding a sparkling waterfall that drops to the valley below.

At glacier's edge the ranger-naturalist tied a long rope around his waist and told everyone to grab hold. "Otherwise somebody would fall into a crevasse before you could say 'Gletschermilch,' " he said. Like a huge snake we shuffled over the glacier, the naturalist probing ahead for soft spots with an ice ax. We skirted crevasses and yawning holes, and explored caves of blue-white ice.

"Glacier Park doesn't get its name from the 40-odd masses of ice here now," our guide said, "but because huge Ice Age glaciers carved its rugged scenery. Half a mile deep, they covered all but the highest peaks—like the Greenland Ice-cap today. They gouged the wide valleys and rocky amphitheaters you see. They scooped out the lake bottoms and sliced some mountains thin—like the Garden Wall up there. Today's glaciers are only ice cubes by comparison. Incidentally, more than 100 feet of snow falls here at Grinnell each year."

High on many a nearby slope are strange tunnels—shafts left from old-time mining booms. Stirred by tales of rich strikes, prospectors probed the region in the early 1890's. Since the land belonged to the Blackfeet, the Great White Father paid his adopted children $1,500,000 for these mountains.

"Crowds of miners rushed in," recalled Blackie, the bearded wrangler at Many Glacier Hotel. "A boom town, Altyn, sprang up here, complete with seven saloons. Not a stick or stone remains today. Just as well, I guess. Like as not there'd be no park if the miners' hopes had really panned out."

OUR DAUGHTERS had been looking forward to visiting Canada, to crossing the "frontier" and entering a "foreign" country. At the Canadian-United States border, the customhouse of each nation flies the flags of both; no ceremony is required as you cross. In 1932 the two nations pooled their scenic treasures, creating Waterton-Glacier International Peace Park, symbol of good neighborliness. The heart of the Canadian park is Waterton Lake, a gleaming sapphire set in rugged mountains. Both countries share this jewel, for it crosses the international boundary.

Like most sightseers, we browsed about Waterton's shops, which featured British china and tweeds, Hudson's Bay blankets, Scottish woolens, and English toffee. Either country's dollars were accepted. With such goods on display, and a wife and two daughters in tow, I found both kinds disappeared like magic.

To sample Waterton's trails, we rode horseback to secluded Crypt Lake, high in a hanging valley on the international border. Many of Waterton's other beauty spots can be reached by car—places like Red Rock Canyon and lovely Cameron Lake. Swimmers sun on the beaches of this sparkling tarn while skiers glide on a snow field draped on its rocky amphitheater.

When we recrossed the border, I realized that September had crept up on us. Evenings were getting short and nights frosty. New snow had dusted the highest peaks; leaves of the mountain maple were turning crimson. We climbed from Lake McDonald's forested shores to mile-high Sperry Chalet to spend a night.

There the world's worries seemed a universe away. A harvest moon silvered the landscape; a breeze stirred, bringing a breath of chill. Soon, I mused, snow would blanket the mountains again. Man would retreat; animals would start their winter sleep or seek the sheltered valleys. For nine months the Ice Age, creator of this land of many splendors, would return to claim its own.

A fallen cottonwood serves young divers sporting in the crystal waters of Lake McDonald.

GLACIER NATIONAL PARK *Northwestern Montana. Area 1,583 sq. mi.*

Features: Superb glacier-carved mountain wilderness similar to central Alaska in climate, flora, and fauna. Some 40 glaciers, 200 lakes; conifer forests, flowered alpine meadows. Moose, deer, bear, coyote, bighorn sheep, mountain goat, cougar, fisher.
Activities: Sightseeing along 50-mi. Going-to-the-Sun Road. 1,000 miles of trails. Day and overnight saddle trips. Boating, trout fishing; wilderness camping. Campfire programs. Guided bus, launch, and trail trips. For all-expense tours write Glacier Park, Inc., East Glacier Park, Mont., or (Oct.–May) P.O. Box 4250, Tucson, Ariz.
Season: Normally June 15–Sept. 10.
Weather: Bracing; occasional rain squalls (elevation at hotels 4,500 ft. or under).
What to bring: Hiking shoes and rough-it clothing; woolens for evening. Raincoat, camera, binoculars.
How to get there: From east or west, US 2. South, US 93 or 89. See map at back of book. Great Northern Railway. Buses from Missoula, Shelby, Kalispell, or Great Falls, Mont. West Coast Airlines serves nearby cities; surface connections to park.
Accommodations: Hotels, motels, and cabins: Glacier Park, Many Glacier, Lake McDonald, Apgar Village, Swiftcurrent, Rising Sun; write Glacier Park, Inc., for reservations. Chalets: Granite Park and Sperry reached by trail, write B. Ross Luding, Martin City, Mont. Trailer and campgrounds at Rising Sun, Many Glacier, Two Medicine, Apgar, St. Mary, Avalanche, Fish Creek; camping only at Sprague Creek. Eight remote campgrounds.
Services: Cafeterias, stores, garages; car rentals at East Glacier Park and Whitefish. Religious services in park.
Park regulations: Fishing by rod in hand only; no license needed; no live bait. Fire permit required for wilderness camping. No molesting wildlife. No pets on trails.

For further information write Supt., Glacier National Park, West Glacier, Montana

Thirsty sightseers split a watermelon along the Continental Divide

Indians crossing the continent's backbone trudged over a trail amid these snowy peaks. Today Trail Ridge Road follows that path through Colorado's Rocky Mountain National Park. For 11 of its miles, motorists ride above the 11,500-foot timber line. Flower-flecked alpine meadows and plunging

canyons invite a pause. Looking west one gazes on a loop of the Continental Divide; one segment follows ridges in the middle distance, another the white horizon of the Never Summer Mountains.

Snows usually block the route, part of transcontinental US 34, from the middle of October to June.

ROCKY MOUNTAIN
NATIONAL PARK

By KATHLEEN REVIS
Photographs by the author

RESTLESS KIT CARSON felt the pull of this scenery when he trapped beaver through these parts in 1840. But you need not be a rugged mountain man to come under the Rockies' spell. Though formidable to look at, these Colorado peaks are friendly and easy to enjoy.

The casual tourist can motor along cloud-drifted Trail Ridge Road, one of the Nation's highest. From 12,000 feet he looks down on seas of alpine wildflowers—and up toward 42 still higher peaks. One-third of the park lies above the timber line.

Whether he goes by car, astride a horse, or on his own two feet, he has a world of sights to see: the works of today's beavers and of ancient vanished glaciers . . . the bounding bighorn ram . . . the swift grace of deer and elk in the afternoon light . . . the grandeur of perpetual snows . . . the petal perfection of moss campion.

To me, this area between Estes Park and Grand Lake makes the best introduction to mountain fun. High point of the park is 14,255-foot Longs Peak.

In 1864, after failing to climb it, one man wrote, "We are quite sure that no living creature, unless it had wings to

Mountaineers' reward: a view and a victory

From a pinnacle as sharp as a conifer, hikers survey the headwaters of the Colorado River. At right, a party returns from Longs Peak through the glacier-gouged Trough, on the Keyhole climbing route.

A youthful posse dodges a highland shower in Beaver Meadow

Rocky Mountain National Park, distinguished by its glacial meadows, evergreen forests, and the raw beauty of the great Front Range of the Rockies, was established in 1915. But neighboring ranches date from homesteading days in the 1860's. Today many throw open their gates to dude guests. Together these ranches and local stables maintain the largest concentration of trail horses in the United States. Within the park mounts are available at Glacier Creek Livery and in Kawuneechee Valley.

These youngsters ride across glacier-formed Beaver Meadow, a favorite haunt for deer. Below, a junior cowgirl dons a slicker in a summer shower.

fly, was ever upon its summit . . . that no man will ever be." But four years later a party climbed to the top.

A few generations later, as a novice, I tried the peak myself. Longs Peak by then had been scaled by hundreds young and old, and I took encouragement from that.

I set out at 6:30 one August morning, weighted by an unfamiliar pack. Two thousand feet above camp we passed timber

line, where century-old trees grow only waist-high. The trail topped a glacial moraine; we caught our first full view of the dizzying cliff that rope-climbers ascend. But we took the easier cable route that lay to the north.

As we climbed over boulders, my lungs seemed about to burst. Once "above burro line," as one climber put it, I got my second wind. Gripping the cable anchored to sheer rock, I pulled myself up. After six and a half exhausting hours I stood on top. Naturalist Enos A. Mills, veteran of some 300 Longs Peak climbs and father of the park, considered this summit "an area sufficient for a baseball game." But to me, baseball held less allure than the superb view, a victorious downward hike—and a night of solid rest.

Fording Big Thompson River, a wrangler brings in horses from mountain pasture. Ice once filled this valley. A row of trees at upper right grows atop the moraine that marks the ancient glacier's edge.

Ground squirrel visits with a friend.

ROCKY MOUNTAIN NATIONAL PARK

Features: Colorado wonderland encompassing 84 peaks above 11,000 feet in its 411 square miles. Moraines, lakes, conifer forests, some 700 wild-flower species, bighorn sheep. Adjoins Shadow Mountain National Recreation Area.
Activities: Moraine Park and Alpine visitor centers, scenic drives, riding, climbing, trout fishing. Nature walks, campfire programs. Winter sports.
Season: Chiefly June–Sept. Park open year round.
Weather: Crisp (elevation 7,800 to 14,255 ft.)
Clothing: Hiking togs and woolens.
How to get there: From east or west, US 34. See map at back of book. Air, rail, bus via Denver.
Accommodations: Hotels, lodges, camps (write park for franchise list; or chamber of commerce at Estes Park or Grand Lake for out-of-park spots). Campgrounds, trailer sites.
Park Regulations: Fires, camping in campgrounds only. Colorado fishing license. No pets on trails.

For further information write Superintendent, Rocky Mountain National Park, Estes Park, Colo.

Grand Lake, adjacent to the park, brims with water sports and boasts the "highest yacht club in the United States."

Chill waters of Chasm Falls crash down a granite flume in Fall River Canyon

DEVILS TOWER

YOU COME UPON IT in the northeastern corner of Wyoming where the Black Hills dwindle into plains. Suddenly the rolling land is rent by a solitary, massive tower of rock, almost shocking in its impact. Devils Tower, a weird volcanic pillar, thrusts like a nubbin of the underworld through the gentle soil. In 1906 President Theodore Roosevelt declared the Wyoming wonder our first national monument, one of nature's legacies to be protected by law.

Devils Tower, soaring 852 feet above the parking circle, rises 1,280 feet above the Belle Fourche River, flowing nearby. Geologists debate its origin. Most agree that molten rock welling up within the earth intruded surface layers, possibly 50 million years ago. Erosion washed away the enfolding soil, leaving the monolith to stand alone. Encircled by majestic stands of ponderosa pine, Devils Tower seems itself like the petrified stump of some gigantic prehistoric tree. The spectacular flutings on its flanks resulted from crack patterns that shot through the buried magma as it cooled and shrank.

Prairie falcons nest among these columns that average ten feet across, while chipmunks scurry through the sage on the flat acre-and-a-half top. At its base, a colony of prairie dogs entertains visitors—some 100,000 each year.

THEODORE ROOSEVELT

NATIONAL MEMORIAL PARK

DARKNESS HID THE BADLANDS of western North Dakota as the transcontinental train panted to a stop. A bespectacled easterner stepped to the platform of Little Missouri depot and gathered his hunting gear. Theodore Roosevelt, not yet 25, planned to shoot a buffalo in this frontierland of 1883.

He got his buffalo. But the starkly eroded, freakishly painted hills and the rugged ways of a ranch captured him for life. Within 20 days of his arrival, T. R. bought 400 head of cattle. Thus began his love affair with the West. He remained a champion of the wilderness, a guardian of its resources.

Teddy Roosevelt would have been "dee-lighted" to know that his Elkhorn Ranch and two huge neighboring areas now form a national memorial park. In these three tracts, totaling 110 square miles, visitors camp and hike among weird buttes, sagebrush plains, grassy bottom lands, cottonwood groves, and scatterings of petrified wood. They walk on reddish clay turned into bricklike rock by the heat of smoldering lignite beneath the surface.

Buffalo were disappearing when Roosevelt came to hunt them. Now, in the protection of his park, they thrive along with antelope and deer.

Devils Tower stands like the stump of a monster tree, talus strewn at its base like chips from Paul Bunyan's ax. Sioux Indians claimed a giant grizzly clawed the formation, causing its fluting. In 1941 a parachutist reached the summit the "easy" way. Unable to descend, he shivered a week until rescue climbers helped him down.

DEAN CONGER, NATIONAL GEOGRAPHIC PHOTOGRAPHER

MOUNT RUSHMORE

By BART McDOWELL, National Geographic Staff

THE PRESIDENT placed a drill in the hands of a stocky, energetic man. The tool bit deep into granite. Thus in 1927 did Calvin Coolidge, self-conscious in a ten-gallon hat, launch the work of sculptor Gutzon Borglum upon the face of Mount Rushmore in South Dakota.

For 14 summers mountain foliage—pine, spruce, silver birch, aspen—shuddered to the blast of dynamite, the chatter of jackhammer. When the last stone fragment tumbled from the mountain, stillness settled over the valley. Carved from this Western Gibraltar stood the world's most heroic sculpture.

"Trained but not tamed," men said of Idaho-born Borglum. A famed disciple of Rodin in Paris, he was a man of many enthusiasms—writer, engineer, an impatient patriot. "There is not a monument in the country as big as a snuff box," he said in 1916. America demanded "an enlarged dimension—a new scale."

Borglum found that scale, and a challenge for all his talents, when historian Doane Robinson suggested a monumental sculpture in the Black Hills. Near the town of Keystone the sculptor examined an exposed granite core. The southeastern face of 5,725-foot Mount Rushmore offered greatest promise. Private funds, then Federal appropriations got the job underway.

Borglum fashioned plaster models, measured them, then dropped proportionate plumb lines from the mountaintop. Faces would be 60 feet tall—as high as a five-story building. Dynamite shots probed reliable rock beneath the deeply fissured surface. Nine times Borglum remade his models to conform to solid stone. He climbed scaffolds training miners to help him; he darted about the canyon to test the effect of shadow upon a cheek or chin.

First face to be completed was, appropriately, George Washington's. Next emerged Thomas Jefferson, eyes fixed on the horizon his Louisiana Purchase had assured. Brow-first, Abraham Lincoln took shape, melancholy in his mission to keep America intact. Last, with a square jaw apt in granite, Theodore

Giants of history—George Washington, Thomas Jefferson, Theodore Roosevelt, and Abraham Lincoln—keep vigil in the Black Hills of South Dakota. The national memorial stands visible for 60 miles.

U. S. AIR FORCE

BLACK HILLS STUDIOS, INC.

Stone eyes look on eternity. When sculptor Borglum learned that this granite erodes perhaps an inch in 100,000 years, he added a foot to Washington's nose. "It will give him another million years!"

Roosevelt's image evoked the vigor of 20th century America. But Gutzon Borglum did not live to see his masterpiece complete; he died at 74, leaving seven months' work to the son he had named for Lincoln.

"I don't intend that it shall be just a three-day tourist wonder," Borglum once said. A million tourists a year testify to his success. They stop in hotels and motor courts in Rapid City and Keystone. They picnic and camp in nearby Black Hills National Forest or feast in the restaurant at the Rushmore site. At the visitor center they listen to a ranger recount the story of the memorial.

They come not to gaze at a giant curiosity, but to observe a monument as large and permanent as the dream these four men made real. Some return time and again to watch morning sunlight move across the faces, to see the figures backed by a Western sunset, to attend the nightly summer ceremony in the amphitheater as floodlights whiten the granite against a black sky.

At whatever time of day, the setting inspires an inward awe. Frank Lloyd Wright left aside all his brilliant barbs when he saw Rushmore: "The noble countenances emerge as though the spirit of the mountain heard a human plan and itself became a human countenance." Vacationers, freshly conscious of the meaning of citizenship, say even more by their reflective silence.

Lincoln's quartz-seamed face dwarfs Park Service men. Eye pupil is four feet across, mouth 22 feet long, head twice as high as that of Egypt's Sphinx. Full figure would stand 465 feet tall. Climbing by visitors is prohibited.

BATES LITTLEHALES, NATIONAL GEOGRAPHIC PHOTOGRAPHER

BATES LITTLEHALES, NATIONAL GEOGRAPHIC PHOTOGRAPHER

Delicate calcite veins lace the limestone chambers of Wind Cave, 46 road miles south of Mount Rushmore.

Millions of years ago a sea that covered this region deposited limestone layers. Pressure from below warped the earth's crust into the Black Hills dome and fractured these ancient beds. Percolating limy waters mortared the cracks with calcite. When subterranean streams dissolved out Wind Cave's chambers, the resistant veins remained as projecting fins and boxes.

"Like the work of a mad set designer for a horror movie," one tourist described the grotesque passages, the frostwork ledges, the pigeonholes on the rust-red walls. Boxwork formations are found in only a few of the world's caverns.

WIND CAVE

TUCKED IN A GULLY on the southeast flank of South Dakota's Black Hills lies a whistling barometer. This rare phenomenon is a hole in the ground, ten inches across, opening to a cave below. As atmospheric pressure changes, air sucks into or blows out from its rocky throat, sometimes with bush-rattling force.

A Black Hills pioneer, Tom Bingham, discovered the mysterious cleft in 1881. But Indians probably knew of it long before, for Sioux legends tell of a sacred cave of the winds through which their forefathers entered the West.

Today hundreds of palefaces daily step into this happy hunting ground of geology—Wind Cave's honeycombed walls and ceilings, in soft, warm hues, are the world's finest known boxwork formations. Electricity lights 1¼ of the 4½ miles of explored passageways that descend some 240 feet. April through October ranger-led tours examine the North Room, Post Office, Rookery, Queen's Drawing Room, and Cathedral. In the Fairgrounds, ultraviolet light sets aglow the calcite fantasies of a frostwork ledge. When the elevator surfaces with visitors, sweatered against the cave's 47° chill, the warm hills seem charged with blues and greens to eyes attuned to reds and browns.

You needn't be a spelunker to savor the cave's setting. The rolling plains, laced with ponderosa pine, forge a treasured link with the sea of grass that once stretched a thousand miles. Then came cattle to overgraze it, plows to break the virgin sod. Wind Cave National Park preserves a lingering segment of the Great Plains where buffalo roam, knee-deep in wind-rippled grass.

A buffalo once charged into a bus in the park. Simply ornery—or perhaps he was stirred by ancestral memories of days when thundering herds stopped transcontinental trains for hours. A century ago more than 50,000,000 roved the heart of America. Wanton slaughter cut their numbers to less than 1,000. Now some 9,000 of the exiled monarchs live in U. S. preserves.

About 350 Great Plains buffalo graze peacefully and freely on the rolling prairie land of Wind Cave's 44-square-mile fenced-in range. In winter they swing massive heads from side to side, battering through deep snow to find forage. They share their domain with elk, deer, pronghorn—and thousands of prairie dogs. These bustling rodents maintain more than a dozen colonies here. Each hummocky town is clear of long grass, for the little fellows combine appetite with a shrewd insistence on a clear view around. A nonvegetarian coyote on the outskirts sends them diving for their burrows.

While observing buffalo, take a tip from Mr. Prairie Dog: be ready to duck for cover. A buffalo is no domestic animal. He can weigh a ton, run 30 miles an hour, and turn on a buffalo nickel. And he's unpredictable. The park highway usually provides a close enough view of the great shaggy beasts.

The park's visitor center is open all year; a campground and lunchroom operate May to October. Nearby Hot Springs and Custer provide accommodations.

JEWEL CAVE

JEWEL CAVE APPEALS to those who like their caves primitive but safe, unadorned with graded walkways, elevators, and electric lights. Ladders join various levels where the hand lantern lights dazzling displays of calcite. Like nearby Wind Cave, Jewel Cave was carved when underground streams invaded fractured Black Hills limestone. Then calcium carbonate in the water spangled the chambers with crystals. With infinite leisure these grew in glittering pyramidal forms, some truncated, others shaped like nailheads or dog teeth.

June through August a park ranger guides hour-long tours through this little gem of a national monument set amid the virgin ponderosa pines off US 16.

The prairie dog, a species of ground squirrel, is named for his barking call.

BADLANDS

A THREE-TOED HORSE once roamed swampy grasslands east of the Black Hills and there he met his death. Perhaps a saber-toothed cat killed him. Or he had a fracas with a rhinoceros, or simply got mired. Layers of silt and volcanic ash covered his bones, which petrified and rested there some 25,000,000 years. Climates changed. The region dried up. Rare but violent rains cut deep into the earth, and ancient sediments again were on the move.

Finally a thunderstorm washed the last bit of clay from a leg bone, and it rattled into the gully below. In the summer of 1958 a man wandering among the Badlands rills spied the fossil bone. He picked it up, mused a bit at the wonder of this ancient world, and, heeding park regulations, put it down where he got it—next to the tooth of an extinct giant pig, near the rib fragment of a tiny deer, not far from two huge turtle fossils.

These relics of the past litter the gullies of South Dakota's Badlands National

Monument, a broad 40-mile strip of eroding clays between the White River and the high plains to the north.

"A no man's land of unimaginable desolation," a journalist once characterized this terrain, and so it seems at first. Tortured pinnacles crowd the highway. Parking turnouts survey a marching sea of buttes, battlements, haystack hills. Fancy sees in them the Pyramids, Great Wall of China, Kremlin, Taj Mahal, and Aztec and Mayan temples. Through them all runs a fugue of color: pastel blues, pinks, greens, and tan compose banded rhythms along the edges of table-flat layers. Kaleidoscopic patterns shift as evening shadows crawl across the crumbling wilderness. In cool moonlight, black shadows lace the luminous ridges and spires; the region's stark beauty almost persuades the observer he has been whisked to another planet.

But all is not desolation. On high ground, prairie dog, cottontail, and coyote scurry through grass that crowds erosion's sharp edge. White-tailed deer and pronghorn sprint through lowland meadows. In spring, wildflowers abound.

More than a million people a year travel US 16A through the Badlands on their way west, to the Black Hills and national parks beyond. Most content themselves with stops at the Cedar Pass visitor center and scenic overlooks along the 30-mile park highway. Many time their visits for early morning or evening to avoid the heat and glare of midday. Children work off energy scampering over ridges and ledges. Parents stretch their legs in fossil-rich ravines that have lured the world's scientists for more than a hundred years.

Some stay in the lodge or campground at Cedar Pass, or in one of two primitive campgrounds. Often the next stop is the South Dakota School of Mines in Rapid City, where an impressive museum display brings to life long-gone Badlands beasts.

In this weird land of long ago scientists hunt big game from Oligocene times. Erosion uncovers rich fossil finds. Here the clay mounds are cracked into millions of inch-square chunks by the hot, dry air; hikers become dehydrated too. Dakota Indians called the area *mako sica*—bad land.

STEWART ANDERSON

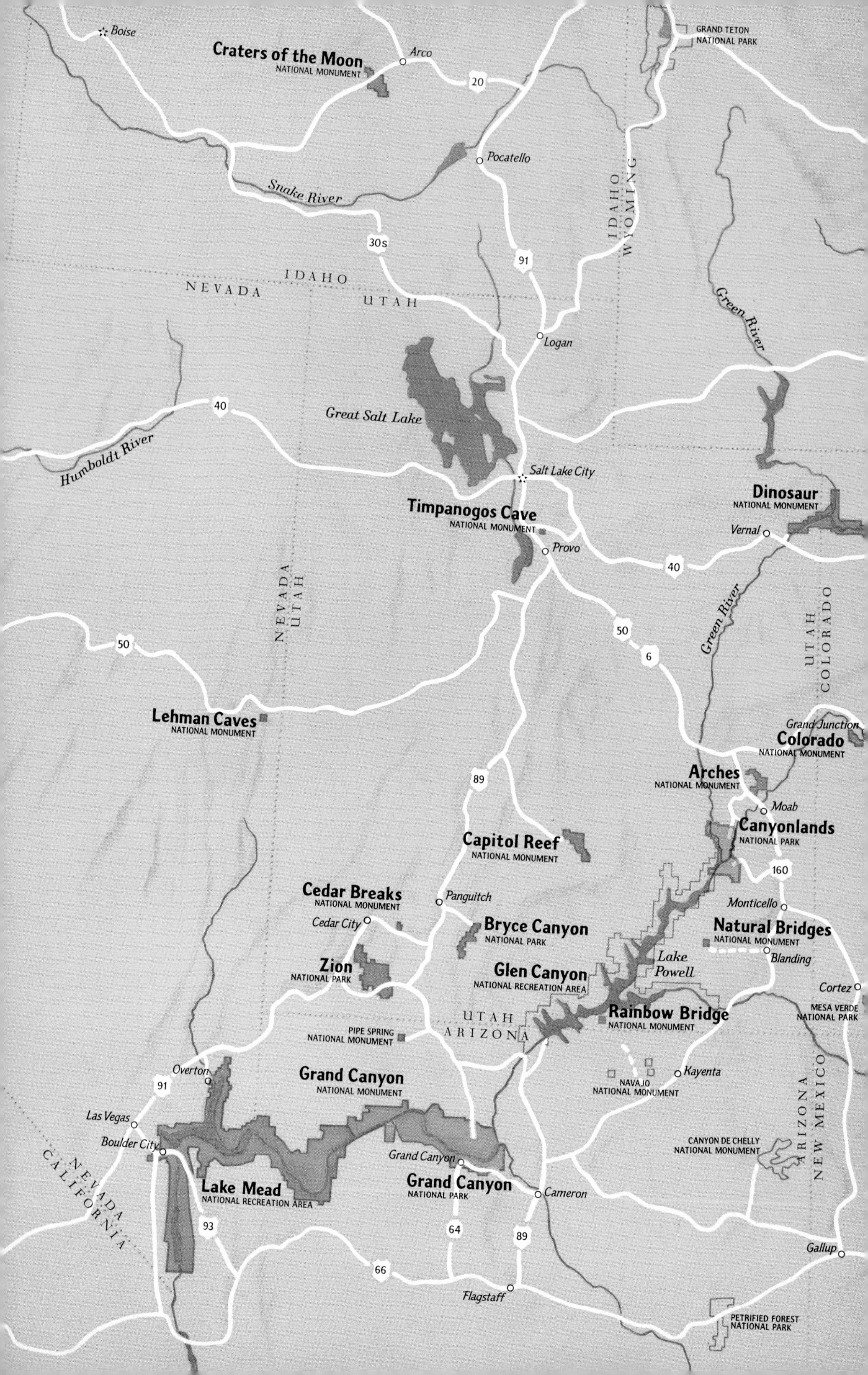

Boise
Craters of the Moon
NATIONAL MONUMENT
Arco
20
GRAND TETON
NATIONAL PARK
Pocatello
Snake River
IDAHO
WYOMING
30s
91
IDAHO
NEVADA
UTAH
Logan
Green River
Great Salt Lake
40
Humboldt River
Salt Lake City
Dinosaur
NATIONAL MONUMENT
Timpanogos Cave
NATIONAL MONUMENT
Vernal
Provo
40
NEVADA
UTAH
Green River
UTAH
COLORADO
50
50
6
Lehman Caves
NATIONAL MONUMENT
Grand Junction
Colorado
NATIONAL MONUMENT
89
Arches
NATIONAL MONUMENT
Moab
Canyonlands
NATIONAL PARK
Capitol Reef
NATIONAL MONUMENT
160
Cedar Breaks
NATIONAL MONUMENT
Panguitch
Monticello
Cedar City
Bryce Canyon
NATIONAL PARK
Natural Bridges
NATIONAL MONUMENT
Lake
Powell
Blanding
Zion
NATIONAL PARK
Glen Canyon
NATIONAL RECREATION AREA
Cortez
Rainbow Bridge
NATIONAL MONUMENT
MESA VERDE
NATIONAL PARK
UTAH
ARIZONA
PIPE SPRING
NATIONAL MONUMENT
Overton
Kayenta
NAVAJO
NATIONAL MONUMENT
91
Grand Canyon
NATIONAL MONUMENT
ARIZONA
NEW MEXICO
Las Vegas
Boulder City
NEVADA
CALIFORNIA
CANYON DE CHELLY
NATIONAL MONUMENT
Grand Canyon
Grand Canyon
NATIONAL PARK
Lake Mead
NATIONAL RECREATION AREA
Cameron
93
64
89
Gallup
66
Flagstaff
PETRIFIED FOREST
NATIONAL PARK

PART TWO

THE GREAT PLATEAU

THIS IS THE LAND of juniper and sandstone. It is a dry and thirsty land, yet water made it what it is.

Water formed its rocks in the beds of ancient seas. Water sculptured the rocks when they rose mile-high. Water gnawed its gorges, carved its square-cut buttes. Water stripped away its flesh, leaving a bright and jumbled skeleton.

Today incredible ribs of stone arch from slickrock walls of hidden chasms. Painted pinnacles raise bony fingers beside red cliffs that mothered them.

"Ours has been the first, and will doubtless be the last, party to visit this profitless locality," one explorer said. But now, a century later, more than a million and a half people each year stand on Grand Canyon's rims. Other millions enjoy parks farther north.

Still it remains a remote, sparsely settled land, of tremendous distances and violent contrasts. Black storm clouds invade the clear air with the clamor of thunder, the quick stab of lightning. Dusty gullies become raging torrents. Then sunset paints the innocent dome of sky in colors which defy the artist's imagination.

One can only gaze in awe at these wonders and hope to return again and again to this stark and lonely land.

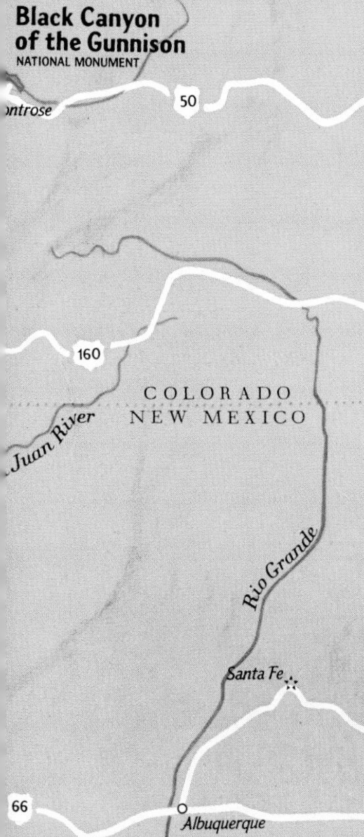

In the mile-deep chasm of the Colorado, one of the world's greatest wonders, rocks reveal nature's story of creation

GRAND CANYON

By LOUIS SCHELLBACH, former Chief Naturalist, Grand Canyon National Park
Photographs by JUSTIN LOCKE

I HAVE LISTENED to thousands of exclamations from awed visitors when first they laid eyes on Grand Canyon. But in my 22 years with this national park I never heard of a more apt comment than that of a cowboy who emerged from a forest to find the colossal abyss yawning before him. "Wow! Something sure happened!"

Averaging eight miles in width throughout its 217-mile length, the incredible mile-deep chasm staggers human senses. Its colors shift like a kaleidoscope as the sun spotlights a different spectacle every hour. Dawn gilds its sculptured pinnacles but leaves the depths in blue shadow. Noon exposes a pitiless desert. Evening sets rock spires afire with alpenglow. Moonlight tints the gorge with mystery, and morning's fog fills it with a river of cotton.

"Something sure happened" to create Grand Canyon. Many visitors want to know just *what* happened. "Did the earth crack open? Did glaciers cut it?"

Not many million years ago northern Arizona stood barely above sea level, and through it ran a sluggish river. Then the region started to rise into an immense plateau. But the ground rose so slowly that it did not change the river's course. Using silt, sand, gravel, and boulders as abrasives, the Colorado scoured its bed. Though the land rose a mile and more, the river held more

Perched on the brink of eternity, a young couple peers into the dark-walled Inner Gorge. Fixed glasses at nearby Yavapai Point (right) pinpoint the canyon's features.

The hungry Colorado River has gnawed Grand Canyon down to earth's primeval rock. Surveyed from Desert View Watchtower, lofty North Rim shows geology's layer cake of sediments laid down eons ago. Rains, frost,

U. S. AIR FORCE

and thaw, and the probing roots of plants have widened the canyon as much as 18 miles. Here the midday sun paints erosion's face in searing reds. The following pages reveal contrasts in Grand Canyon's ever-changing moods.

Etched by morning's cool shadows, white-throned temples of Deva, Brahma, and Zoroaster guard

a crumbling wasteland. Bright Angel Point (left) looks down its namesake canyon to South Rim's banded wall.

Alpenglow at sundown bathes the canyon's heights. The Battleship, foreground, sails on a

blue-shadowed sea below South Rim's Hopi Point. Bright Angel Canyon joins the Colorado's gorge on the left.

or less its original level. If we liken the earth's crust to a layer cake, then the river, by analogy, becomes a cake knife. But instead of the knife's slicing downward, the cake rose against the blade.

Erosion ate away the chasm walls. Wind carved caves in soft cliffs. Pelting rains washed away soil. Water ran into cracks, froze, and split off fragments. Water undercut ledges, which eventually tumbled down. Rain on the plateau to the north runs into the canyon. As a result the North Rim has been cut back 2½ times as far as the South, where water drains away from the rim.

RECENTLY I JOINED some tenderfoot riders on a mule trip into the canyon. "Keep the reins in your hands at all times," our guide counseled. "Keep your feet in the stirrups, your mind in the middle. Never dismount unless I am at your side. Obey those rules and your mule will take care of you."

With these words we rode off the brink of the South Rim and down Bright Angel Trail toward the Inner Gorge, almost a mile below. Our party was taking a ride back through the ages that were required to form the earth's crust. But at this moment they were indifferent to geology; they thought only of mules and heights. Most had never ridden a mule in their lives.

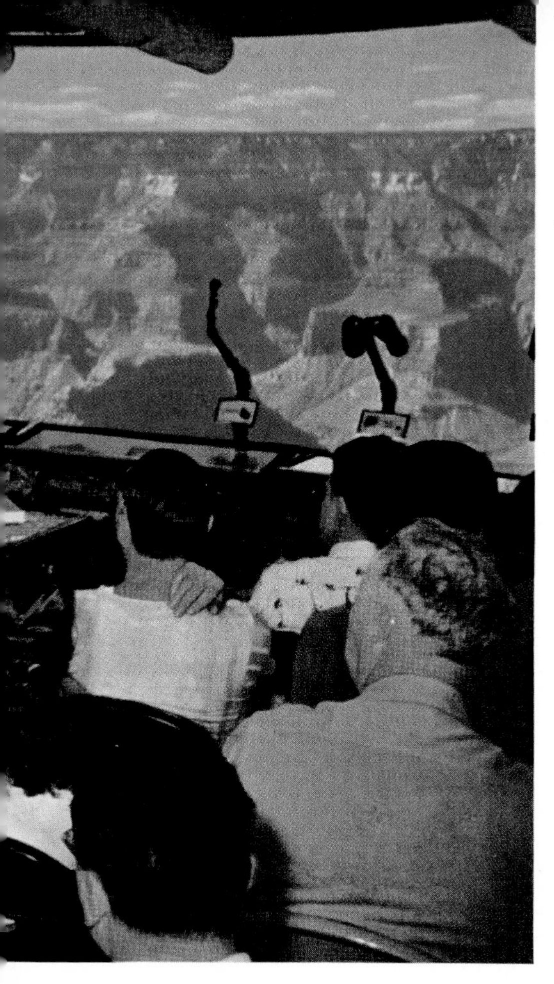

"Earth's history from the beginning lies exposed before you," says the ranger-naturalist

At Yavapai Lookout on South Rim, visitors learn of their planet's violent, convulsive past, laid bare by the relentless gouging of the Colorado River. Exposed rock layers reveal a story of mighty, age-long cataclysms: of mountains buckling skyward and wearing away; of molten rock welling up; of seas sweeping over the land and laying down vast deposits, then disappearing.

Trail riders read geology's open book closer at hand. Returning from the canyon floor, they mount the ladder of the ages. Here in a gigantic cross section of the earth's crust (below), nature has written the story of life's development and illustrated it with fossils of extinct animals.

Older Pre-Cambrian walls of the Inner Gorge, formed some 1,500,000,000 years ago, show no trace of life. But primitive algae left their mark in Younger Pre-Cambrian rocks. Climbing past layers that tell of life's growing complexity in the Paleozoic Era, riders see fossil remains of trilobites, then, higher up, tracks left by amphibians as they ventured from ancient seas.

The record of the Age of Reptiles has washed away. It would have towered far above the present rim. Our own Age of Mammals has left no sedimentary deposits here.

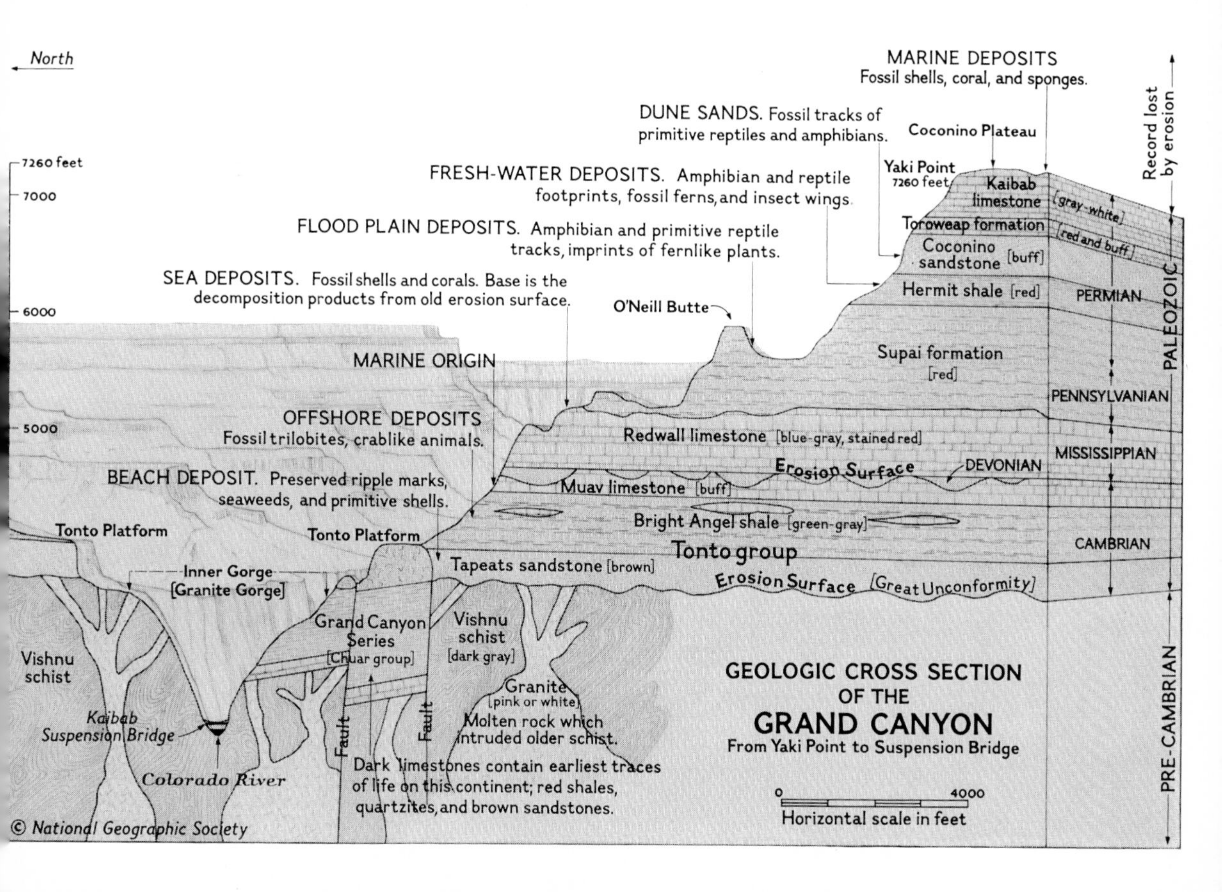

Smiles in the corral hide many a fear

Banter prevails on the South Rim every morning as visitors saddle up for a swing down the switchbacks. "Don't fall into the canyon," nonriding friends counsel.

The quaking tenderfoot shrugs off the joshing with an air of bravado. But the moment his mule ambles to the canyon's lip and steps off into space, he clutches the saddle horn, leans away from the abyss, and lets the animal take charge.

Chosen over horses because of strength and stability, the trail mule gets weeks of rigid training before passengers are entrusted to his broad back. Trainers get on and off the wrong side, clap hats over the mule's ears, bang cameras against his flank, and otherwise imitate tenderfoot ways. The result is a mount esteemed for his patience, endurance, sagacity.

A rider should not weigh more than 200 pounds, nor be under 12 or "too advanced in age." Veterans of the trip swear they wouldn't have missed it for anything.

As long as the mules headed straight down, the trail seemed a comfortable four feet wide. Newcomers got their first shock when we halted for the traditional group picture. Each mule did as he was trained: he put his tail to the wall and let his head hang out over space. Nothing but mule intervened between rider and thin air. Frightened tenderfeet clutched saddle horns and leaned back toward the rock.

"Wish I'd written my will," muttered one.

Riders were scarcely adjusted to saddles when the caravan abruptly entered a dizzy series of switchbacks cut into sheer cliffs. Approaching a turn, the mules leaned so far over the precipice it seemed they intended to step off into the abyss. Then, so slowly that to novices the fateful seconds lasted forever, our mounts pivoted, one foot after another.

Appearances to the contrary, the animal is not bent on suicide. In more than 50 years, Grand Canyon mules have yet to lose a customer to accident.

"The first few hundred yards always seem the worst," our guide told us. "A

Snaking down Jacob's Ladder, mules give dudes' nerves a test on Bright Angel Trail. Tonto Plateau lies beyond green clumps of Indian Garden.

woman may get scared or her husband may decide he has 'heart trouble.' They can dismount and hike to the rim, but very few do."

Riders turned in their saddles to see the fault line that Bright Angel Trail follows; the broken and shifted rocks on one side stand 180 feet above matching strata on the other. Some of our party observed that they had journeyed a thousand feet below the canyon's rim. Confidence partly restored, they began to enjoy the marvelous view. Earth's strata changed colors before their eyes. The gray-white top layer of sea-formed limestone gave way to buff-colored sandstone, hardened wind-blown dunes of an ancient desert landscape.

At last we entered the 550-foot Redwall, a magnificent pink façade whose blue-gray limestone had been stained red by iron oxides. The trail down this cliff follows Jacob's Ladder, another series of switchbacks. Our mules chose this alarming stretch to display their appetites. For any clump of green they stuck their heads way out over the trail's edge.

A pocket of luxury within the canyon wilderness, Phantom Ranch offers trail-weary riders a refreshing dip and a good night's sleep

Wildlife trespassers wander freely among rustic cabins and central lodge in this oasis watered by Bright Angel Creek. Here the air is 20 degrees warmer than on the South Rim, towering nearly 4,400 feet above. Maj. John Wesley Powell camped near here on his epic 1869 journey down the muddy Colorado through what he named the Grand Canyon.

"Hold your reins tight; yank his head up," advised our guide. "If you let him, your mule will eat anything—sticks, straw hats, old ropes."

We stopped for lunch and to stretch numbed legs at Indian Garden, a cottonwood oasis on the Tonto Platform, a wide plateau two-thirds of the distance from rim to river. Long ago the Havasupai Indians irrigated their farm plots from springs here. Today those springs supply most of the water used by Grand Canyon community, site of park headquarters on the South Rim. Pumps lift the sparkling load three-fifths of a mile.

Leaving the platform, we followed another zigzag trail cut into the rocks of Inner or Granite Gorge to the Colorado River, 7.8 trail miles from our starting point. Here we stood 4,500 feet below the South Rim and 5,700 below the North Rim. Manhattan Island could be tucked into a 13-mile stretch of the canyon. If the 1,472-foot Empire State Building were set down on the river bed, only its television tower would stick out of the Inner Gorge.

Held between sheer walls only 300 feet apart, the river roared in fury as boulders in its grip crashed against one another and bedrock. When the wind is right its mighty voice can be heard as far as the South Rim. Living up to its Spanish name, *colorado* (red), the river seemed more mud than water. Half a million tons of soil a day were moving before our eyes. "Too thick to drink and too thin to plow," is the way old-timers describe the Colorado's water.

Conqueror of the Colorado was Maj. John Wesley Powell, one-armed Civil War veteran and geologist. Undeterred by frightening tales of underground channels, he left Green River, Wyoming, on May 24, 1869 with nine men and four boats to explore and chart the river.

Mile after mile the boats twisted through whirlpools and crashed against rocks. Day after day the men endured skimpy rations, damp clothing, and weary

From Toroweap Overlook a cliff plunges 2,802 feet into the Colorado in Grand Canyon National Monument, a wilderness area adjoining the park.

portages. Early in August the voyagers entered the Grand Canyon. On the 28th of that month three men gave up rather than face further perils. Making their farewells, each party felt sure the other had chosen certain death.

Powell and his remaining boatmen triumphantly emerged from the canyon the very next day. The three who quit were killed by Indians.

As highways of commerce, many rivers are servants to man. But the 1,450-mile-long Colorado with its hundreds of dangerous rapids posed a threat even to the most experienced boatmen until a few years ago. Today the river is so well charted and its caprices known that many organized parties have boated and rafted in relative safety through the maelstrom of the Grand Canyon itself.

KAIBAB SUSPENSION BRIDGE, just wide enough for a pack mule, led us to the north bank and on to Phantom Ranch, only resort in the canyon, for a cool dip in the pool, dinner, and relaxing sleep in a guest cabin. Bright Angel Creek, as clear as the Colorado is muddy, made the ranch an oasis.

We were in another climate—20 degrees warmer than on the South Rim. It can be snowing on North Rim, raining on South Rim, and merely misting at Phantom Ranch. Daylight is shortened by canyon walls rising high on every side.

Daredevil driver Jon Hamilton rams his jet boat against the 20-mile-an-hour Vulcan Rapids, Grand Canyon's wickedest water, in a 1960 run upstream. In 1949 Otis Marston piloted the first motorboat through downstream.

WILLIAM BELKNAP, JR.

"The man who works only from sunup to sunset wouldn't have much of a job here," said the manager of Phantom Ranch. "During a busy summer week we have to pack in 3,500 pounds of supplies. Dirty laundry goes out, fresh linen, food, fuel oil—even mail—comes in by mule express.

"This is a sanctuary for wild animals," he continued, "and they know it. My wife found a bull snake in the house the other day and had to carry it by the tail out to the rocks. We drove a beaver away because he was felling our trees, two a night. A bobcat used to promenade past the ranch house every evening. Deer steal the mules' hay and ring-tailed cats prowl for garbage."

As our party rode on from Phantom Ranch to the North Rim we climbed through four life zones—all in 14 miles. To pass through these zones at sea level would take us from Mexico's Sonora Desert to southern Canada. Snows close the North Rim in winter. The South Rim, 1,000 to 2,000 feet lower, is open all year.

Canyon cliffs rim Supai, home of the Havasupais

Havasu Creek, born of gushing springs, nurtures the remote valley settlement of Supai, a true "fortress built by Nature" at the western end of Grand Canyon National Park. Diversion ditches water fruit orchards, farms, and pastures, turning some 175 acres into a green paradise amid an inferno of sun-blistered buttes and savage gorges.

Cheerful Havasupai Indians woo the tourist dollar, even appoint a tribal tourist manager to greet guests. They arrive down eight-mile Hualpai Trail on horseback along with mail and supplies, for no wheels roll into this hideaway Eden.

The marked climatic differences in the canyon make it a barrier to many small animals. Those on one rim are now of different species or subspecies from their relatives on the other. Classic examples are the Kaibab squirrel, found only on the North Rim, and its South Rim counterpart, the Abert squirrel. Both have tufted ears and a chestnut stripe down the back. But the Kaibab has a white tail and black belly; the Abert, white belly and gray tail.

Grand Canyon's barrier deflects north-south highway and rail traffic too. By muleback, the ten air miles from rim to rim take two days. By automobile via Navajo Bridge is a day faster but some 200 miles longer.

SHELTERED in a side canyon of the park is the most isolated Indian reservation in the United States. Here live some 200 Havasupais. Havasupais are not celebrated as warriors, philosophers, dancers, or artists, but they know a good

WILLIAM BELKNAP, JR.

thing when they see it, and that is Supai, the tribe's adopted home. In a green valley surrounded by red stone walls, Supai is a lotus-eaters' land where no one worries much about H-bombs or anything else. Avoiding the heat of the day, the Havasupais till their farms no more than they have to, but they work hard at having a good time. Rodeos, card games, sweat baths, and idle talk fill their days. They seem to suffer just two indignities: youngsters must go to school and their fathers must buy licenses to hunt. Many Havasupais, neighboring Hopis, Walpais, and Navajos work in Grand Canyon hotels as bellboys and maids.

Hopis guided Don García López de Cárdenas and his 12 Spanish followers to

Havasupai boys lead a life Huck Finn would envy

Around the age of two, young braves learn to ride by hanging on to Dad. Football, baseball, and Wild West movies later absorb them. Restrictions are few, discipline practically nonexistent, since parents believe harsh words shrivel young souls.

Every day finds boys swimming in Havasu Creek or shouting against the roar of 220-foot Mooney Falls (right). From the color of the pools the tribe takes its name—Havasupai, the Blue-green Water People.

GRAND CANYON NATIONAL PARK
Northern Arizona. Area 1,052 sq. mi.

Features: World's mightiest gorge, cut by the Colorado River. Finest open record of earth's history. Varying color moods. Desert wildlife. Four distinct climatic and plant-life zones from canyon bottom to North Rim.
Activities: *South Rim.* Visitor center at Grand Canyon Village, interpretive talks at Yavapai Point. Rim drives, mule and horse rides, bus tours, scenic flights. Campfire programs, Hopi dances. *North Rim.* Bus and saddle trips, nature walks, evening programs. Two-day mule trips to canyon floor via North Rim's Kaibab Trail and South Rim's Bright Angel Trail. Day trips into canyon also start from both rims.
Season: South Rim open all year. North Rim, about May 15–Oct. 15.
Weather: South Rim (elev. 6,900 ft.) bright, warm days, pleasant nights. North Rim (elev. 8,100 ft.) cooler; snow in winter. Canyon floor 20 degrees warmer than South Rim.
What to bring: Cottons, hat, hiking shoes. Rough-it clothing, long-sleeve shirt for trail trips. Sunglasses, sun lotion, binoculars, camera and light meter.
How to get there: See map at back of book. *South Rim.* Ariz. 64 from US 89 or 66. Santa Fe Ry. from Williams, Ariz., to park in summer. Frontier Airlines to Flagstaff. Buses from Williams, Flagstaff. *North Rim.* Ariz. 67 from US 89. Union Pacific RR, Western Airlines to Cedar City, Utah. Bus to park.
Accommodations: *South Rim.* El Tovar Hotel, Bright Angel Lodge, Phantom Ranch in canyon (all open year round); Yavapai Lodge, auto lodge (both summer only); write Fred Harvey, Grand Canyon, Ariz. Camp and trailer grounds. *North Rim.* Grand Canyon Lodge (June–Sept.), auto camp (May–Oct.); write Utah Parks Co., Cedar City. Camp and trailer ground at Bright Angel Point.
Services: Hospital at South Rim, nurse at lodge at North Rim. Restaurants, stores, garages, post offices at both rims. Church services in park.
Park regulations: Camping, fires in designated areas only. Hiking on trails only. *Don't overestimate your endurance; the hike uptrail from the canyon floor is strenuous.* Pets allowed on leash, not in canyon.

For further information write Supt., Grand Canyon National Park, Arizona

Hopis pirouette for clicking cameras on South Rim

Swirling like gaudy birds on the plaza outside Hopi House, Indians gyrate through centuries-old dances. Here the Hopis stage evening performances all year round.

They come from mesa-top pueblos in a nearby reservation, where some 4,000 Hopis follow a way of life little changed since the Spaniards found them 400 years ago.

Guests at El Tovar Hotel gape at the Hopi bellboy in blue velveteen jacket and bright headband vacuuming the lobby carpet. Scores of other Hopis serve in the park as maids and kitchen help.

the South Rim in 1540, sixty-seven years before Englishmen settled Jamestown, Virginia. Instead of finding the fabled golden Seven Cities of Cíbola, López, a lieutenant of Coronado, found a mighty canyon that barred further progress.

Before retreating, some of his soldiers ventured into the gorge. The Spanish chronicle records that those who went down discovered that the rocks which had seemed "about as tall as a man" when viewed from the rim were actually "bigger than the great tower of Seville."

Like many visitors today, the Spaniards did not appreciate the canyon's size until they descended into it. Gazing toward the North Rim across miles of clear Arizona air, one feels he can reach out and touch Wotan's Throne, Deva, Brahma, and other formations named for Old World deities.

As I look upon this incredible chasm I experience an uplifting of the spirit and a deep sense of humility. Like all who savor Grand Canyon's majesty, I find endless freshness in what naturalist John Burroughs called "the world's most wonderful spectacle, ever-changing, alive with a million moods."

JAMES P. BLAIR, NATIONAL GEOGRAPHIC PHOTOGRAPHER

LAKE MEAD

LEGENDS OF DESERT MIRAGES pale before the startling reality of Lake Mead and Lake Mohave. Walled by the painted mesas of Arizona and Nevada, they lie deep, blue, and inviting beneath the brazen summer sun.

Formed by 726-foot-high Hoover Dam, itself a wonder of the modern world, Lake Mead stretches 115 miles up the Colorado River into Grand Canyon's western end. Downstream 67 miles from Hoover Dam's spillways, Davis Dam backs up the long, bent finger of Lake Mohave.

These huge man-made lakes are the heart of a 3,000-square-mile oasis, Lake Mead National Recreation Area, enjoyed all year by holidayers, many arriving via nearby Las Vegas. Boats and water skiers crisscross the lakes, hundreds of feet above the old river channel explorer John Wesley Powell braved in 1869. Yet the gaunt shore's scene remains little changed. Bighorns bound down from lava cliffs for a drink in waters where large-mouth black bass swim.

You can fish year round, hunt game birds and animals in season, hike and explore in fall's crisp weather, or delight in desert floral displays February to June. Though summer temperatures soar, nights usually call for a blanket.

WILLIAM BELKNAP, JR.

Beaches and marinas that now ring Lakes Mead and Mohave would have made old-time rivermen rub their eyes. Though the stark shores lack trees, campers harvest driftwood, often too decorative to burn.

U. S. AIR FORCE

Hoover Dam, linking Nevada (left) and Arizona, impounds a desert sea that lures vacationists and wildlife.

Threading the little-known Narrows, adventurous hikers trace Utah's Virgin River amid the mighty walls of Zion

ZION NATIONAL PARK

By LEWIS F. CLARK

Photographs by JUSTIN LOCKE

MY BROTHER'S LETTER breathed enthusiasm. "Let's go through the Virgin River Narrows this summer," he wrote. We had long dreamed of such a trip into the wilds of southwestern Utah's Zion National Park. Here the North Fork of the Virgin River has carved one of America's greatest stone miracles. Like an endless belt of sandpaper, grit-bearing water has scoured through layer after layer of sandstone to create fantastic Zion Canyon.

Great monoliths, blazing with color, guard the course of the Virgin as it tumbles southward along Zion's green floor. From the park's south entrance a highway skims past eight miles of these rock sentinels—Bridge Mountain, the Altar of Sacrifice with its white summit streaked with crimson, Mountain of the Sun, Lady Mountain, the Great White Throne, a dozen others—to the Temple of Sinawava. Alcoves, broad amphitheaters, magnificent arches indent these majestic cliffs. Slender pilasters stand everywhere.

A mile north of road's end the canyon shrivels to a writhing gorge; in places only a few feet separate walls half a mile high. Here the Virgin has a fall of 90 feet to a mile, 10 times that of the Colorado in Grand Canyon. Though more than half a million visit Zion each year, only a few have penetrated this chasm. Perhaps the first was Grove Karl Gilbert, geologist, map maker, and early Trustee of the National Geographic Society, who explored the North Fork in 1872 and named these twisting miles the Narrows.

Zion's chief ranger was dubious when we registered for our unconventional two-day hike early in July. "Our flash floods come between now and the end of August," he told us. "Thunderstorms could start any day." But trusting our ex-

Like Wall Street skyscrapers, cliffs of the Narrows soar above the Virgin River's flood-scoured bed; they sometimes hide the sky. In one side canyon in Zion the author could touch both walls at once.

LEWIS F. CLARK

A celestial skyline evoked the name of Zion from Mormons who discovere

the canyon in 1858. Today buses bring park-bound pilgrims into Sinawava's amphitheater to see its "towering temples of stone." The Great White Throne rises at center.

perience and equipment, he granted permission. We would camp on the plateau above the gorge that night. If skies were clear in the morning, the three girls in the party would drive back to Zion Canyon and meet us late the following afternoon at the south end of the Narrows. We nine men would try the river.

We took the Mount Carmel Highway to the park's east gate. From the canyon floor, six great switchbacks climb in easy grades some 800 feet in three miles—all contained in an area of less than one-third square mile! Then the highway plunges into the north wall of Bridge Mountain and through a 5,607-foot tunnel continues its climb to the summit of Zion Canyon's east wall. Six galleries gouged in the rock enable travelers to view such scenic wonders as the Great Arch of Zion, one of the largest natural

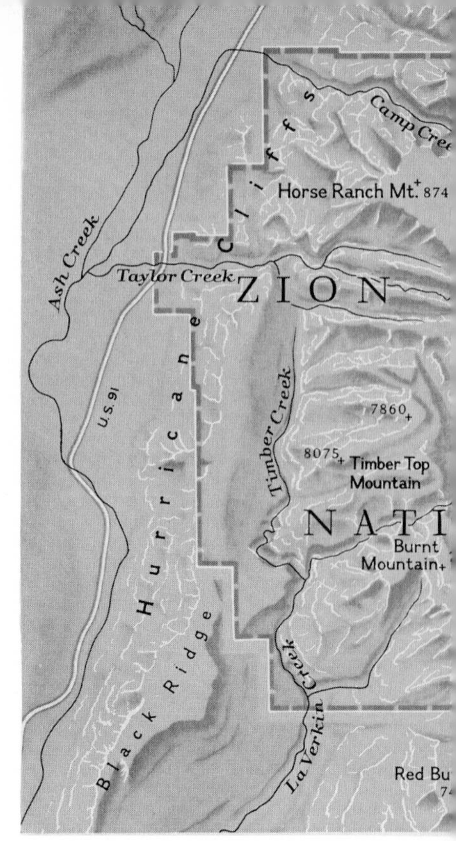

JAMES P. BLAIR, NATIONAL GEOGRAPHIC PHOTOGRAPHER

On the track of nature, a ranger-naturalist leads visitors to the mouth of the Virgin River Narrows, pausing to point out the splendors along the way. From road's end in the Temple of Sinawava thousands hike the easy mile north, past trickling streams and the Hanging Gardens of Zion. Ferns soften the canyon floor; in late summer scarlet lobelia brightens the trail. Even in the Narrows vegetation thrives on the sun's brief daily penetration.

Giant amphibians and three-toed dinosaurs roamed the Zion of yesteryear. Cougars and coyotes still lurk here. In the evening mule deer slip out of side canyons to browse in the meadows. Golden eagles rest on the crags and pinnacles, and desert birds like the roadrunner scuttle across the lowlands. Reptiles abound; all except the rattlesnake are harmless.

In the canyon depths the white, trumpet-shaped blooms of the sacred datura, or "Zion moonflower," open at night and wilt in the morning sun. Indians once made medicine from the showy, two-foot-high plant.

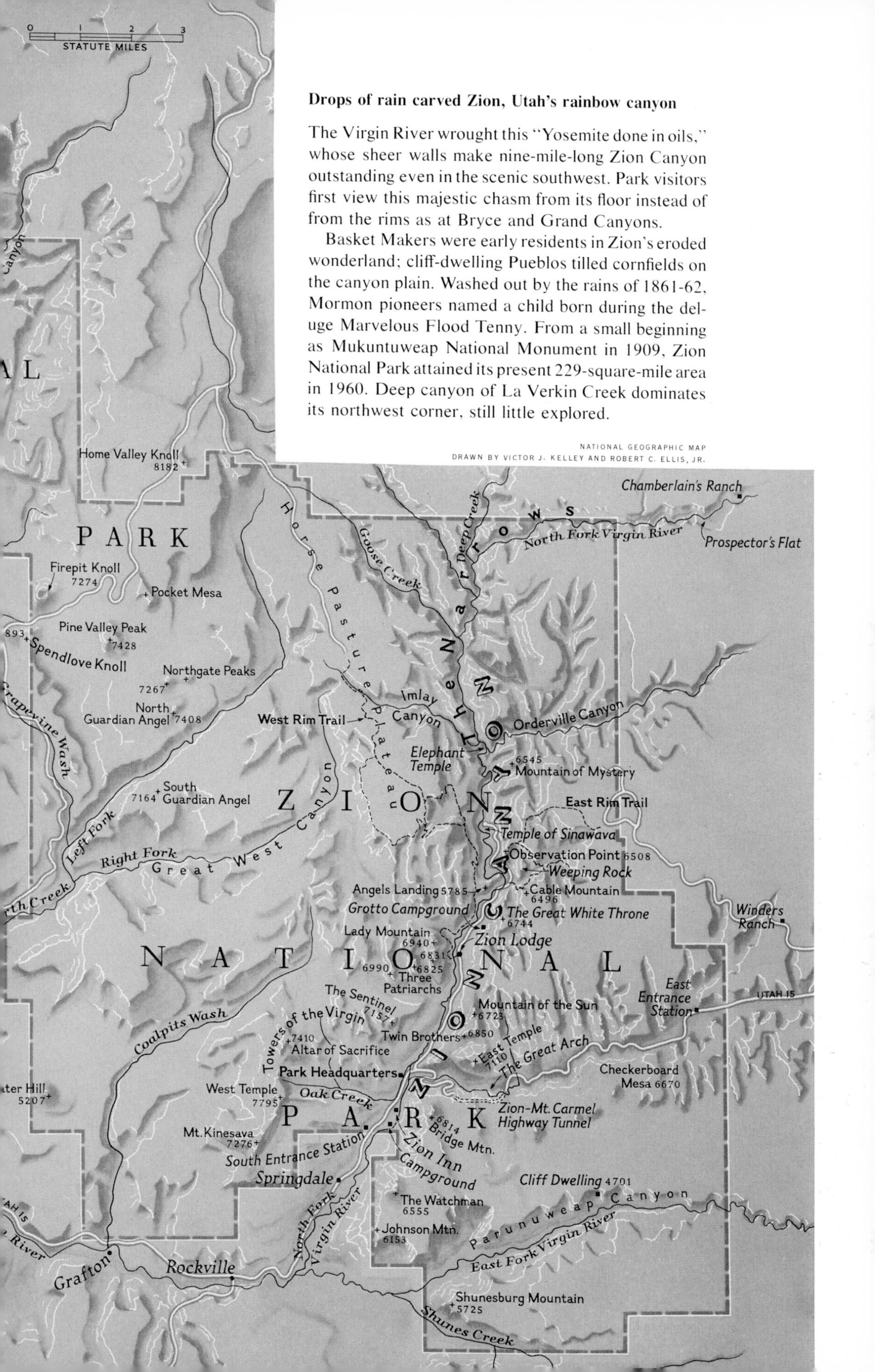

Drops of rain carved Zion, Utah's rainbow canyon

The Virgin River wrought this "Yosemite done in oils," whose sheer walls make nine-mile-long Zion Canyon outstanding even in the scenic southwest. Park visitors first view this majestic chasm from its floor instead of from the rims as at Bryce and Grand Canyons.

Basket Makers were early residents in Zion's eroded wonderland; cliff-dwelling Pueblos tilled cornfields on the canyon plain. Washed out by the rains of 1861-62, Mormon pioneers named a child born during the deluge Marvelous Flood Tenny. From a small beginning as Mukuntuweap National Monument in 1909, Zion National Park attained its present 229-square-mile area in 1960. Deep canyon of La Verkin Creek dominates its northwest corner, still little explored.

NATIONAL GEOGRAPHIC MAP
DRAWN BY VICTOR J. KELLEY AND ROBERT C. ELLIS, JR.

A pony's step from thin air, East Rim trail-riders skirt Navajo sandstone cliffs on the climb to canyon top. The seven-mile round trip takes about five hours. Longer, more strenuous West Rim Trail spells a full day in the saddle. Riders pack food and water.

arches in the world. After emerging from the tunnel, the highway winds along Clear Creek, past Checkerboard Mesa with its weather-lined façade.

To see anything more dramatic one must take to the park's many trails. From East Rim Trail the climber has an eye-popping view the full length of Zion Canyon. No less spectacular is the longer trail to the west rim. One of its steeper stretches—"Walter's Wiggles"—was built by custodian Walter Ruesch in 1919, the year Zion became a national park. Twenty-one switchbacks in 600 feet of canyonside trail mount to a shelf on the cliff. "It's the only place in the world a horse is going two ways all the time," one rider remarked.

Symbol of Zion Canyon is the Great White Throne, rising 2,450 feet above the Virgin River foaming at its base. In two days we would see this stupendous flat-topped rock—if all went well.

We camped outside park boundaries, not far from the top of the Narrows. Light clouds in the west made a beautiful sunset. Next morning there were no clouds—a good omen. We forded a stream, followed a tortuous road, and two miles east of the park boundary we took our leave of the girls. To their shouts of "Good luck!" we strode off toward the river. Our map showed 12 miles of water-grade route between us and our goal. This would take us through the gradually deepening upper gorge and between the towering walls of the Narrows to the Temple of Sinawava—the end of the canyon road.

The creek bed dropped steadily before us. The defile tightened around us. We watched for possible escape ledges where we could climb beyond the high-water mark. We recalled rumors of gorge waters rising 100 feet in 10 minutes, stories of the musty downdraft that precedes a flood, photographs of a wall of water plunging down like a wave crest. The thought that we could be trapped never left our minds.

In one passage the walls rose sheer and smooth, like the hull of a ship in dry dock. In another the waters evidently cut through harder rock, overhanging and twisted. As we looked up, no sky at all was visible.

Thirsty mounts drink from La Verkin Creek in Zion's wild northwestern ell. Hurricane Fault's 2,500-foot cliffs jut nearby.

Abruptly the cavernlike passage led into a hall which looked deceptively simple. But on the shallow side of the stream we stepped onto soft footing.

"Quicksand!" someone warned. We waded noisily into deeper water and found firm bottom. Farther on the walls parted again and we passed into a natural temple. Sculptured cliffs of many hues rose above us.

ZION NATIONAL PARK once lay under fathoms of water. Water pressure and chemical action changed layers of gravel, sand, and lava ash into solid rock, cemented and colored by iron oxides and lime. Embedded in this slowly upthrust rock are fossilized fish, shells, and plant life; here are found the bones and tracks of dinosaurs which disappeared 70 million years ago.

Formations of six geologic epochs are prominently displayed in the park.

Youngest, and therefore the uppermost, is the Carmel limestone which caps the East Temple, West Temple, and the Altar of Sacrifice. This 200- to 300-foot layer was the floor of the shallow sea, perhaps 120 million years ago. Beneath is the Navajo sandstone, more than 2,000 feet thick. From these mighty beds Zion's rainbow canyon has been carved.

The lower sandstone walls, predominantly red, run a full range of purples, blues, and browns in changing light. Higher up, the spectrum pales through pinks, lilacs, and buffs to the limestone's gray-white. Above all a cap of green forest touches the brilliant blue sky.

Such scenic riches inspired one Mormon, Isaac Behunin, to reason: "These great mountains are natural temples of God. We can worship here as well as in the man-made temples in Zion. Let us call it Little Zion."

So it came to be known. But Brigham Young was not satisfied. "It is not Zion," said he. Some of the faithful thereafter called it "Not Zion."

Mormon pioneers sent to live in the canyon protested the lack of timber for construction. "Lumber will soar down from the cliffs like an eagle," Brigham Young is said to have told them.

Some 30 years later the prophecy came true. In 1900 David Flanigan hit upon the idea of a 2,600-foot cable from canyon rim to floor to bring down the fine yellow-pine timber that stood above the cliff. Today's visitor can see the upper tower of Flanigan's cable, still perched atop Cable Mountain, northeast of the Great White Throne.

There is no evidence that Escalante, the Franciscan Father, or Jedediah Smith, the fur trader, ever saw Zion Canyon, though Escalante crossed the Virgin River in 1776 and Smith traversed La Verkin Canyon in 1826.

Nephi Johnson, a young Mormon missionary and interpreter among the Paiute Indians, was probably the first white man to see its depths. Called by

Lunching on tableland, a trail party gets an eye-level view of 6,744-foot Great White Throne (left), long a challenge to climbers. Zion Canyon's west wall rises on right.

Zion: "The most wonderful defile it has been my fortune to behold," said explorer Grove Karl Gilbert.

Brigham Young in the fall of 1858 to explore the upper Virgin River, he persuaded the Paiutes to guide him over the rugged escarpment of the Hurricane Cliffs and up the Virgin River as far as the Narrows. His Indian guide refused to go any farther than Oak Creek because Wai-no-pits, the Evil One, might lurk in the shadows of the narrow canyon.

That night, camped on a rocky bar in Deep Creek, I almost agreed with the Paiutes. From a sandy couch I gazed at the darkening sky. To the north, stars disappeared behind thin clouds. Could it be raining in Cedar Breaks? I heard a roaring sound like distant thunder or a great waterfall. Then I saw winking lights—a plane. Relaxed now, I watched moonlight outline the chasm walls. Then I dozed.

The next time my eyes opened the sky was paling. A fire blazed and the doubts of the night had fled. The canyon that had looked so forbidding in evening shadow now beckoned with the sunrise.

We climbed over the debris of a fresh-looking avalanche. Tons of rock had poured through a notch high in the cliff. The hurtling boulders had torn branches from canyon pines. Over all lay a blanket of fine rock dust.

We passed by hanging valleys where intermittent tributaries poured their waters into the canyon in cascades and clear falls. We walked through a beautiful green meadow filled with grasses and wildflowers. Tall pines stood against the cliffs that enclosed this amphitheater.

As we rounded a turn, the walls closed in. Water filled the gorge from side to side. Often the walls overhung the stream. In places we couldn't see even a patch of sky to judge if the weather was still favorable. We seemed to be splash-

The Virgin River tumbles from the Narrows (foreground), named by Gilbert, dodges Angel's Landing, and rolls on between giant altars of stone. Each year it gnaws away 300,000 tons of rock. Eventually erosion will wash away the cliffs one elderly lady found so magnificent—"but they do shut off the view!" Right: Appetites are keen at Grotto Campground.

ing through high, vaulted tunnels. For 40 or 50 minutes at a stretch we saw no possibility of climbing up if the waters should rise. Eerie walls echoed and re-echoed our voices. With the help of walking sticks, we found fairly secure footing on the round stones that covered the riverbed.

At one point I heard a low gurgling—mysterious and ominous. After a search, I found its source, a spring higher than my head, pouring into a dark pool. The chasm widened, but each side was blocked by immense rocks fallen from the heights. The only way was through the pool, which was too deep to wade. Putting cameras and wrist watches into plastic bags, we plunged into the water and swam across, towing our buoyant packs.

We were surprised to find several water ouzels, seemingly unconcerned at our approach. Whether through fear or lack of it, one of these small slate-gray birds sat quietly on a branch while we petted it. Another we gently picked up and carried a quarter of a mile. Rather than frightened, it seemed merely curious when we placed it on the limb of a tree.

Again the walls closed in. The water became deeper, the course more winding. Then, at an almost closed horseshoe bend we glimpsed the Mountain of Mystery jutting skyward. We knew that not far from this 6,545-foot peak lie well-known park landmarks: Weeping Rock, Angel's Landing, and Cable Mountain, all easily reached from Zion Lodge and Grotto Campground.

The canyon widened, and on the gravelly shore we saw horseshoe tracks and a gum wrapper. Civilization was near. At last, seven great bends beyond Orderville Canyon, we heard voices. Across the river were the girls. They had walked up from the Temple of Sinawava.

As we emerged dripping from the river at the trail's end, a group of park visitors looked toward the Narrows behind us as a ranger told of its hazards.

That night it rained lightly.

Several weeks later we heard that a flash flood had inundated the upper canyon. The river had increased its volume 50 times, mostly within 15 minutes.

ZION NATIONAL PARK *Southwestern Utah. Area 229 sq. mi.*

Features: Vertical Zion Canyon, cut from forested tableland by Virgin River. Eroded back country. Desert wildlife. Indian ruins.
Activities: Visitor center at park headquarters. Scenic drives; 155 mi. of hiking, climbing, riding trails. Nature talks.
Season: Open all year. Roads snowfree.
Weather: Summer days hot, nights cool.
What to bring: Hiking shoes, rough-it togs, cottons, light jacket. Sunglasses, camera.
How to get there: US 89 or 91 to Utah 15. Union Pacific RR or Bonanza Airlines to Cedar City, Utah; bus connections to park.
Accommodations: Zion Lodge (June 15–Sept. 10), Zion Inn (May 15–Oct. 1); write Utah Parks Co., Cedar City. Camp and trailer ground open all year. Motels in Springdale.
Services: Restaurants, stores, garages in park. Nurse, church services at Zion Lodge.
Park regulations: Camping and fires outside campgrounds by permit only. Stay on trails; no hiking or climbing alone. Pets on leash.

For further information write Superintendent, Zion National Park, Springdale, Utah

Planed by the floods of time, cliffs of Zion's remote Hop Creek Valley rival the Narrows.

Enchanted castles of Bryce Canyon were carved by the artful fingers of frost and rain. Northeast from Sunset Point the visitor views a spectrum ranging from flaming yellow to the purple of Utah's distant Table Cliffs. From Sunrise Point a trail descends to the fiery hues of the Queen's Garden (opposite).

BRYCE CANYON

Photographs by
WILLIAM BELKNAP, JR.

JAMES P. BLAIR, NATIONAL GEOGRAPHIC PHOTOGRAPHER

On a thawing spring day, visitors can actually hear erosion: the trickle of water, the tumbling of rocks, the rattle of gravel. In the 56 square miles of Bryce Canyon National Park, geology is as current as a newspaper, and far more sensational. For the traveler planning an easy three-park vacation—Grand Canyon, Zion, and Bryce—geologists promise a cross-section history of the planet earth. Rocks deep in Grand Canyon, formed some 1.5 billion years ago, are perhaps twice as old as life itself; the Canyon's youngest stones are still about 180 million years old. Zion continues from there with the Age of Reptiles. Bryce belongs to the timely Age of Mammals, the last 60 million years.

These iron-stained rocks, hardened from ocean sediment and desert drift, were once lifted two miles above sea level. The mass cracked, so that on the faulted eastern side of a plateau in southern Utah water and ice could pry into crevices and carve what Paiute Indians called "red rocks standing like men in a bowl-shaped canyon."

Capt. Clarence E. Dutton, an early surveyor, described a bewildering landscape of "standing obelisks, prostrate columns, shattered capitals, panels, niches, buttresses . . . the work of giant hands, a race of genii once rearing temples of rock, but now chained up in a spell of enchantment while their structures

Javanese spires rise from a silent city: the view from Inspiration Point. Bryce is not a true canyon but the cracked eastern face of a green plateau. "A cavern with the roof stripped away," some describe it. Varying tints come from iron and manganese oxides in the rock.

Hikers thread Navajo Loop Trail into a magic world of temples, palaces, and sculptured figures. Paiutes believed these were creatures who fell into evil ways and were turned to stone. Science calls it erosion.

are falling in ruins." Imaginations run riot as visitors today delight in naming thousands of these eroded fantasies. Perhaps the only person to escape Bryce Canyon's spell was the Mormon homesteader who gave the place his name. Ebenezer Bryce called it "a hell of a place to lose a cow."

Some 300,000 travelers a year judge Bryce a wonderful proof that nature is still an artist, and still at work on the Great Plateau. After feasting on its magnificent scenery, one lady said: "Zion was the fruit cocktail, and Grand Canyon the main course. But I had to come to Bryce to get my dessert!"

Queen Victoria (left and right) serenely surveys her garden of stone. The Three Wise Men (above) eternally seek the road to Bethlehem. One teen-ager imagined them guided missiles, all set to blast off. Hikers below rest in the depths of Wall Street, a chasm that seldom gets direct sunlight. Faces reflect the glow of flaming rock.

Nature's giants dwarf puny mortals pressing for a look from Bryce Point. Colors in the canyon range from red and pink to gold and frosty white, with touches of blue and lavender. Throughout the day patterns and hues shift constantly with the moving sun. Some rocks seem to glow as if lit by internal fires. By moonlight they appear almost phosphorescent.

BRYCE CANYON NATIONAL PARK

Features: Some of world's most fanciful and richly colored formations, carved from 20 miles of southwestern Utah's Pink Cliffs. Bryce Canyon itself is the most spectacular of a dozen basins, or amphitheaters, in the 56-sq.-mi. park.

Activities: Visitor center. 17 mi. Rim Drive (go first to Rainbow Point, stop at Bryce, Inspiration, Sunset, Sunrise, and other overlooks on way back). 61 mi. of hiking and riding trails. Guided walks on Navajo Loop Trail. Illustrated talks.

Season: Visitor center open all year. Rainbow Point road, April–Nov.

Weather: Summer days warm, dry; nights nippy. (Rim elev. 8,000 to 9,100 ft.) Winters cold, snow.

What to bring: Hiking shoes, rough-it clothing; woolens for evening. Sunglasses, camera, binoculars.

How to get there: US 89 to Panguitch, east on Utah 12. (Zion National Park is 85 mi. southwest, Grand Canyon's North Rim 160 mi. south.) Union Pacific RR, Bonanza Airlines to Cedar City; bus to park.

Accommodations: Lodge (June 15–Sept. 6), Inn (May 15–Oct. 12); write Utah Parks Co., Cedar City. Camp and trailer ground.

Services: Restaurants, stores, gas. Nurse at lodge, hospital in Panguitch. Church services in park.

Park regulations: Camping and picnicking in campground only. Do not disturb formations or wildlife. Stay on trails. *Don't overdo: you are at high altitude.* No pets on trails.

For further information write Supt., Bryce Canyon National Park, Utah

CEDAR BREAKS

BETWEEN BRYCE CANYON and Cedar City, drivers can pull up at a two-mile-high overlook in Cedar Breaks National Monument and get a hawk's-eye view of formations even more colorful than Bryce offers close up.

In this huge amphitheater, cut from Utah's Pink Cliffs, mineral-stained ridges radiate toward the cliff arc like painted spokes of a circus wagon wheel.

A lodge (write Utah Parks Co., Cedar City), a campground, a visitor center, and often a committee of deer welcome summer travelers. Rangers answer the inevitable question: Cedar Breaks was named by Mormon settlers who thought junipers were cedars. "Breaks" are cliffs at a mesa's edge.

CAPITOL REEF

A BARE CENTURY AGO westbound wagons were halted in south central Utah by a sudden escarpment. The cliff—layered in chocolate, green, and ivory—ran about 150 miles; horsemen could cross it in only three places. This was the famous Waterpocket Fold.

Polygamists took refuge here and bequeathed a name to Cohab Canyon. Even after 61 square miles were set aside as Capitol Reef National Monument in 1937, the area remained incompletely explored.

Motorists can put in at nearby villages and ranches or at private facilities within the monument. Some may bed down at the monument campground beside eroded domes, cliffs, pinnacles, and petrified forests. Around them stirs the "night life" of the canyons—the distant hoot of the horned owl, the nearby bustle of the "trade" rat who is said to leave an offering for every item of camp gear he steals.

Superintendent: Torrey, Utah.

LEWIS WAYNE WALKER

Sparrow hawk eats mice and grasshopper

DR. SPENCER R. ATKINSON

Pack or trade rat gives baby a ride.

MARVIN H. FROST

Jack rabbit needs little water.

Indestructible coyote, the West's commonest predator, brings home a jack rabbit.

Wildlife on a Thirsty Plateau

"What could possibly live here?" the parks visitor asks, gazing at the stark canyons that scar the Great Plateau. The answer: everything from the cougar stalking a mule deer among the rocks to a tiny chipmunk bravely raiding picnic crumbs.

For wherever water gathers—along canyon floors, in desert potholes, amid the plants atop mesas—wilderness creatures enact their drama. Bobcats prowl the piñon forest for ground squirrels and cottontails. Foxes and coyotes roam the sagebrush for jack rabbits. Soaring overhead, hawks, owls, ravens, and eagles search for marmots and mice.

Lizards scamper over rocks where an occasional rattlesnake suns itself. The skunk parades in lonely majesty, and a yellow-haired porcupine waddles into an empty tent to chew on the salty handle of a hatchet.

DON A. GILCHRIST, HEARST MOVIETONE NEWS

Protected in parks, mountain lion helps keep nature in balance.

E. R. KALMBACH, U. S. FISH AND WILDLIFE SERVICE

RAINBOW BRIDGE

By RALPH GRAY, National Geographic Staff
Photographs by the author

Amid a jumble of slickrock canyons that crease the Utah-Arizona border rises Rainbow Bridge, one of the world's wonders. Lake Powell motorboats now churn to within an easy walk of this hidden gem. Planes fly over to give sightseers a view of it, like half a butterscotch Life Saver lodged in a crevice. I saw it the old way—from the back of a tired pony after 14 jarring miles.

I saddled up with a party of riders near Navajo Mountain Trading Post. All day our sweating mounts picked their way across the northern ridges of Navajo Mountain, the whale-backed landmark of the state boundary. We saw water only three times, at the bottom of great gulches down whose sides our blowing horses lurched. On the heights again, their shod feet slid on polished sandstone.

Shadows had cooled Rainbow Bridge Canyon by the time we reached it. We clopped over a shoulder of talus, then drew rein to stare. Ahead, partly hidden by an intervening cliff, an incredible arch of stone gracefully curved across the evening sky.

Rainbow's arch of stone spans the creek that carved it. Ages ago, digging its channel in southern Utah's desert, Bridge Creek cut into necks of sandstone. The stream wore away other formations, but this one it penetrated, leaving a looping rib of rock in air.

EDWARDS PARK, NATIONAL GEOGRAPHIC STAFF

Thousands of tons of sandstone soar gracefully across the sky

The world's largest natural bridge spans 278 feet and arches 309 feet above Bridge Creek. Seen from below, it reveals its immensity. From atop Rainbow Bridge Canyon, the span

is dwarfed by the wilderness around it. In 1909, spurred by Indian rumors about *Nonnezoshi* (Stone Rainbow), a party first saw it after days of parched travel through red rock and yellow sand. Presented in the *National Geographic* by Byron Cummings, one of its discoverers, Rainbow Bridge was made a national monument by President Taft in 1910.

Roping down onto the bridge from its western abutment, Geographic staffman Ted Park lashes onto a spike driven into the rock.

Rainbow Bridge! Seeing it, I felt that lifeless matter had been caught in dramatic action. From high on one canyon wall the solid rock seems to stream up, out, and down in fluid motion.

Nature has fashioned hundreds of arches and bridges in Utah and Arizona; new ones are found almost every year. Yet Rainbow overshadows them all. It spans 278 feet and rises 309 feet—large enough, lacking only inches, to frame the United States Capitol.

The job of making camp barred me from closer acquaintance until next morning. Then, joined by two companions, I hiked down the canyon and stood under the vaulting rock. In its shadow we found the registry book, kept since earliest days for the visitors who have reached Rainbow, among them Theodore Roosevelt and Zane Grey. I became signer number 10,741. That's less than the number of people who visit Grand Canyon on two summer days. I read scribbled reactions of awe, relief, frivolity. One girl claimed

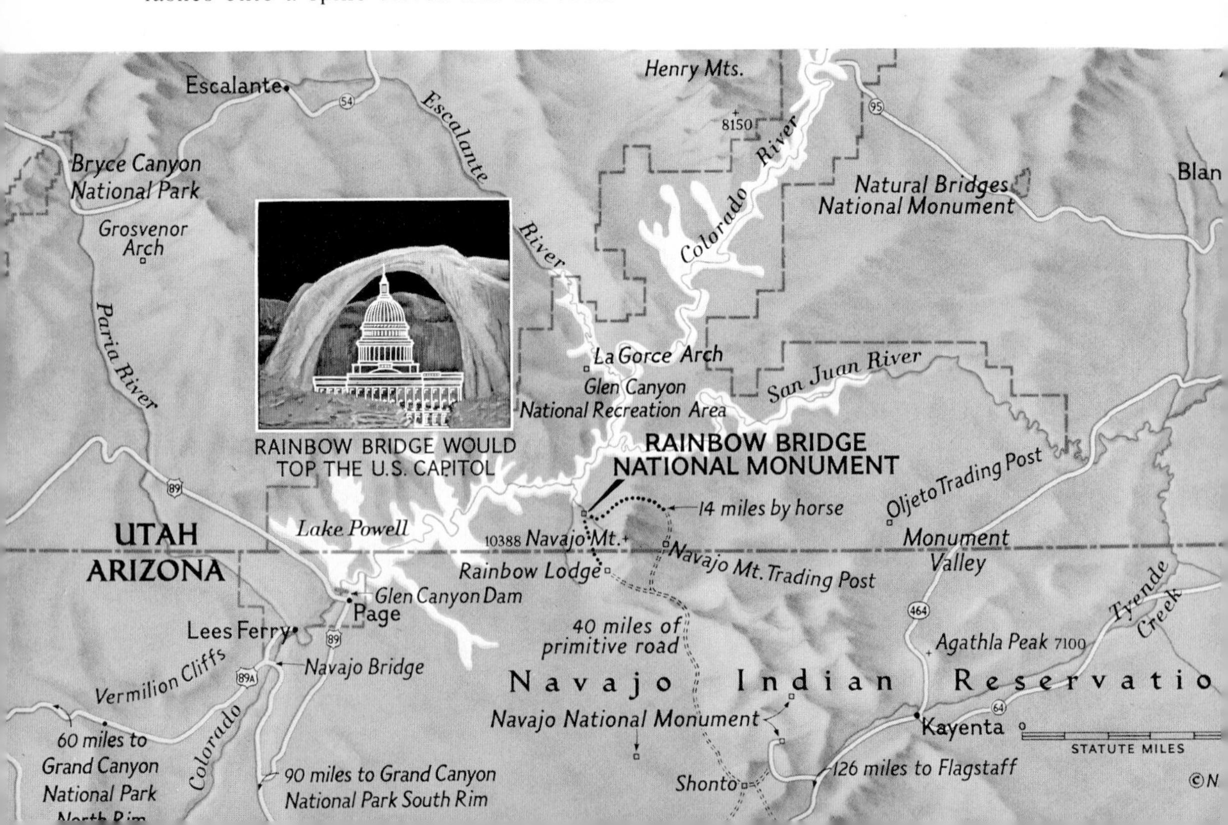

Blustery wind greets author's party atop Rainbow. "It seemed crowded with just us three."

to be "first to sleep all night on the bridge." Farther along, in the "Method of Transportation" column, a man wrote, "hands and knees."

With full canteens and a 40-foot rope, three of us set out to climb Rainbow Bridge, something few attempt. Clinging to toe holds, we inched up the canyon's west wall and reached the great shoulder that rises almost level with the rounded top of the bridge. From this abutment we roped down to the arch—slender looking from afar, but actually 42 feet thick at its top, and as wide as a high-crowned country road. We felt the thrill of achievement as we stepped to the apex of the Rainbow. We exchanged triumphant handshakes, spread a National Geographic Society flag to the gusty breeze, then walked to the edge and peered down. Cutting far beneath our feet, the canyon floor looked no wider than a footpath. Instinctively, we recoiled from gaping emptiness.

Certainly we had conquered Rainbow Bridge. But as we huddled on that age-old, weathered crest, surrounded by the austere cliffs of its hideaway, we felt puny and uncertain—like trespassers in a world of giants.

At Glen Canyon National Recreation Area boaters on Lake Powell now skim across the dammed-up waters of the Colorado to within shouting distance of the bridge. Much of the wild trail from the river is submerged.

NATURAL BRIDGES

EVERY SUMMER a few uranium hunters wander into Natural Bridges National Monument, geiger counters in hand. A ranger soon sets them straight—prospecting is forbidden on park lands. Some linger to see what our Nation values more than radioactive ore: three huge bridges, hewn from buff sandstone, all within four square miles of southeastern Utah's tangled canyons.

Each spotlights a different phase in nature's leisurely bridge-building. Kachina, youngest of the trio, seems at first glance to block its stream bed like a 206-foot dam. The waters that ate away its flank broke through only in comparatively recent times. Winter's frosts and thaws are still slenderizing the 93-foot-thick span. Springtime visitors taking the trail to Kachina usually find fresh flakings of stone scattered beneath it.

From Kachina, hikers follow a two-mile trail to the largest and most perfect bridge, a flat-topped spur of rimrock leaping its gorge in a 268-foot stride. So gracefully arched is its underside that it was named Sipapu after the Pueblo's sacred entrance to the underworld.

Close by the monument's main road, a tendril of rock, Owachomo Bridge, soars 180 feet. Oldest of the three, its span has weathered to a mere nine feet in thickness. Zeke Johnson, an early custodian, recalled that a geologist pronounced Owachomo ten million years old. "That was July, 1926," Zeke said, "so if he's right, it will be 10,000,040 years old in July, 1966."

ARCHES NATIONAL MONUMENT

By PAUL JENSEN

WHAT'S THE DIFFERENCE between a natural bridge and an arch? Bates Wilson, superintendent of Arches, gave me the answer. "Simple," he said. "A bridge bridges a watercourse and an arch doesn't. Anywhere in Utah's redrock country a canyon stream might cut itself a bridge. But all 88 arches here are on high ground away from streams. All were cut just by weather from stone fins."

"Fins?" I asked. We had driven up from the visitor center, near Moab on US 160, and stopped at Courthouse Towers. Park Avenue's sandstone skyscrapers stretched before us—only the doormen and poodles were missing. Beyond sprawled The Windows, a reef rising in turrets, spires, and balanced rocks.

"Fins," said Bates and pointed to a fresh crease in my fender. The paint had cracked along lines of stress. "That's what happened to this whole area. Only

Like a viaduct for some forgotten city, Sipapu strides 220 feet above its cottonwood-crowded gorge. Cass Hite, a prospector, discovered the bridges in 1883, but not until 1904 were they fully reported—in the *National Geographic*. Natural Bridges became a monument in 1908.

JACK BREED

here the 'paint' is a 300-foot-thick layer of Entrada sandstone. The earth humped and the Entrada cracked clear to the bottom in regular rows ten to twenty feet wide."

"And these isolated rocks?" I looked down Courthouse Wash.

"Flukes of erosion," said Bates. "Over millions of years the elements have worn most of the fins away, leaving solitary formations like the Organ, Sheep Rock, the Three Gossips. Then there's Delicate Arch. But that's one you'll want to see alone. Some things are better without people talking all the time."

The West abounds in marvels of nature: the world's grandest canyon, its biggest trees. But Delicate Arch is not the world's biggest anything. It doesn't have to be. Alone, it would be lovely. Combined with its setting, it is incomparably beautiful.

Here nature's hand has chiseled a great amphitheater and on its rim left standing a spraddle-legged colossus. I saw not a speck of dust or even a lichen clinging to this pink stone arc or to the coliseum it embellishes, whose polished sides plummet to the valley. Beyond the gorge of the Colorado River rise the snow-capped La Sal Mountains.

The sun went down and an eerie pall fell over the lifeless scene. Wisps of a breeze hissed across the grainy surface. Swept by a sudden chill of loneliness, I hurried down the trail.

Whereas Delicate Arch impressed me with its weird beauty, Landscape Arch, carved from an enormous fin in the middle of Devils Garden, struck me as just plain impossible. Coming up the

Delicate Arch, star of the 53-square-mile preserve, stands 85 feet high and 65 wide on the lip of a slickrock bowl. Wind and rain carved it from a sandstone reef. Old-time cowboys called it "Old maid's bloomers."

Hearty desert blooms like the claret-cup cactus (right) and yellow cactus (above) defy Arches' blistering summer sun.

JACK BREED. OPPOSITE: W. ROBERT MOORE, NATIONAL GEOGRAPHIC STAFF

trail, I didn't see it at first, for it blended into the high wall behind. Then suddenly it seemed to snap into place—a 291-foot band of black and red stone, the world's longest natural span.

Mathematically speaking, Landscape Arch can't stay up. It's all wrong—far too long, far too flat. One end is only six feet thick, while in the center the arch humps its back, spreads 20 feet wide, and weighs thousands of tons. But there it stands. Bates Wilson worries over the cracks that pierce Landscape. When it falls, as surely it must, it will be a black day for him.

Go see it soon, and spend some time among the other marvels. Hike through Fiery Furnace, where slender fins, blazing red in sunset's glow, tower 200 feet above a labyrinth. It's rough going, but deep within the Furnace fresh water awaits in potholes and there are cool coves where the sun never penetrates.

CANYONLANDS

By W. ROBERT MOORE

National Geographic Staff

On and on it stretched below our wings: a vast city of towering skyscrapers, massive domes, and bridges beyond an architect's dreams. But this was a city without a blueprint—the work of nature, not of man. And it had taken hundreds of thousands of years to build.

"It's one of the most spectacular spots in all Utah," said Harlon W. Bement, Director of the Utah State Aeronautics Commission, as he nosed the Beechcraft down for a look at long-deserted cliff dwellings.

From this height the erosion-clawed land reminded me of a maze into which a scientist might place white mice to test their abilities to find their way out. Next day we would become the mice—seeking our way in and out of these kinking canyons by Jeep, by horseback, and on foot.

This rugged wonderworld lies in the most southern and inaccessible part of Canyonlands, which in 1964 became our 32d national park. Today a visitor can take a guided tour of the park's central region by boating from Moab down the Colorado to where it meets the Green and their silt-laden waters become one of the wildest rivers on the continent. Beyond that point, bold river runners can shoot the rapids of Cataract Canyon and continue south to Lake Powell.

Tourists also drive their cars across the narrow, cliff-edged Neck onto Island in the Sky, the plateau that dominates the northern area of Canyonlands between the rivers.

Sandstone colossus hewn by wind, rain, and frost, Druid Arch towers in monumental grandeur amid Utah's canyons.

W. ROBERT MOORE, NATIONAL GEOGRAPHIC STAFF

Grandview Point on this mesa, nearly 3,000 feet above the confluence, provides a magnificent 75-mile panorama of southeastern Utah. Below rimrock, vacationists explore remote arches, buttes, and spires.

But on our trip, before Canyonlands became a national park, we blazed a tortuous trail. Cold rain whipped around us at Monticello as our party of 11 stowed supplies into three Jeeps and a station wagon. Heading northwest, we drove toward Dugout Ranch, surrounded by irrigated fields and massive red buttes. Until a few years ago this cattle ranch was isolated. But not now. Uranium and oil seekers have combed the desert valleys. So much traffic passes through the ranch holdings that on one gate I saw a sign reading: "It takes only a minute to close the gate, but it may take hours to pick the shot out of your hide if you don't."

Opening—and closing—several gates, we continued into wilder canyon country. By lunchtime we reached Cave Spring. Though now an entrance to the park, it is no imposing landmark. The cave is an eroded undercut in the base of a cliff, the spring only a drip that forms a puddle in a stone depression. But for centuries Cave Spring has afforded refuge and fresh water for Indians and others roaming the canyons. Prehistoric natives ground corn on hollowed floor stones, and their many fires smudged the roof black. From here we turned south into Salt Creek.

"If you fall into this creek you'll get mighty dusty," somebody said. We got dusty without falling in. The Jeeps plowed through a salt crust and threw up choking clouds of sand as we bucked our way through tangled brush and along dry stream beds that in rainy seasons can become raging torrents in the space of minutes. Wherever we found a shallow puddle or a small stream, we had to be alert against quicksand.

W. ROBERT MOORE, NATIONAL GEOGRAPHIC STAFF

We followed the Salt for three miles before turning off to explore a large tributary in Horse Cañyon. Though our course led upstream, the cliffs thrust higher and higher. Suddenly, rounding a bend, we spied the triangular window of Gothic Arch high above the canyon floor.

As we vainly sought a way up the cliff to Gothic, we came upon a small cluster of Indian storehouses nestled in a ledge. Though abandoned perhaps 800 years ago, their stone-and-adobe walls still stand almost intact. On the dusty floors we discovered corncobs, dry and hard as bone. The primitive Indian farmers obviously gained no bumper yields from the flint corn they planted in the canyons: no cob was longer than three inches. Potsherds strewed the ground. A rock wall displayed a row of pictographs; one portrayed a hunter drawing a bow.

A mile or so beyond Gothic Arch we came to a canyon stricture, The Narrows. Here the stream has cut a

Quicksand! A treacherous bend in Horse Canyon traps a Jeep. Gun the motor. No use. The author's party and a Jeep that made it strain to free the mired one.

Canyonlands campers drive their cars on improved roads to primitive sites at Island in the Sky and Squaw Flat. The trail to Chesler Park and The Needles, like most trails in this rugged 402-square-mile preserve, requires a four-wheel-drive vehicle. Supplies, lodgings, scenic flights are available at Monticello and Moab. Rangers assist visitors all year at The Neck and Cave Spring. The Park Service plans permanent facilities to handle an expected half-million people a year by 1974—a torrent compared to the trickle of first arrivals in 1964.

OTIS IMBODEN, NATIONAL GEOGRAPHIC PHOTOGRAPHER

Like a great grasshopper leaping over stone sentinels, Secretary of the Interior Stewart Udall's copter invades Chesler Park during a 1961 inspection. In Devils Lane Mrs. Udall and daughter Lynn match palms with the painted prints of prehistoric Indians. Near Dead Horse Point the Secretary savors pancakes hot from the griddle.

W. ROBERT MOORE, NATIONAL GEOGRAPHIC STAFF

If Newspaper Rock ever carried a scoop, it's unreadable today. Scientists speculate that Indian artists used hard stones to cut figures in the "desert varnish"—a dark crust of iron and manganese oxides. The slab lures visitors on the southern approach to Canyonlands.

channel through cliffs, forming a gap scarcely wider than our Jeeps. A little farther springs filled several pools and gave birth to a pleasant little stream. We set up camp on a grassy bank and spent the night serenaded by croaking frogs. Next morning, and every morning after that, we were awake at five o'clock. Harlon Bement saw to that—by firing his pistol. Then, fortified by breakfast cooked on an open fire, we hit the trail again.

Returning from upper Horse Canyon, we headed up Salt Creek once more. Soon we switched from Jeeps to horses, then left the mounts and scrambled up gullies and over massive broken boulders to reach Angel Arch. From the purple shadows of a rocky defile, I gazed up in wonder at the great rock band rising from a high cliff shoulder, one of the most striking formations we had seen.

Later, on a second exploration of Canyonlands, we pushed farther west. From Cave Spring we drove to Devils Pocket, a pleasant hollow lined with green spring-

Canyon country hikes build hefty appetites. Campers must haul food and fuel. Blankets, too. Daytime temperatures in midsummer soar to over 100°, but nights in this high, dry land are cool.

time grass and massed patches of flowering beeweed, as yellow as mustard. We clambered out of Devils Pocket and down into Devils Lane, a quarter-mile-wide corridor extending several miles. To the west lay The Grabens, fantastic sunken valleys formed by faulting sandstone. We turned into Chesler Canyon, named after a stockman who ran cattle there, then climbed into a spectacular oval meadow. This is Chesler Park, rimmed by sandstone eroded into red spires 50 stories high—The Needles.

And finally, at the head of Elephant Canyon, we stood on a slickrock ledge and looked across a canyon at our goal: Druid Arch. The resemblance of this craggy titan to England's Stonehenge, popularly associated with the Druids, is remarkable. This was one of the arches that Harlon Bement had found on his flights. I am not surprised when I hear that he has found others. Our trips had probed only a portion of this erosion-gouged landscape. And it may be years before visitors succeed in cataloguing all the arches of Utah's cliff-hung canyonland.

While we were photographing Druid, white, fleecy clouds scudded across the sky. Within minutes they massed into a solid cover, turned black, and spat flurries of snow. The wind honed itself to a cutting edge. Back in camp, we huddled by the fire and ate an early dinner. Tomorrow we would head for home. After all, who wants to risk the ire of a Druid nature deity.

Angel Arch glows in the glare of a setting sun; its yawning cavity—150 feet high and 130 feet wide—makes men appear as Lilliputians. Head of the graceful figure which gives the arch its name projects at upper left; body shows on the opposite side. The fractured face

BURNETT A. HENDRYX

of Canyonlands began to take shape ages ago when the sandstone crust cracked during a general uplift of the earth. Seeping ground water widened the cracks; swirling streams gouged canyons, faulting formed valleys. Weather erosion applied the finishing touches.

BLACK CANYON OF THE GUNNISON

ANGLERS SEEKING RAINBOW TROUT in the gorge of the Gunnison River have reported that in full daylight they could see stars gleaming in the strip of sky overhead. Rangers label this a fish story—but do confirm that, except at midday, an eerie twilight shrouds the depths between the sheer walls.

Knifing through a plateau in the San Juan Mountains region of western Colorado, the Gunnison has cut as deep as 2,700 feet through base rock. Black Canyon of the Gunnison National Monument, established in 1933, includes the deepest 10-mile stretch of this stupendous chasm. And black is the word for the canyon. Cliff bottoms reveal ebonylike schist, millions of years old. Overhangs cast long shadows on frowning walls banded by coarse gneiss and granite ranging from somber gray to pink.

To stand at the lip of the abyss and peer straight down at the tiny, writhing river is enough to raise the hackles on summer sightseers.

Small trees crowd the plateau, among them piñon patriarchs whose 700-odd years are chronicled in the rings of their gnarled trunks. Vacationers who pitch tents at the north and south rim campgrounds may glimpse the rare Rocky Mountain bighorn. Elk often winter in the 21-square-mile sanctuary.

COLORADO NATIONAL MONUMENT

DRAMATIC RED SANDSTONE FORMATIONS unfold before visitors to this western Colorado preserve. A 22-mile scenic drive, open all year, skims the edges of canyons that cut deeply into the escarpment above the Colorado River near the cities of Grand Junction and Fruita. Overlooks and self-guiding trails give motorists and campers close acquaintance with Window Rock and the pot-bellied "coke ovens" of Monument Canyon, the arrow-straight vista down Red Canyon, and such columns and spires as 500-foot-tall Independence Rock.

Juniper, piñon, and flowering plants dot the red-rocked land. Formed during the Age of Reptiles, the red strata lie directly on black granite dating from earth's nearly lifeless infancy. No vein of stone exists here between the two layers to record the passage of a half-billion years. Rangers call this strange geological missing link the great hiatus.

Where brontosaurus, the "thunder lizard," once shook the ground with his tread, a small herd of bison now grazes within the monument's 28 square miles.

"Place of high rocks and much water," Ute Indians described the gorge of the Gunnison. Scenic drives parallel north and south rims.

EDWARDS PARK, NATIONAL GEOGRAPHIC STAFF

JACK BREED

High cliffs and high adventure mark the 75-mile raft run down the Yampa and Green Rivers across the monument. Many of Dinosaur's most spectacular sights are known only to those who ride its rivers.

Daring "river rats" shoot the rapids through Colorado-Utah borderlands where monstrous reptiles met a mysterious end

DINOSAUR NATIONAL MONUMENT

By JACK BREED

"THIS RIVER IS STRICTLY A ONE-WAY STREET," said Bus Hatch. "Once we enter the canyon of the Yampa, there's no turning back. So if any of you fellows want to reconsider. . . ."

His glance traveled deliberately over each member of the little group. Our three rubber life rafts, loaded with camp equipment, were drawn up on the muddy shore near Lily Park, Colorado. Ahead lay 75 miles of white water twisting into Utah through some of the West's most spectacular gorges, the bright-hued cliffs of Dinosaur National Monument. We grinned back at Bus.

"Well, don't say I didn't warn you," he said. "Let's shove off."

I clambered aboard Bus's raft. This jolly, plump contractor from Vernal, Utah, and his son Don were "river rats" of no mean skill. The rest of us—Conrad Wirth and four Park Service colleagues, a local rancher, and I—made up in high spirits what we might have lacked in experience.

Our boats looked ugly but dependable. Navy craft designed to hold ten men each, their rubbery buoyancy gave them an obvious advantage over wooden skiffs. Our 4½-day trip downriver would take us to the Dinosaur Quarry, where paleontologists unearthed more than two dozen complete dinosaur skeletons.

For the first few miles of our journey down the Yampa we had leisure to study the country. Here the river, yellow and brown with

Indian warrior has guarded Dinosaur's cliffs 1,000 years or more. The monument is rich in such petroglyphs.

In reptilian coils, two rivers course through Dinosaur land

Carrying Colorado's silt toward Utah, the slender Yampa (right) joins the Green River for a promenade around 700-foot-high Steam-

JUSTIN LOCKE

boat Rock. In this cliff-barricaded meadow a hermit, Pat Lynch, took refuge for 50 years; oldtimers called the site Pats Hole. Today a road enters from US 40. Echo Park, in shadow at right, is named for Steamboat's resonance. Spanish explored the region in 1776.

silt, was a sluggish stream less than a foot deep; we used oars more than outboard motors. But our placid drifting drew to a close with the distant roar of white water ahead. We tipped up the propellers to avoid concealed rocks; the canyon walls converged. It looked as if the river were turning into a broad staircase, each step capped by curling spray.

I flinched as the first ripple glistened ahead. But nothing happened. Our rubber boat simply buckled, folding itself over rocks like a caterpillar.

On a sandbar beneath Yampa Canyon's walls we ate a typical river rat's lunch of bean stew and sandwiches. No one needed to tell us how the Yampa had earned its title, "River of no return." We could not possibly have climbed its 1,400-foot cliffs or hiked back upstream. I was glad I had no appendix.

Back on the river, we saw Canada geese placidly swimming. Beavers moved close to the banks; deer occasionally bounded up the talus slopes. "You can see why early trappers liked this country," Bus said. "Mountain men camped here in the 1830's and '40's. We'd better pick a spot ourselves."

It was only 5 p.m., but the sun sets early and rises late in narrow canyons. We pitched camp on a grassy slope in Starvation Valley, at the head of Big Joe Rapids. Soon steaks were sizzling and we were ready for sleeping bags.

In the morning we made a reconnaissance of the rapids below. The water raged with whirlpools and waves 8 and 10 feet high. Don tossed in several logs. We watched one swirl past—and disappear into a foaming caldron.

"Stay clear of that one!" yelled Bus.

He took his raft first. Standing in the stern, Bus gunned his engine and pointed the bow toward midriver, seeming to head for the worst waves of all. He shot into them—and vanished.

He reappeared skimming the crest of a wave, his raft bending around a stubborn rock. Spume drenched him, but he never took his eyes from the river. In an instant he had cleared the rapids. Cheers from all hands.

Storm clouds threaten as raftsmen pit their skill against Green River rapids in Split Mountain Canyon. Channels change day to day as the rampaging stream shifts boulders.

JACK BREED

The rest of us followed. Now the river widened and we entered the amphitheater called Harding Hole. From here the Yampa threads white sandstone cliffs. Drifting, we lounged and looked up at the blue ribbon of sky.

"Steamboat round the bend!" Tom Vint sang out, and we saw massive Steamboat Rock, marking the Yampa's wedding with the Green. We camped here in the meadow of Pats Hole and next day rode the Green River through Whirlpool Canyon. Rock slides strewed the banks; juniper and scrub pine clung to crevices.

On our final day, Bus cautioned us. "I've run boats through Grand Canyon, the San Juan, the Snake. None has worse stretches than you'll find in Split Mountain Canyon today." And indeed we had close calls. Once Bus lost control; in a wooden craft, we would have cracked up. Then the canyon opened up, and twilight found the river more peaceful. We were at voyage end: Dinosaur Quarry.

I tried to imagine this country when dinosaurs roamed it, back in the Jurassic

"Where can we see the dinosaurs?" eager visitors ask. "You're about 120 million years late," rangers reply. "But our new visitor center tells about ones that used to live here." Bones of this 70-foot-long diplodocus at the National Museum in Washington came from Dinosaur.

BATES LITTLEHALES, NATIONAL GEOGRAPHIC PHOTOGRAPHER

New roof joins an ancient wall at Dinosaur Quarry Visitor Center

Open all year, the building encloses a fossil-filled cliff, allowing spectators to watch as workmen chisel away at barren rock to expose petrified remains of prehistoric animals. Expanded to 322 square miles from the original 80 acres set aside in 1915, the monument has picnic areas, summer campsites, trails, wilderness roads. Permit or guide required for river trips. Lodgings, supplies at nearby communities on US 40. For further information write Superintendent, Artesia, Colorado.

HAROLD J. BRODRICK AND (ABOVE) LYLE FORREST, NATIONAL PARK SERVICE

period. No Rocky Mountains, no canyons; just tropical marshland, with a fringe of volcanoes showering ash and dust. Several kinds of dinosaurs lived here—some no bigger than a turkey; others, like the brontosaurus, 80 feet long. All were a bit stupid, averaging one pound of brain to 40 tons of bulk.

What killed these dinosaurs? Perhaps a blizzard of volcanic ash or a bacterial plague. Rivers washed their carcasses against a great sandbank where they were covered by sand and silt. Silica impregnated their bones. Sand and bone became stone. In 1909 Dr. Earl Douglass, of Pittsburgh's Carnegie Museum, discovered the paleontological treasure trove, one of the world's richest.

Today this cliff makes an exhibit unique in our national parks. From a balcony within glass walls visitors view fossil bones as they were uncovered and glimpse vistas of life history more exciting even than canyons and rapids.

LEHMAN CAVES

PIONEER RANCHER Absalom Lehman stumbled upon a small cave in 1885 and thus gave his name to an intimate, exquisite cavern system in the flank of 13,063-foot Wheeler Peak near Baker, in eastern Nevada. Ninety-minute tours, conducted by park rangers the year round, lead past "bacon-strip" draperies, twisting helictites, and rare, geologically puzzling formations called shields or pallettes, thin disks of calcite angled on the floors and walls. In spring, summer, and fall the scenic square-mile monument offers refreshments. Campers pitch their tents amid the aspens along trout streams nearby.

TIMPANOGOS CAVE

LEAVE HIGH-HEELED SHOES in the car when you visit Timpanogos. The cave lies at the end of a mile-and-a-half trail that switchbacks up the side of American Fork Canyon in Utah's scenic Wasatch Mountains. Don't forget a sweater, for cave temperatures hover around 42°. But the delights of these little chambers outweigh the chill. Stalactites are jeweled with drops of water, for this is a living cave, its formations still growing. Pale colors tinge coral-like helictites, fragile structures whose crystals grow every which way. Only 35 miles from Salt Lake City, the 250-acre monument closes in winter.

CRATERS OF THE MOON

YOUNGSTERS EXPECT MOON MEN in pressurized suits and fishbowl helmets. Instead they find in this 83-square-mile national monument in southern Idaho one of the world's most complete displays of volcanism. Here the earth's crust was weak, and for thousands of years lava bubbled from wounds along the Great Rift. Hot magma lapped around living trees, turned them to torches, and left molds of their burned-out trunks. Molten blobs, hurled from spatter cones, hardened in mid-air to the teardrop shape of bombs.

Today all is black desolation with an austere beauty of its own. Rivers of rock seem still to flow around cinder cones and lava domes. Visitors tentatively touch ropy lava to see if it's still warm. Playing Superman, they hoist overhead fantastically heavy-looking chunks of volcanic froth.

A loop road and trails explore these pockmarked wonders. Campers pitch tents on the cinders and slake their thirst on cold spring water piped from mountains to the north. In winter skiers sport on the cinder slopes.

To explore Boy Scout Cave at Craters, youngsters lug a sled through midsummer heat (above), then pull themselves across the cave's watery ice with prospector's picks. Hard hats guard against jagged lava that insulates this once-molten tube, keeping temperatures near freezing.

WILLIAM BELKNAP, JR.

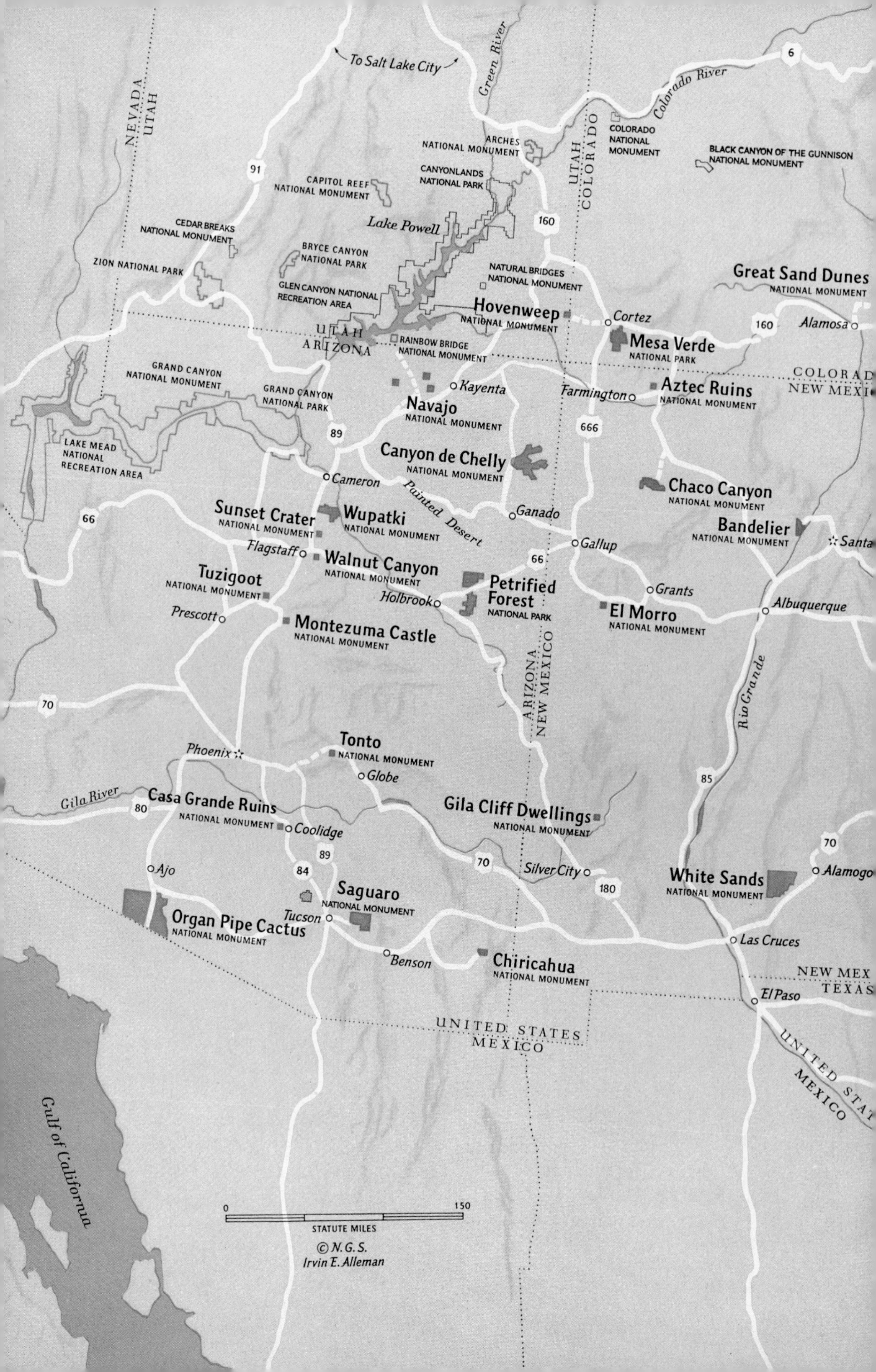

To Salt Lake City
Green River
Colorado River
NEVADA
UTAH
UTAH
COLORADO
ARCHES NATIONAL MONUMENT
COLORADO NATIONAL MONUMENT
BLACK CANYON OF THE GUNNISON NATIONAL MONUMENT
CAPITOL REEF NATIONAL MONUMENT
CANYONLANDS NATIONAL PARK
CEDAR BREAKS NATIONAL MONUMENT
Lake Powell
BRYCE CANYON NATIONAL PARK
ZION NATIONAL PARK
NATURAL BRIDGES NATIONAL MONUMENT
GLEN CANYON NATIONAL RECREATION AREA
Great Sand Dunes
NATIONAL MONUMENT
Hovenweep
NATIONAL MONUMENT
Cortez
Alamosa
UTAH
ARIZONA
RAINBOW BRIDGE NATIONAL MONUMENT
Mesa Verde
NATIONAL PARK
GRAND CANYON NATIONAL MONUMENT
COLORAD
NEW MEXI
Kayenta
Farmington
Aztec Ruins
NATIONAL MONUMENT
GRAND CANYON NATIONAL PARK
Navajo
NATIONAL MONUMENT
LAKE MEAD NATIONAL RECREATION AREA
Canyon de Chelly
NATIONAL MONUMENT
Cameron
Painted Desert
Chaco Canyon
NATIONAL MONUMENT
Sunset Crater
NATIONAL MONUMENT
Wupatki
NATIONAL MONUMENT
Ganado
Bandelier
NATIONAL MONUMENT
Santa
Gallup
Flagstaff
Walnut Canyon
NATIONAL MONUMENT
Tuzigoot
NATIONAL MONUMENT
Petrified Forest
NATIONAL PARK
Grants
Holbrook
Albuquerque
Prescott
El Morro
NATIONAL MONUMENT
Montezuma Castle
NATIONAL MONUMENT
ARIZONA
NEW MEXICO
Rio Grande
Tonto
NATIONAL MONUMENT
Phoenix
Globe
Gila River
Casa Grande Ruins
NATIONAL MONUMENT
Coolidge
Gila Cliff Dwellings
NATIONAL MONUMENT
Ajo
Silver City
White Sands
NATIONAL MONUMENT
Alamogo
Saguaro
NATIONAL MONUMENT
Tucson
Organ Pipe Cactus
NATIONAL MONUMENT
Las Cruces
Benson
Chiricahua
NATIONAL MONUMENT
NEW MEX
TEXAS
El Paso
UNITED STATES
MEXICO
UNITED STA
MEXICO
Gulf of California
6
91
160
160
666
89
66
66
70
85
80
89
84
70
70
180
0
150
STATUTE MILES
© N.G.S.
Irvin E. Alleman

PART THREE

THE SOUTHWEST

In the Painted Desert a silent ocean of mesas and buttes rolls to the horizon. Sunwashed colors play on their wrinkled skins, setting afire chunks of petrified wood. Amid the gesturing saguaros of Arizona, the sweeping range lands and vast caverns of New Mexico, there is the same grandness—and seeming emptiness. It is as though this broad Southwest heard no voice but the dry whisper of its winds, saw nothing but the glare of its sun. It is as though man had never intruded on this communion of land and sky.

Yet for thousands of years men have come, one migration elbowing aside its predecessor. In forgotten canyons stand crumbling villages that once rang with life. On cliff walls Indian sketches show helmeted conquistadors astride monstrous horses. Each age has left its mark on this dry and sunny land where nothing seems to perish.

Descendants of early pit-dwellers live in adobe pueblos and sell pottery to Spanish-American ranchers—and "Anglo" tourists. Singing a high-pitched dirge, the Navajo trots home to his hogan. Serenely unconcerned with humans, the Southwest has absorbed them all, preserved their cultures, and thus enriched itself.

244 **Limestone cascades in a frozen Niagara;** stone parachutes hang motionless in Carlsbad's Big Room. Dripping water patiently fashioned these translucent stalactites. Tubular, they resound like bells if struck, but, since knuckles may break them, the practice is forbidden.

Beneath sunbaked cactus lands where conquistadors marched and outlaws ambushed wagon trains of California gold, Carlsbad's cool caverns reveal a vast and gleaming fairyland

CARLSBAD CAVERNS

By MASON SUTHERLAND, former Assistant Editor, National Geographic
Photographs by E. "TEX" HELM

NEW MEXICO RANCHERS in the 1880's noticed sky-darkening flights of bats that spiraled like a tornado funnel from a cave in the foothills of the Guadalupe Mountains. But not until 1901 did a young cowboy, James Larkin White, light a kerosene torch and descend to explore deeper recesses of the bats' home.

White discovered a world of hidden wonders, a network of corridors and vaulted chambers, ornate with magical formations. From then on he made Carlsbad Caverns his life's work and hobby. He found with each trip a new fantasy that had been wrought through ages of darkness by drops of water. Fragile chandeliers, folds of mineral drapery, pillars, domes, make-believe birds, and fanciful flowers lurked whereever his torchlight fell.

Yet this enchanted underworld remained rel-

Queen's Draperies burst into flame as a torch shines through them. Absorbing light, they glow for seconds after it has been doused.

"You are entering the world's most spectacular caverns," announces the tour leader at the start of the three-mile hike. Elevators await those who can't make it. At summer twilight bats stream out entrance.

atively obscure until 1924 and 1925 when the National Geographic Society put it on the map. Backed by a grant from The Society and guided by Jim White, Dr. Willis T. Lee of the United States Geological Survey explored and mapped portions of the caverns, which he described in two *National Geographic* articles. "The most spectacular underground wonder in America," Lee wrote. "For spacious chambers, for variety and beauty, [the cave] is king of its kind."

Thus Carlsbad Caverns achieved their first nationwide publicity. They were established as a national park in 1930.

In the days when Dr. Lee was supervising the recently explored caverns, yearly visitors were counted in the hundreds. Within 30 years annual attendance soared above the half-million mark. Today rangers lead four-hour trips along three miles of paved trails. For my tour I had the company of Col. Thomas Boles, the park's first superintendent, who served 19 years at the caverns and spoke to more than two million visitors. "I have made 5,071 complete trips and enjoyed every one," he told me.

FOR A MOMENT we paused at the caverns' natural mouth. The ranger leading our tour told how Carlsbad Caverns were hollowed out of a 1,600-foot-thick limestone formation called the Capitan, deposited in a shallow sea some 200 million years ago. When the Rockies started growing, about 70 million years ago, the Carlsbad area was uplifted. Between that era and the Pleistocene, a million years ago, ground water entered fissures and dissolved the less resistant stone. Finally the water table fell, air filled the cavities, and collapse hastened water's work to completion.

Then the decorative phase of cavern building set in. Rain water, seeping from the surface, picked up limestone. Wherever drip was slow enough, evaporation squeezed out the water and deposited minerals which, layer by layer, formed stalactites and stalagmites. Nature sought to fill the chambers she took so long to hollow out.

Starting down the switchbacks, a series of winding ramps descending 829 feet, the height of an 80-story building, we passed the entrance to Bat Cave. No place in the caverns seems gloomier than this passage, illuminated only by natural light and seldom shown to visitors. Shortly after the turn of the century miners descended to the cave to remove the nitrate-rich bat guano. In 20 years they hoisted out 100,000 tons of this valuable fertilizer.

As many as nine million bats at a time have slept by day on Bat Cave's walls and ceilings, hanging head down. At night they feed on insects outside. Leaving at the rate of 300 a second, more than a million an hour, they fill the evening air with their sweet and musky odor.

"I recall one morning," said Boles, "when a party got caught in the bats' return flight. Women screamed and raised skirts above their heads."

But the 14 species of bats found in the park are harmless to humans. Most

numerous from April through October, they migrate to warmer climes when cold cuts down the supply of night-flying beetles and moths.

Beyond Bat Cave we entered the Main Corridor, a cathedral-like hall a mile long that descends deep into the earth. We saw natural sculptures such as the American Eagle, with a 12-foot wingspread; the Whale's Mouth; the Three Little Monkeys, perched high above the trail; and the Baby Hippo. My attention was drawn to millions of tons of material which had fallen from the ceiling.

"Don't be alarmed," said Boles. "You couldn't be in a safer place. No collapse has taken place in thousands of years." One spectacular collapse has been named the Iceberg. Despite its 100,000 tons, the Iceberg slipped so gently that its stalactites received no injury.

"Remember you can destroy in an instant what nature took centuries to build," tour leaders counsel. "Please don't touch the formations. Stay on the trail at all times and make your trip quietly."

I heard the silence rule broken at the Iceberg. Snapping off the lights to give us a taste of the utter blackness in which the caverns grew, our guide asked us not to speak lest we destroy the illusion. A creepy interval followed. Then some man pinched his wife, she giggled, and the crowd roared.

In the Green Lake Room, first of the scenic rooms on the first half of the tour, floodlights threw the Veiled Statue into relief. This shrouded column resulted when stalactite met stalagmite. Nearby the Frozen Waterfall spilled out of a tunnel, and a small enchanted pond explained the room's name. It turned reflected light an emerald green.

We entered the King's Palace, perhaps the caverns' most ornate chamber, where the trail leveled off under thousands of stalactites, glittering like chandeliers. Each of these downward-hanging stone lances was formed by water seeping from the ceiling and leaving a mineral trail in tubular form. One seven-foot pendant as slender as a soda straw is known as the King's Bellcord.

Generally, when droplets roll off a stalactite and hit the floor, they build a stalagmite. But few of these reach upward in the King's Palace. One stalagmite, however, comes within a knife's blade of kissing its corresponding stalactite. Doomed never to touch, since no water now drops between them, they are called the Frustrated Lovers. These two guard a keyhole entrance to the Queen's Chamber. There we found the famous draperies, masses of stalactites grown together like curtains. We saw no sign of the Queen herself, but the King's Boots hung in her chamber.

Baby of the royal chambers is the Papoose Room, its low ceiling gleaming with porcupine-quill stalactites. No one has described them better than the little girl who said, "That's just how my foot feels when it goes to sleep."

Nature fills its cavities with limestone marvels. Shapes vary from swirling stone portieres at the Dome Room entrance (opposite page) to the Dolls' Theater (right), a tiny forest of stalactites and stalagmites that looks like a brilliantly lighted stage. This exquisite formation shows how the decorative phase of cavern building tends to reverse the dissolving process by filling passages with secondary growths.

Some pillars, gleaming like candle wax, are wet—still growing. "Popcorn" studding them shows they were immersed in water. Broken stubs bear witness to the Park Service rule: "Don't touch the formations!"

Mountains of stone dominate the Hall of Giants in the Big Room, relegating surrounding stalagmites to foothill status. Giant Dome (right), rising 62 feet and connected to the ceiling by a thin band of stone, suggests to many the Leaning Tower of Pisa. Twin Domes (center) are not identical and were not necessarily born at the same time. Smaller Rock of Ages stands at far left.

Other caverns may be more vividly colored than Carlsbad, but none matches the immensity of its spectacle. The Park Service shuns colored floodlights, insists on showing the formations in their natural state.

DAVID S. BOYER AND ARLAN R. WIKER, NATIONAL GEOGRAPHIC STAFF

At one time Colonel Boles used to halt touring parties in the scenic rooms for lunch. They would drink pure, cold drip water caught on the spot. Now Carlsbad's guests break their tours for lunch before tackling the mile-and-a-quarter trail around the Big Room. We mounted Appetite Hill, 80 feet of rugged switchbacks, walked past the Boneyard, where partly dissolved rocks illustrate the first stages of the caverns' formation, and took a passage to the huge subterranean lunchroom where we bought coffee and sandwiches and sat at a picnic table. Though hikers can sit for a moment along the trail, this 40-minute rest was welcome. Reminiscing, Boles spoke of the Rat Hole trip that parties used to take before tours grew too unwieldy.

"That narrow tunnel made an interesting detour," he said. "Everybody had a laugh when fat men got stuck in a tight gap. One guide used to save an old starched collar for the occasion. Just as the visitor's trousers grew taut under the strain, the guide would rip the collar. It sounded like the seams giving way!"

At last we hiked to the Big Room, the world's largest known underground chamber. Like a vast, richly ornamented cathedral, the Big Room has the ground plan of a cross, one arm measuring some 1,800 feet, the crosspiece stretching 1,100. The ceiling at its highest point rises 232 feet.

We caught a distant view of the Rock of Ages, one of the caverns' most famed formations. At this monumental stalagmite, Colonel Boles used to stop tour parties and call the roll of states. He saved the Texans until the last, because, "cheering the mention of their state, they made further roll call impossible."

We marched past Crystal Spring Dome, fastest growing formation in the caverns. Though some 95 percent of the formations are dry, and hence dormant, here the eye easily picks out splashing drops of water that spread a thin coat of limestone paint. The

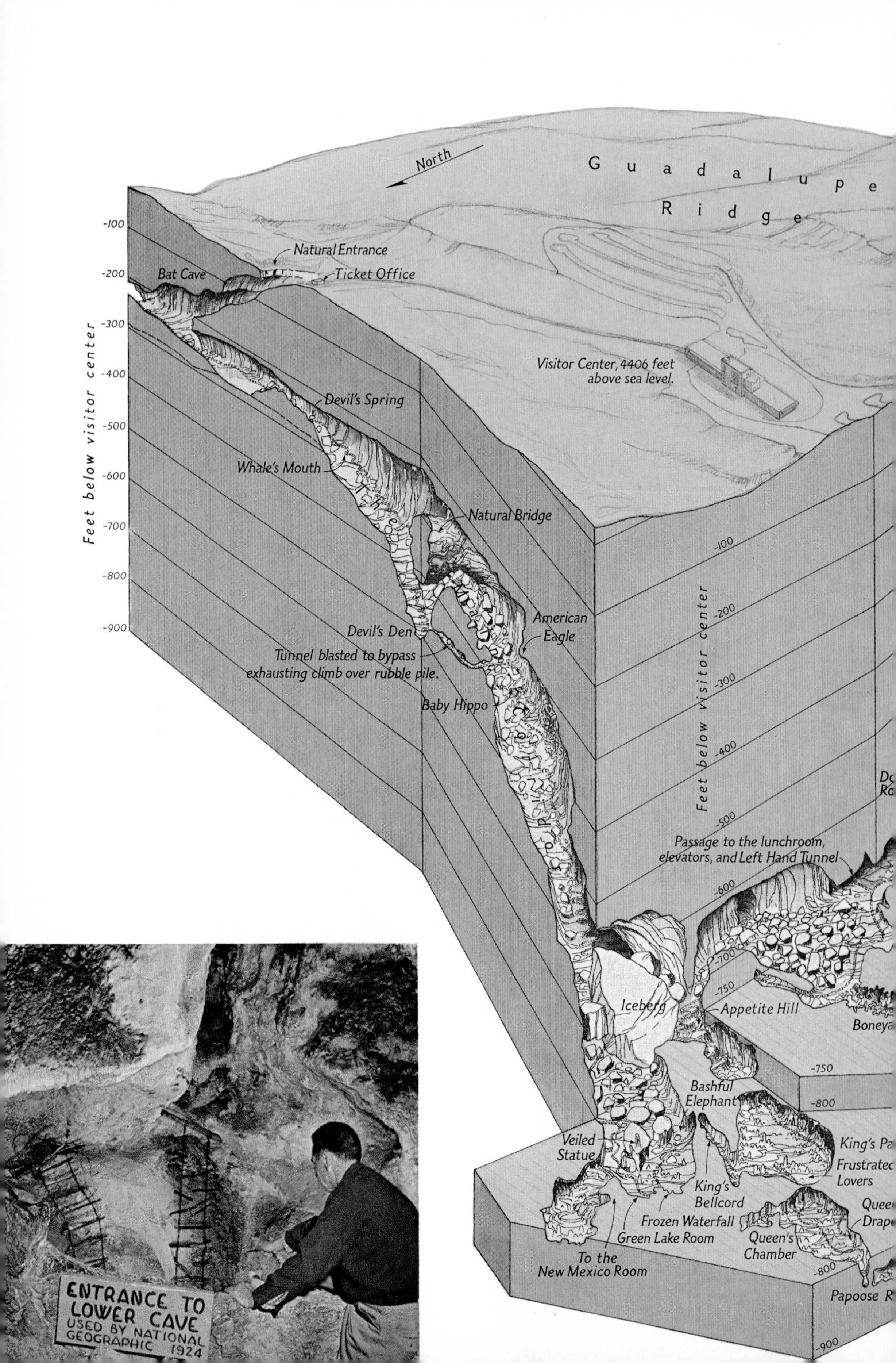

North
Guadalupe
Ridge
Feet below visitor center
-100
-200
-300
-400
-500
-600
-700
-800
-900
Natural Entrance
Bat Cave
Ticket Office
Visitor Center, 4406 feet above sea level.
Devil's Spring
Whale's Mouth
Natural Bridge
American Eagle
Devil's Den
Tunnel blasted to bypass exhausting climb over rubble pile.
Baby Hippo
Passage to the lunchroom, elevators, and Left Hand Tunnel
Iceberg
Appetite Hill
-700
-750
-800
Bashful Elephant
Veiled Statue
King's Bellcord
Frozen Waterfall
Green Lake Room
To the New Mexico Room
Queen's Chamber
Frustrated Lovers
ENTRANCE TO LOWER CAVE USED BY NATIONAL GEOGRAPHIC 1924

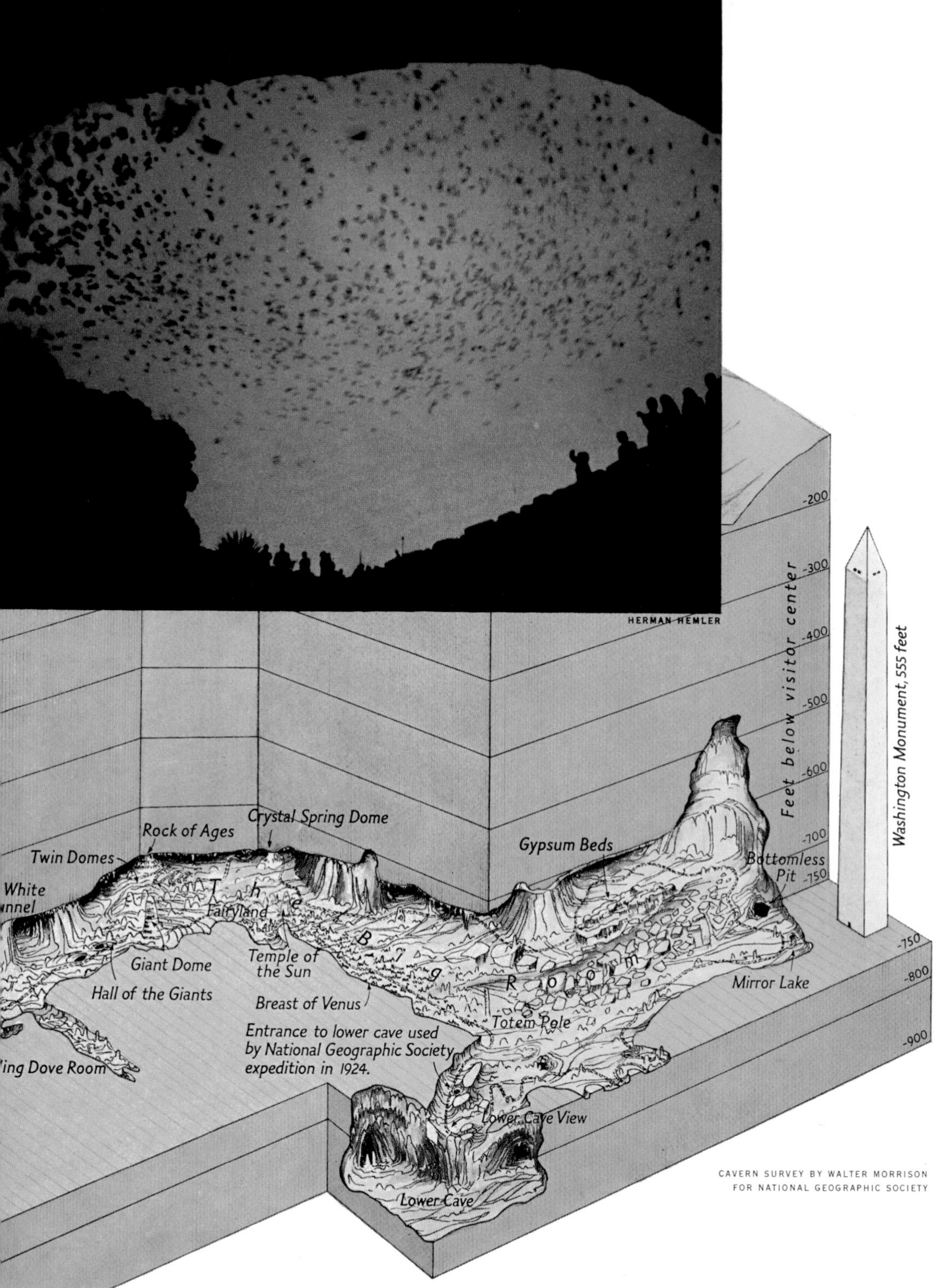

HERMAN HEMLER

CAVERN SURVEY BY WALTER MORRISON FOR NATIONAL GEOGRAPHIC SOCIETY

Carlsbad Caverns unroofed: a depth map reveals the cave's enormity

In contrast to National Geographic explorers who clambered over loose rocks and even scaled a rickety ladder to probe Lower Cave (opposite), today's visitors follow a paved trail. After walking a mile down the Main Corridor they gaze in awe at the Green Lake Room, first of the decorated chambers. Appetite Hill readies hikers for the lunchroom, halfway point of tours. The second half is spent circling the Big Room. Elevators then return parties to New Mexico's sunlight. From April to October they can watch millions of bats spiral out of Bat Cave into the twilight (upper). Most bats migrate for the winter.

Of Carlsbad's eight miles of explored passages only the three paved miles are shown. Some tunnels have never been entered. Deepest pit reaches 1,013 feet below the surface.

For a mile and a quarter hikers wind beneath Big Room's bearded ceiling

So vast is the Big Room and so twisting the trail that most visitors fail to recognize it as a single chamber. A stroll through it takes 30 minutes, the average walking time between the White House and Capitol in Washington, D. C.

Its stalactites resemble soda straws, ribbons, needles, atomic clouds, chandeliers. One, poised over the path, is aptly named the Sword of Damocles. Stalagmites of every shape grope upward from the 14-acre floor. One of the most celebrated of all, the Rock of Ages, occupies a niche in the dark central window.

Sometimes stalactite and stalagmite meet and merge into a pillar or column. Most of Carlsbad's formations have stopped growing, reflecting climatic changes overhead in semiarid New Mexico.

To take these pictures, photographer Tex Helm used multiple-flash gear and a bank of 13 mounted cameras, each set at a slightly different lens opening. Bulbs and reflectors bathed the caverns in a blinding, crucible glow for one-thirtieth of a second.

For one over-all shot of the Big Room, Helm used 2,400 huge bulbs and bombarded the great sanctum with light four times as intense as New Mexico's sun.

EUGENE HILL

Cave pearls spun for centuries in watery nests. The calcium carbonate spheres grew around grains of sand or pieces of bat bone.

The Society's 1924 expedition caught flash-powder shots of cave wonders

Probing the caverns for the National Geographic, Dr. Willis T. Lee and his men were lowered into Bat Cave in a guano bucket. They struggled down unknown tunnels, into yawning pits, and over blocks of fallen limestone "like a train of ants making its way through a brickpile." Feeble torches were almost helpful since they lit "only one difficulty at a time." Like Tom Sawyer, the men strung twine as they explored; if one lost his way, he followed the twine back to the main trail.

Lee returned (right) to photograph formations like the gnarled, popcorn-coated stalactite that reminded him of a cave man's club.

Dome is accumulating about 2½ cubic inches of mineral a year. A small pool, Crystal Spring, collects at its foot.

We peered down the Bottomless Pit, whose bottom actually can be seen by flashlight, 138 feet below the trail. Here the ceiling of the Big Room reaches its apex, so the vertical drop from ceiling to pit bottom covers 370 feet—largest in the caverns.

The trail skirted Mirror Lake, which correctly reflects its own inverted signpost. The Totem Pole, tallest of several skinny stalagmites, lacks a parental stalactite because water dripped too fast to deposit a big growth overhead. The Temple of the Sun has never seen its namesake's light. Tinged with delicate pastel hues by iron oxides, the decorative formations here turn the ceiling into an inverted pincushion.

Passing the Temple, we walked into

Algae growing under lights tint stone grapes green. Cave fungi thrive in dark. Carlsbad would make a good mushroom garden.

the Hall of Giants where the Onyx Draperies hung above the trail and three huge stalagmites rose beside it. These were Twin Domes and Giant Dome, the latter reaching 62 feet above us to stage the Big Room's smashing climax.

In 1924 Dr. Lee and his aides explored and mapped Lower Cave. Actually no deeper than the scenic rooms, it may be seen 90 to 100 feet below the main trail in the Big Room. Two abysses look down into it. One is the Lower Cave View or the Jumping-off Place (no one has jumped yet), the other the site of a rusting ladder used by the 1924 National Geographic expedition. Today's guides know five other ways of entering Lower Cave.

In the caverns' dim lighting one loses all sense of time. Passing a park ranger, I said "Good night." His answering laugh sent me to my watch: 2:30 in the

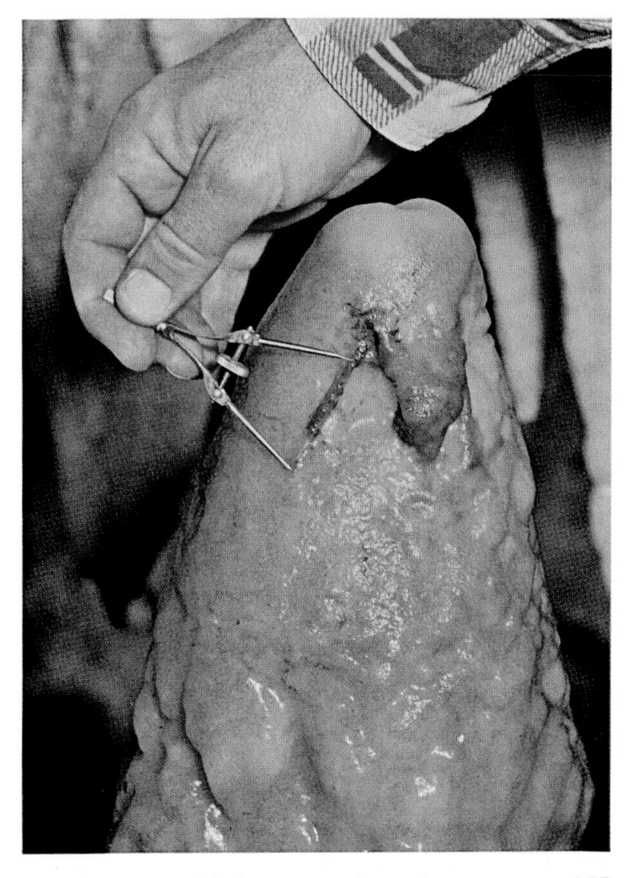

Unlucky bat tumbled on a growing stalagmite; now it's a fossil. As many as 300 bats roost head down on a square foot of Bat Cave's ceiling. Guano miners took 100,000 tons of fertilizer from the floor.

afternoon. Floodlights give many areas a fairly even illumination, and skillful lighting accents big formations. But I took equal pleasure in some lesser sculptures that had to be picked out with a flashlight.

I saw a stone hen that had sat on her nest for thousands of years without laying an egg. The Statue of Liberty held a torch in her left hand. Abraham Lincoln brooded with furrowed brow and bearded chin; and a life-sized Santa Claus, complete with stocking cap, perched atop a totem pole.

I was enchanted by a miniature city with Gothic cathedrals and castles standing on a bluff beside the Big Room trail. Long stone faces recalled Easter Island sculptures. There were stalagmites that looked like fire hydrants, giant candlesticks with melted wax running down their sides, and tombstones in a Moslem cemetery. I even spotted a stalactite growing from the girder of an elevator. And

Hungry hikers welcome a 40-minute rest in the domed lunchroom, 754 feet below the surface. Box

like every tired sightseer, I felt grateful for those elevators that waited near the lunchroom to whisk us to the surface.

Though all attention is usually focused on the caverns, the national park embraces 72 square miles of semidesert near the Texas border. Some of the thousand mule deer that roam this sanctuary have been spotted apparently reading a sign, "U. S. park boundary. No hunting allowed." My car's headlights picked up glow from the eyes of deer idling in the park highway.

About 30 known caverns lie within the park. A guide showed me one, New Cave, or Slaughter Cave. It cannot match the size or beauty of Carlsbad Caverns, but boasts such gigantic formations as a 100-foot pillar, 18 feet in diameter, decorated by fluted draperies that resound like organ pipes. If Carlsbad continues to grow in popularity, new wonders may be opened to the public.

unches feed 2,000 an hour. Elevators are nearby.

CARLSBAD CAVERNS NATIONAL PARK
Southeastern New Mexico. Area 72 sq. mi.

Features: World's most spectacular limestone caverns; colorful stalactite-stalagmite formations in fanciful shapes. Big Room is world's largest known underground chamber.
Activities: Visitor center. Four-hour cavern trips start in morning all year; extra afternoon trips in summer. Elevator service down to lunchroom and second half of tour, to surface at tour's end. Special photographic tours. Naturalist talk on bats each summer evening.
Season: Park open year round.
Weather: Surface temperature varies from near zero in winter to above 100° in summer. Cave is a constant 56°. Elevation at entrance 4,350 ft.
What to bring: Sweater or jacket for cave; low-heeled shoes with rubber soles or heels. Camera for flash or time exposures on photo tour.
How to get there: US 62-180 and 285 (see map at back of book). Trans-Texas Airlines, Sante Fe Rwy. to Carlsbad, New Mex. Major air and rail service to El Paso, Tex. Carlsbad Cavern Coaches from Carlsbad and El Paso to park.
Accommodations: None in park. Hotels, motels, trailer parks in Carlsbad and nearby towns.
Services: Restaurant, curio shop, nursery, kennel adjoin visitor center. Lunchroom in caverns. Garages, car rentals, hospital, church services in Carlsbad, 27 mi. NE.
Park regulations: No camping or fires; lunching in designated places only. Walking sticks in caverns by permit. Pets on leash, none inside.

For further information write Superintendent, Box 1598, Carlsbad, New Mexico

BIG BEND

By BART McDOWELL, National Geographic Staff

TEXANS HAVE A large superlative for the park they gave to the Nation. "It's not the biggest or newest," said a gun-toting U. S. marshal from San Angelo. "But it is the *wildest* national park in the U.S.A."

Texans make a flamboyant case for their claim. Even today parts of Big Bend National Park are unexplored. Law and order are still uneasy newcomers; on some risky patrols, park rangers are carefully dispatched in pairs. Yet for comfort-loving travelers, Big Bend offers safe and varied action, shirt-sleeve weather in the dead of winter, and blanketed beds on summer nights.

This authentic wilderness owes its unspoiled state to freaks of geology. Mountains here are turned upside down, and the Rio Grande has dug itself a formidable system of moats. Spanish conquistadors, even after their triumphs in the Andes, never succeeded in exploring the Rio Grande around its great U-shaped bend. Later men also failed—U. S. boundary surveyors, Texas Rangers, everyone until Robert T. Hill came in 1899. Paddling ten hours a day, six men in Geological Survey boats bested the canyons. "Every stone," wrote Hill, "was closely scanned for men in ambush."

Violent men indeed took refuge behind the Big Bend barricades. Comanche warriors trailed through Persimmon Gap (where motorists from Marathon now enter the park) going to and from their raids in Mexico. Train robbers, smugglers, revolutionaries, bandit gangs all hid in the Chisos Mountains. A gold mine lost, a damsel kidnaped, a rancher slain—such events are still

Cool cottages, at an elevation of 5,400 feet, offer pleasant summers in the Chisos Mountains Basin.

Big Bend National Park, established in 1944, hugs the Mexican border where the Rio Grande makes a sweeping 100-mile turn. Here in Boquillas Canyon the river courses between Texas (right) and Mexico.

WILLIAM A. BARDSLEY AND (RIGHT) W. RAY SCOTT

Big Bend bigness sprawls northward from Burro Mesa. Pioneers said every plant here "either sticks,

recalled by local folk. Crusty Judge Roy Bean, "the law west of the Pecos," claimed dominion over this land. Mexican raiders during Pancho Villa's time invaded U. S. territory here as late as 1916.

Times change, and the real violence is now mainly confined to the struggle of river against rock and to the colors of high desert. Here nature is balanced upon contrasts. The great river waters a warm, fertile strip along its banks; beneath cottonwoods, park visitors run trotlines for 10-pound catfish and sometimes wade abroad into Mexico. Nearby, lunarlike mesas display the austere beauty of classic desert. Beyond, the 7,800-foot Chisos Mountains stand abruptly cool and green.

Campgrounds in each environment give Big Bend a year-round use. Roads and trails lead to the habitats of white-tailed and mule deer, the cranky javelina or peccary, the pronghorn, mountain lion, beaver, and to the only known U. S. nesting place of the lyric-voiced Colima warbler. With horse and guide or on marked hiking trails, the visitor can share the same Southwestern vistas seen by the earliest explorers—and perhaps find spots untrod before.

Cliffs of two countries, pried apart by the Rio Grande, face each other at Santa Elena Canyon. This shaded picnic spot is 94 miles south of Alpine, Texas, served by Solar Airlines and Southern Pacific Railroad. For information write Superintendent, Big Bend National Park, Texas.

W. RAY SCOTT AND (BELOW) WILLIAM A. BARDSLEY

stings, or stinks." But today's city-weary vacationists find the 1,107-square-mile park a feast.

Slat sails set to the desert breeze, a family embarks on picnic delights.

WHITE SANDS

By WILLIAM BELKNAP, JR.

Photographs by the author

STAY ON THE ROAD, folks. Watch our speed limits," said the ranger as he handed us our permit, "and have fun!"

We had turned off US 70 at the monument visitor center, and the country looked flat and unpromising. Have fun doing what? I began to wonder if there would even be anything to photograph. My family, like most others, had come little suspecting the surprises in store.

As we drove along White Sands Drive, my disappointment quickly faded. Shimmering white dunes loomed ahead. Our 12-year-old son Buzz and our daughter Loie, 10, called a halt at the first drifts and shot from the car as if spring-ejected. They scampered up a slope, dropped to their knees, and scooped up great handfuls. Then the magic hit Fran and me as we ran our fingers through the incredibly soft stuff, cool and delightful. Off came our shoes and we raced up a snowy mound.

"I had no idea it could be this lovely," Fran said. "It's like fairyland!"

Enchantment, disbelief, puzzlement—ours were typical reactions to White Sands. We strolled along the roadside dunes, fascinated by the way desert plants—yuccas, sumacs, and even cottonwoods—fought to keep their heads above the sugary tide. Just sand? Not quite. It was like nothing we had ever seen, great rolling waves of it, white and fresh as a wilderness snowfall.

Children have a three-ring circus in New Mexico's 146,000-acre sandbox.

At sunset, shadow islands float on an amethyst sea. After a day busy with people and loud with

Like three million visitors before us, we began to appreciate White Sands' uniqueness. Later, at the museum, we learned it is the world's largest known surface deposit of gypsum sand. Utah and Australia have some, but neither deposit rivals New Mexico's 275-square-mile display. Dunes at White Sands are not only the largest in area; they move faster, pile steeper, look whiter, and are just plain more fun than any others.

How does pulverized gypsum differ from ordinary beach sand? If you heat quartz sand, it melts into glass, but gypsum bakes into pure plaster of Paris. Also, gypsum is much softer and, being white, stays cooler in the sun. It rubs to powder between your fingers, and its wind-driven crystals will not pit the

WESTERN WAYS FEATURES
›lay, peace comes to the desert.

finish of your car. You can even taste the difference. Unlike sand, gypsum dissolves in water and has a definite flavor—mineral and unpleasant.

Late on our first day a windstorm arose, and we saw nature's construction force at work building the gypsum dunes. Fran and Loie stayed snug in the car but curiosity sent Buzz and me struggling up a powdery hillside.

Amazingly, once on top we walked through the storm without getting sand in our eyes. The heavy gypsum traveled as "bed load," rolling, skipping, and bouncing, instead of flying. Braced against the blast, with heavy particles peppering our legs, we saw White Sands come to life. Wind undermined our shoes when we stood still, letting us sink slowly. Air turbulence started small dunes as we watched. Feet first, we slid down the steep dune—and got sandblasted as our faces passed the crest.

The chief ranger has his hands full. His job is an odd combination of protecting a natural wonder and running an amusement park.

"Traffic is our number one problem," he explained. "People like to race and cut corners on the Loop Drive. Some ignore the no-dune-driving signs; they don't realize the danger. If they don't bog down near the road, the bigger dunes beckon. Usually they leave the car imbedded and hitchhike for help."

Perhaps the busiest Park Service man is the road man, who puts in endless hours aboard a grader. The more the wind blows the harder he works. Often he's hard at it by dawn, using his grader like a snowplow.

"We used to fight the sand," he said. "Now we cooperate with it. If a dune wants to cover the road, we bulldoze another route around the dune."

White Sands National Monument occupies part of New Mexico's Tularosa Basin. Because of its relative isolation, natural barriers, and clear atmosphere, this 100-mile-long valley was used as a practice bombing range during World War II. Fifteen miles from monument headquarters lies the fast-growing city of Alamogordo, a name that still rings a bell the Nation over for its connection with the first atomic bomb. The historic blast was set off in a wasteland nearby. Between Alamogordo and White Sands is Holloman Air Force Base, home of the Air Force Missile Development Center. The Army, Air Force,

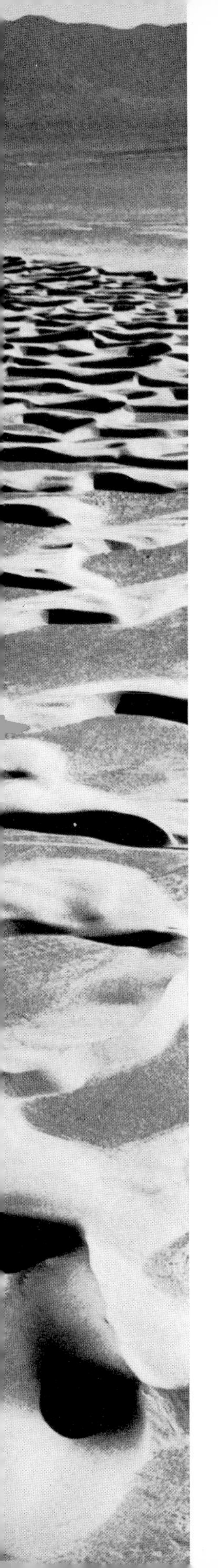

An automobile threads dunes like a mouse in a monstrous maze

Swinging around the Heart of Sands, the monument's recreation center, a car rides the Loop Drive, a track graded wherever fickle nature directs. Dunes constantly lope over it and change its course.

Shallow ditch gouged at center shows how near ground water is to the surface. High mineral content makes it too strong to drink, but it supports more than 100 plant species that have adapted to Tularosa Basin's arid and alkaline life.

Cloudbursts and melting snows dissolve gypsum beds in the distant mountains. Runoff collects in marshy Lake Lucero (mid-distance), for the basin has no outlet. Evaporation leaves transparent selenite crystals (below). Wind pulverizes and whirls them into gleaming patterns. Drifts rise in slopes before the wind, drop off as cliffs to the lee.

An odd adaptation to this snow-white wilderness is the bleached earless lizard (right). Its *Holbrookia* clan is normally brown. But for centuries only lighter members blending with the sands escaped enemies, and a white race arose. Another dunes dweller is the Apache pocket mouse. It wears a white coat too.

A billowing sea of dunes, bound by shores of the San Andres Mountains,

washes over a patch of stunted yucca. Restless as the winds that whip them, dunes rise 50 feet.

and Navy use the Tularosa Basin range to test missiles and research rockets.

Missiles have long been associated with White Sands. Several fluted stone projectile points—spearheads used by Folsom man some 10,000 years ago—have been found in the area. Campsites, arrowheads, and implements of later nomadic Indians show up along its margins. But modern missiles seldom affect visitors at White Sands. Proving grounds officers may restrict traffic along the highway during important "shoots," purely as an ultra precaution. The rockets land many miles away and are almost never seen from the road.

Recreational hub of White Sands is the picnic area. We thought the palette-

White Sands' feathery dunes play host to some 450,000 visitors each year. The national monument, proclaimed by President Hoover in 1933, encompasses one-third of the dunes area in the world's largest gypsum desert. Remoteness deters commercial development of the gypsum.

Proudly calling itself "The Rocket City," nearby Alamogordo takes its name from the Spanish for "fat cottonwood."

Soon after sunrise or before sunset are the best times for taking photographs. Dusk throws a blue shroud over a group (right) relaxing in the coolness of the dunes.

shaped arena had been carved by bulldozers, but these creamy flats are natural. Their moist floors are surprisingly solid. Shelters and grills await picnickers, but wood and water are strictly bring-'em-yourself. There's no camping.

Unlike most other parks, recreation is stressed more than conservation. The moving sands bury more plants than visitors can pick. Even litterbugs can't mar their beauty for long, though the litter of yesteryear sometimes surfaces.

"We don't condone breaking regulations," the superintendent explained. "'Take only pictures, leave only tracks' is as good a rule here as anywhere. But our feature attraction, being in motion, is just about indestructible."

WESTERN WAYS BY RAY MANLEY

Spiny symbol of the southwestern desert, the saguaro may top 50 feet and wave 40 oddly curved arms. Yet early growth is slow. It takes 30 years to stand a yard tall and 75 years for the first branch to sprout. The cactus may live two centuries.

SAGUARO NATIONAL MONUMENT

STRANGE ARMIES of towering, gesturing figures stand rooted to the southern Arizona soil. Stately saguaros, mightiest cacti in the country, raise bristled arms above the 123-square-mile national monument that bears their name.

These green giants belie the image many have of the desert as a dun-colored waste. Visitors to the monument's major area, 16 miles east of Tucson, picnic amid a pastel preserve abounding in wildlife. En route to the new section, 16 miles west of Tucson, many stop at the famed Arizona-Sonora Desert Museum.

Saguaros live off moisture stored in spongelike tissue. After rain, their broad, shallow root systems may suck up a ton of water. The plant's ribs widen like accordion pleats, its tough skin distends and sometimes bursts. Indians harvest its scarlet fruit. The creamy blossom is Arizona's State flower.

ORGAN PIPE CACTUS

THE DESERT PULSES with life as spring touches Arizona's Organ Pipe Cactus National Monument. Wildflowers parade their colors all through this 516-square-mile preserve along the Mexican border. Lavender-tinged petals open during night's coolness at the ends of the 20-foot organ pipes, some 30 stalks clustering in a single plant. Blossoms tip fluted saguaro columns. Barrel cacti tilt toward the afternoon sun.

Bighorn sheep, white-tailed deer, and peccaries forage amid this unusual desert. The gilded flicker drills a nest hole in the moist cactus fiber and the elf owl roosts among its spines. Coyotes howl—and campers feel that beyond the hiss of their cookstoves civilization has slipped centuries away.

CHIRICAHUA

RISING ABRUPTLY from southeastern Arizona's yellow desert, the Chiricahua Mountains look misplaced. Their purple crests and green forested flanks recall New England; their tortuous canyons and grotesque rock sculptures seem to belong on the moon. Layers of ancient lava, cracked and eroded, form Punch and Judy, China Boy, and other likenesses in the 17-square-mile monument.

Campers, hikers, and trail riders from nearby ranches see Arizona white-tailed deer and coatimundis roaming deep gorges that once sheltered the Chiricahua Apaches. From these mountains, Geronimo swept down with his warriors and Big Foot Massai staged one-man raids. Cochise Head, a mountaintop profile nearby, honors the wily chief who held off Fort Bowie's troopers a dozen years.

PETRIFIED FOREST

By EDWARDS PARK
National Geographic Staff

As THOUGH DROPPED by a negligent giant, thousands of jewel-like logs lie scattered across the blistered, mile-high desert in northeastern Arizona. In the Triassic Age, these were living trees. But 190 million years saw their wood turn to stone, glowing with rainbow colors. The world's biggest, brightest collection of petrified wood now clusters within the 147 square miles of Petrified Forest National Park.

US 66, "Main Street of America," slices across the forest's northern section, tempting travelers to swing off the highway for a look at one of nature's strangest revelations. I followed their lead. Like many visitors (nearly a million come each year), I planned to spend an hour or two but ended up staying all day.

Like broken jackstraws, the shattered stone trees lie clumped in four distinct areas.

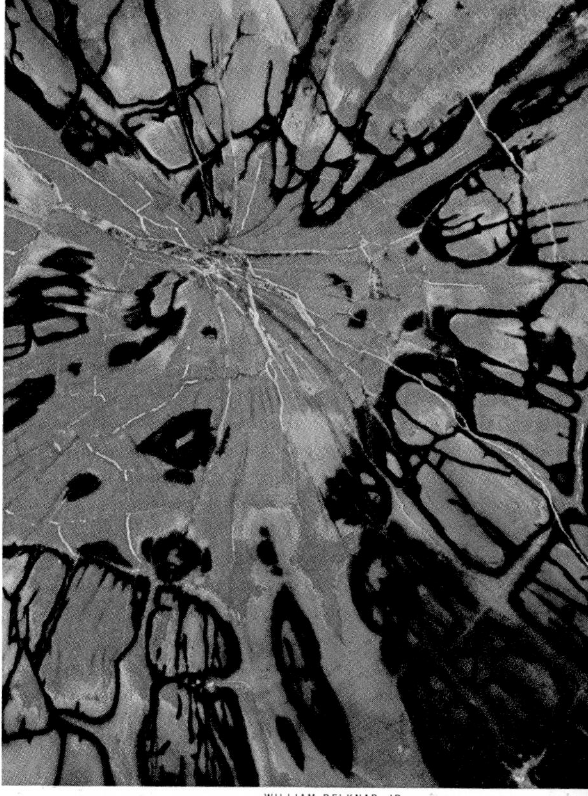

WILLIAM BELKNAP, JR.

Polished cross sections reveal beauty locked in stony hearts of primal trees.

Colors come alive as a petrified slab gets its face doused.

Erosion gnaws at Chinle, age-old mud that swallowed a log jam

Rain and wind nibbling at the claylike earth of Blue Mesa leave some petrified logs stranded on slender pedestals. Each stone

RALPH GRAY, NATIONAL GEOGRAPHIC STAFF

chunk acts as a cap and slows further erosion of its support. But eventually it will crash, as thousands have before it, and roll into the gully to join them in magnificent clutter. Here banded pyramids and cones clearly show the ancient marsh layers.

Paved roads lead to three of these forests, each with its special features. At Rainbow Forest visitors wind through a garden of tumbled 160-foot trunks to snap pictures of Old Faithful, a sprawling forest monster that looks as if it crashed to the ground perhaps a dozen years ago. Actually, its huge gnarled trunk belongs to no familiar species—none but a dinosaur would recognize it. At Crystal Forest, short logs seem to have been left for pulpwood. But no woodsman cut these glittering chunks. Petrified wood is harder than steel.

"The only trees we don't have are upright ones, though we have found a few stumps," a ranger told me as I gazed at Jasper Forest's prostrate trees. He explained that they probably grew along a wide, primeval river. Most were a long-extinct type of conifer. Falling from natural causes, they were swept off by floods and grounded here, in what was then a marshy area. "These petrified trees have lost their branches and most of their bark," he added, "supporting the theory that they tumbled downstream and came to rest stripped of boughs." The stranded trunks were buried by layers of marshy sediments geologists call the Chinle Formation. The land sank. Then an upheaval, some 70 million years ago, produced

A fossil bridge still stands where other logs fell to pieces

When a gully opened under it, the petrified conifer (left) braced itself like a keystone arch. Mineralization of the forest, begun 190 million years ago, was so thorough that even the knotholes remain (below).

Centuries ago, Indians built Agate House (right) entirely of petrified chunks. Partly restored, it overlooks Rainbow Forest amid a jumble of exposed trunks. Some logs lie 300 feet underground.

First reported in 1851, the "stone trees" came close to disappearing forever. Gem hunters carried away agate and even blasted open whole logs for the amethyst crystals often found inside. Erection of a stamp mill to crush the fossil wood into abrasives brought Government action. Petrified Forest became a national monument in 1906, a park in 1962.

WILLIAM BELKNAP, JR. BELOW AND OPPOSITE: RALPH GRAY, NATIONAL GEOGRAPHIC STAFF

the Rocky Mountains—and raised the 400-foot-thick Chinle to the surface. Erosion laid bare some of the trees. But now they were stone.

The magic was performed by silica and other water-carried minerals that filled each wood cell, duplicating its structure like plaster in a cast. Over the centuries, every detail of the wood was retained. Traces of iron, manganese oxide, and carbon added color. At Rainbow Forest Museum I saw cross sections of agatized logs that glowed with all of Arizona's brilliance: the deep reds and orange of sunrise, the purple of a thunderstorm, the blazing blue of the desert sky.

Where plain silica infiltrated the cells the logs look exactly like yellowed trunks lying half-shattered and rotting. The scattered chips surely flew from an ax only yesterday. The grain stands out; splinters protrude. I picked up a sliver, expecting the spongy feel of old wood. But what I touched was cold stone—heavy, brittle, dry. Weathering and earthquakes caused the chipping, and the fracturing that makes many long trunks look as if they had been sawed.

Although geologists foresee more agate wood cropping up as the Chinle wears down, the law imposes severe penalties for removing any of our present heritage of petrified wood. Rangers told me why. If each visitor should pick up just one piece and lug it home, there would be no Petrified Forest left for our grandchildren to see. But you needn't go away empty-handed. Souvenir polished wood from outside sources can be purchased at the concessions.

Part of the Painted Desert falls within Petrified Forest. A rim drive leads to views of bright, eroded mesas extending to the northern horizon. The park includes Indian ruins; petroglyphs cram Newspaper Rock, near Blue Mesa.

Painted Desert Oasis and Rainbow Forest Lodge offer meals, gasoline, and souvenirs. You can picnic but not camp, and the road linking US 66 and 180 is closed at night. Nearest lodgings are at Holbrook, 20 miles west.

EL MORRO NATIONAL MONUMENT

REARING 200 feet from the western New Mexico plain, El Morro (the Headland) beckoned generations of travelers. For at the foot of this sandstone crest gleams the desert's priceless treasure—a pool of water. Weary men made camp beside it. Then, painstakingly, they scratched their marks on El Morro's smooth face, scarring it with history in the raw. Indians cut pictures of hunts. Conquistadors carved haughty reports of triumph in the new land. Juan de Oñate, New Mexico's Spanish colonizer, left an engraved calling card dated "the 16th of April of 1605" —the first European inscription in the Southwest.

Today's travelers picnic amid El Morro's wild scenery, 56 miles from Gallup. And many search the rock for names of pioneer ancestors, dusty cavalrymen, and wagon-train drivers who pulled up at the old landmark, quenched their thirst, and gratefully signed the stone register.

Weather chiseled El Morro's buttress; men carved hundreds of inscriptions on its sandstone base. Atop the mesa lie ruins of Zuñi Indian pueblos, thriving communities in pre-Columbian days.

WILLARD R. CULVER

GREAT SAND DUNES

"THIS IS ONE national monument where you can write your name all you want—in the sand, that is!" The superintendent of Great Sand Dunes enjoys dropping this remark to visitors whose "Kilroy was here" instincts have been frustrated by "Do not deface" signs in other national park areas.

"Write it in letters a yard high! And put in your home town, if you like. The wind will erase it all by morning anyhow."

Here in southern Colorado, where desert meets mountain, the winds give and the winds take away. From the southwest, from the heat-hazed expanse of San Luis Valley they come, driving the loose sands along. As the airs rise to surmount snow-capped 14,000-foot peaks of the Sangre de Cristo Range, they lose velocity and drop their gritty burden. After untold centuries, these sands of time now smother some 50 square miles, with crests soaring a staggering 800 feet above the valley floor, highest dunes in the inland United States.

The dunes are at their loveliest during the changing light of dusk or at sunrise, when the picture below was made. Visitors are encouraged to tramp and play to their hearts' content. Open all year, the 57-square-mile monument provides picnic and camping facilities, including wood and water. Alamosa, Colorado, 36 miles southwest, is the nearest town with accommodations.

CAPULIN MOUNTAIN

FROM MAY THROUGH JULY, Capulin Mountain National Monument presents the contradictory spectacle of a once-raging volcano seemingly tamed by wildflowers. The spurting lava is stilled, the choking ash has drifted away, and gay bluebells, daisies, Indian paintbrush, and lupines mask the black slopes.

Seven thousand years ago, northeastern New Mexico reeled with its most recent subterranean churnings. Capulin Mountain, formed then, is a perfect example of a cinder cone, created by welling lava which sputtered and popped like grease in a pan as trapped gases burst free. Cooling as it fell back, the frothy cinder debris slowly built Capulin's cone.

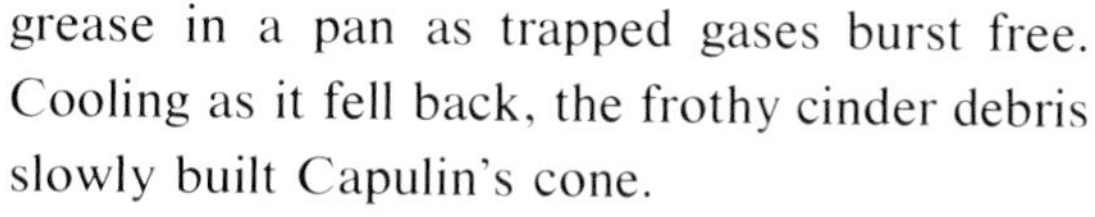

Today the peak's serene symmetry belies its furious birth. And its lush vegetation continually surprises travelers who reach it across the dry expanses of the High Plains. Deer, porcupines, and squirrels abound, and bird song fills the air. Over the summit, 8,215 feet above sea level, golden eagles soar.

A good all-year road spirals the cone, ziggurat-fashion, passing through moist climate zones supporting juniper, piñon, and ponderosa pine, and higher, squawbush and chokecherry (for which the Spanish gave Capulin its name). The crater rim, 1,000 feet above the surrounding plains, affords a five-state view. Foot trails circle the one-mile lip and descend to the crater bottom 415 feet below.

Capulin has a picnic area and visitor center. Raton, New Mexico, 29 miles west, offers accommodations. The famous Folsom site is nearby. Here finely chipped projectile points have been found with the bones of extinct bison hunted by Stone Age Americans.

First footprints of day mark Colorado's Great Sand Dunes, a stormy sea of drifts held restless captive by the towering Sangre de Cristo's giant curve.

RALPH GRAY, NATIONAL GEOGRAPHIC STAFF

PAUL COZE

THE SOUTHWEST REVEALS A PANORAMA OF ANCIENT INDIAN CULTURES

A KACHINA stands on a kiva roof, bearing a bough of evergreen, symbol of eternity. Kachinas, incarnations of the gods, come to reward the good, punish the evil, and bless a semiarid region with rain and fertility.

The people we call the Pueblo (Spanish for village) intently follow the ritual, already ancient when gold-hungry Coronado came seeking the Seven Cities of Cíbola. These Pueblo Indians of Arizona and New Mexico—the farmers, cowboys, filling-station attendants, and students who live in 31 dusty, flat-roofed villages of the Hopi, Zuñi, and Rio Grande tribes—are the Southwest's true aristocrats. Their ancestors were Basket Makers who settled amid these mesas and canyons before Christ was born.

They had no metal tool, no wheel, no beast of burden. Yet these peaceful, democratic farmers learned in time to build compact villages of cut stone. Their cities rose in terraces from canyon floors, and clustered high in cliffside caverns. They made and traded fine pottery, cloth, exquisite turquoise jewels. Then these cities fell empty, their ladder poles sticking like fingers from underground kivas that no longer throbbed with ceremonies. Mountain lion and mule deer inherited the silent realm.

When the 19th century world began to hear of vanished "cliff dwellers" and their strange fortresslike homes, fancy ran riot. A highly civilized non-Indian race built them 20,000 or 30,000 years ago, then grew effete, and was vanquished by barbarians, some people said. Or perhaps dwarfs built them, because the windowless chambers (actually granaries) were so small!

Only when archeologists began to bare these ruins, the National Park Service to protect them, and the National Geographic Society to date them by deciphering tree rings locked in their ancient beams did the true prehistory of the Southwest emerge into light.

The following 48 pages show the ancient cities as they look today, and describe the lives, joys, trials, and migrations of their builders.

Pueblo Bonito, still a "beautiful village," spreads its ruined grandeur beneath the north rim of

CHACO CANYON

By RALPH GRAY, National Geographic Staff

"LET'S BYPASS THE SUBURBS and head straight for the big city."

Edwards Park and I were on a tour of a dozen national parks and monuments containing gloriously preserved dwellings of vanished Southwest Indian villagers. Ahead, near New Mexico's northwest corner, lay Chaco Canyon with its Pueblo Bonito, the largest single ruin in the National Park System, and the mother city of many of the sites we would visit.

RALPH GRAY, NATIONAL GEOGRAPHIC STAFF

Chaco Canyon. Like Greek city-states, Indian towns flourished along the floor 1,000 years ago.

During our years with the National Geographic we had heard a lot about this extraordinary prehistoric apartment house that The Society had excavated in the 1920's. Now we were to see it for ourselves.

Through empty range land northeast of Gallup our car raced a chain of blue-black thunderstorms. Lightning danced around us. Rain cascaded. An unbridged arroyo filled fender high with raging runoff. Afraid to cross it, I stopped. Ted grumbled at the delay.

"Pueblo Bonito has waited a thousand years to greet us," I told him. "Another hour won't matter."

By sunset the wash had drained, and we drove on through gathering twilight to Chaco Canyon National Monument. It was too dark to see Pueblo Bonito as

Neil Judd, Curator of American Archeology at the U. S. National Museum when he led the National Geographic expeditions, reconstructed Bonitian life from buried fragments. He described the villagers as backyard farmers who raised corn, beans, and squash, and hunted rabbits atop the mesas.

Women ran the home; they made pots, wove baskets, tanned skins, plaited sandals, and swept with grass brooms. They were also the master masons. Children fashioned tiny ladles and pitchers—the clay still bears imprints of small fingers.

Bonito, Neil Judd and his helpers laid bare the secrets of pre-Columbian civilization for all to see, understand, and enjoy. Troweling amid crumbling stones, Judd uncovered a genuine—and beautiful—treasure. He glimpsed a flash of color and carefully removed a magnificent turquoise necklace while his Indian workers, lured by some telepathy, gathered silently to watch. With infinite patience, a Bonitian craftsman had polished and drilled the 2,500 stones.

Big as Pueblo Bonito is, it is but one of more than a dozen sizable ruins along an eight-mile strip of Chaco Canyon. Within the monument's 32 square miles rose a little empire of separate villages, supporting some 6,000 people—the largest concentration of population in the prehistoric Southwest. Major sites

O. C. HAVENS AND (RIGHT) B. ANTHONY STEWART, NATIONAL GEOGRAPHIC PHOTOGRAPHER

Turquoise treasure emerges from the dust of centuries

Indians of the Southwest prized turquoise as a mystic symbol of water and sky. Judd shared their awe the day his trowel cut away earth to reveal this breath-taking ceremonial necklace. His tiny brush delicately swept away the sand. At last the blue-green stones shone in all their ancient splendor.

What labor went to mine the precious stones, what patient hours to shape the 2,500 beads and four pendants by rubbing on sandstone, to pierce each with sharpened flint! Marauders missed this prize during Pueblo Bonito's decline.

Thousands of visitors to National Geographic headquarters in Washington inspect the necklace yearly.

accessible most of the year include Pueblo del Arroyo, Hungo Pavi, Una Vida, huge Chettro Kettle, and Casa Rinconada, where pit houses date from A.D. 700.

Two centuries later, Pueblo Bonito started to rise, reaching its zenith about the time William the Conqueror invaded England. By 1299, Chaco was deserted. Droughts, raids, overworked soil, all had worn down the thriving culture. The people drifted off, probably planning to return. But they settled instead in better-watered regions, and the sands blew into the empty windows of their once-loved home.

Saddened at the thought, Ted Park and I pulled stakes and drifted off, too. We felt that somehow we had made friends with these proud Bonitians—a people white men had never seen.

This desert citadel in its heyday sheltered 1,200 in 800 terraced rooms. Four stories tall at outer wall, Pueblo Bonito was America's largest apartment house until 1882.

W. LANGDON KIHN

Tree rings, a link between climate and human history, give archeologists the key to the past.

As excavations progressed in the '20's under Neil M. Judd's direction, more and more became known about the pre-Columbian civilization at Pueblo Bonito, but one question hung tantalizingly unanswered. How old was this supreme example of Pueblo culture?

Dating by tree rings (dendrochronology) was then in its infancy. This method is based on nature's practice of adding concentric growth rings to the outer edges of tree trunks each year. Specific years and cycles of years can be identified in different trees by thick and thin rings. A good year with lots of rain adds a wide growth ring, a drought year adds little.

The rings can be read long after cutting, sometimes even after charring. Thus the pines Bonitians felled with their Stone Age axes provide the key to dates of their home-building. Comparing these Chaco beams with those in other areas, Mr. Judd found the Chaco beams were cut years earlier. But what would the date be in our calendar?

To anchor Pueblo Bonito's floating tree-

E. F. CARPENTER AND (RIGHT) A. E. DOUGLAS

With nature's calendar, they trace the wax and wane of Indian cultures in the Southwest.

ring chronology to the calendar, the National Geographic Society sent out three expeditions led by Dr. A. E. Douglass of the University of Arizona. No living trees could be found locally that had stood in Pueblo Bonito's time, so Dr. Douglass worked back from living trees, dead stumps, and beams from Spanish missions, Hopi pueblos, and ancient Pueblo sites. Painstakingly matching the tell-tale rings, he pieced together an unbroken chronology from the present back to A.D. 700. This told him when the Bonitians started to build (919) and when they reached their peak (by 1066).

The final link of present to past appears below. The upper chart is tied to the calendar; the lower, at the end of the undated chronology, records tree rings of a beam from Showlow, Arizona. Drought years (long lines) match perfectly! At left, a core from a beam in Oraibi, Hopi town still inhabited, reveals 24 narrow rings (white arrows) of the Great Drought, 1276-1299, that saw Pueblo Bonito abandoned to the sands.

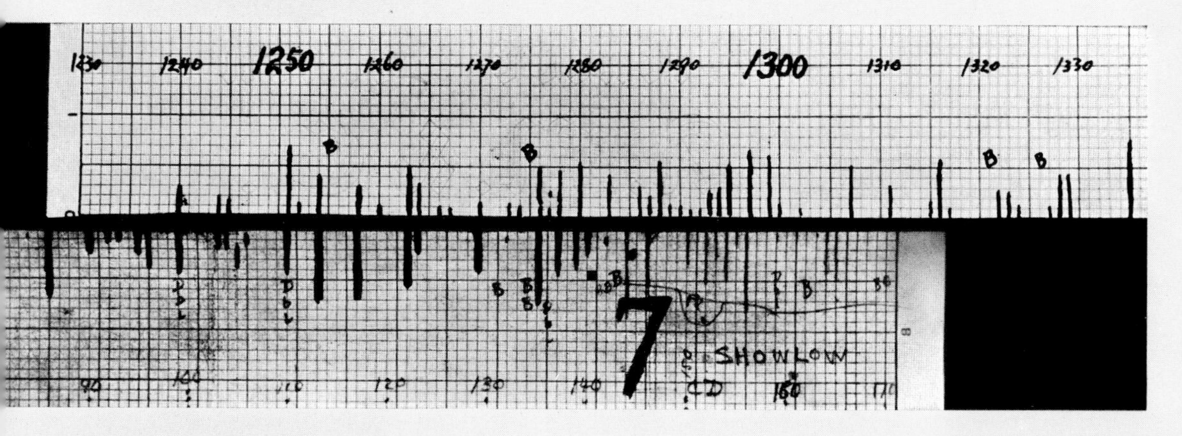

WILLARD R. CULVER

Impregnable Balcony House yields to sightseeing invaders. Cliff cities in this 81-square-mile national park display unusual access: Scientists speculate that the shape of a Mug House door (opposite) offered handholds to a dweller burdened with a backpack but forced raiders to enter stooped and in single file.

MESA VERDE

By DON WATSON, former Park Archeologist, Mesa Verde National Park

On a snowy day in December, 1888, two cowboys rode across little-known, canyon-sliced Mesa Verde in the southwestern corner of Colorado. Suddenly Richard Wetherill jerked his horse to a stop.

"Charlie, look at that!" He pointed. Charles Mason's eyes went wide. Across the canyon a silent stone city lay sheltered by an enormous cave. Stone houses, piled story upon story, rose to the arched cave roof. It reminded the two men of a cliff palace, and thus they named it. Swirling snowflakes hid some ruins; rubble and bushes concealed others. But in all, ten ruins lay cold and silent within their range of vision.

If the cowboys could have stood here two and a half centuries before Columbus, they would have seen Chapin Mesa bustling. Hundreds of Indians lived in Cliff Palace, protected from enemies and elements. In courts and on terraced housetops women bent over cooking fires. Old men and women toasted their aching bones and talked of bygone days when "things were better." In the mealing rooms young women and girls plied grinding stones, reducing brightly colored corn to precious meal. The constant rasping of stones was made bearable only by the melodious notes of the grinding songs. Chanting priests, in underground kivas, added a deep undertone.

At Balcony House, an adobe-paved court spreads beneath another vaulted roof. On three sides stand beautifully built two-story houses; under their upper doors are narrow walks, or balconies, that lead from one room to the next. Along the fourth side of the court lies a low wall that kept children from falling 700 feet down the sheer cliff to the canyon floor. In the rear of the cave flows a beautiful spring of clear, cold water.

WILLIAM BELKNAP, JR.

CITY IN A CAVE *prepares for winter. An autumn day about 1250 finds residents hard at work in Cliff Palace, largest of the Mesa Verde cave pueblos. Masons patch a crumbled corner; others hoist building materials atop a towerlike dwelling. Ears of corn are spread on rooftops, and squashes, cut in coils, hang on sticks to dry (right). Some 400 Indians lived in Cliff Palace.*

PAINTING BY NATIONAL GEOGRAPHIC ARTIST PETER V. BIANCHI © N.G.S.

BIANCHI

Beneath a sullen brow of sandstone Cliff Palace still stands, a cave metropolis containing

Each family had a simple, rectangular room for a home. Here Mesa Verdeans—short, heavy-set Indians with brown skins, straight black hair, prominent cheekbones, and slanted eyes—slept and stored their family possessions.

The floors of these rooms seldom exceed 8 by 10 feet. Few dwellings have window openings. The doors average approximately 16 by 24 inches, and the sill rises two or three feet above the floor. Some walls are plain; some are plastered; a few display paintings in red and white. The pole-and-adobe roofs often sit so low that a person cannot stand completely upright in the room.

Small storage rooms, frequently mere bins, rest in odd nooks and crannies.

MARGARET DURRANCE, RAPHO GUILLUMETTE

23 circular kivas and 200 family rooms. Sightseers also visit earlier pit houses and crude pueblos.

Here were stored the corn, beans, and squash that each harvest produced. Balcony House also has two kivas. These circular, subterranean chambers served as men's clubs and workshops as well as ritual centers; a small hatchway in the open court was the only indication of the compartment below.

Seven or eight centuries ago, this was a simple farming hamlet of perhaps 80 people. During growing season men trotted up toe holds cut in the cliff and cared for crops on the great green mesa above. Crafts took much time. Women shaped pottery by hand; from plants and minerals they concocted paints. When the firing was over, only a heap of ashes remained, but from within those ashes came black-

on-white pottery of superlative beauty—mugs, pitchers, ladles, canteens, jars, and bowls, gracefully shaped and artistically decorated.

Men produced cloth, weapons, tools, and the all-important ceremonial objects. Each man could make any of these, but he preferred to specialize. Here lived a flint chipper; there a rope maker; across the court a weaver. Exchange of goods was by barter, often by gambling. At any time of

Flying fingers fashion ancient Mesa Verdean wares in a smoke-filled kiva

The busy underground shop of seven centuries ago (right) finds a weaver at left looming cotton, spun by the man beside the ladder. Youth above emerges from a tunnel. Man in center creates a blanket by twining yucca cords wrapped in turkey feathers. Indian at right chips an arrowhead; woman on ladder brings in corn gruel. Hole in the floor is the *sipapu,* gateway to the spirit world. Kivas served both as ceremonial chambers and workshops.

Cliff dwellers vanished mysteriously but left many clues, including the bowl being passed through a kiva door in photograph above. Scientists guided artist Bianchi in his portrayal of pre-Columbian pueblo life.

day a group of men were betting on some game of chance: arrowheads against sandals; a feather blanket against a necklace. An inch of beads would buy a bow; a foot of beads, almost anything a man needed.

The sun, rising over the opposite canyon rim, awakened Balcony House. After a simple breakfast of corn bread and meat, villagers went to their tasks. Women changed the juniper-bark diapers of babies, bound the infants to their cradleboards, and hung them on the ends of roof poles to swing in the breeze. Long days on the pillowless cradleboard flattened the back of every cliff dweller's skull. This strange deformity lasted throughout life.

PETER V. BIANCHI, NATIONAL GEOGRAPHIC STAFF ARTIST, AND (OPPOSITE) ALBERT MOLDVAY, NATIONAL GEOGRAPHIC PHOTOGRAPHER

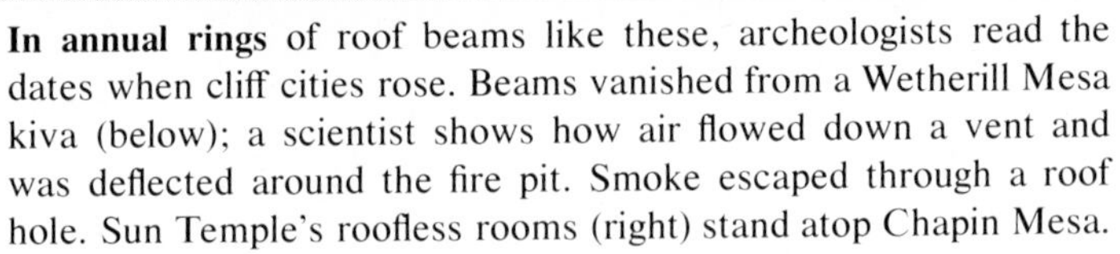

In annual rings of roof beams like these, archeologists read the dates when cliff cities rose. Beams vanished from a Wetherill Mesa kiva (below); a scientist shows how air flowed down a vent and was deflected around the fire pit. Smoke escaped through a roof hole. Sun Temple's roofless rooms (right) stand atop Chapin Mesa.

RICHARD H. STEWART, NATIONAL GEOGRAPHIC STAFF, AND (ABOVE) WILLARD R. CULVER

Turkeys were driven out of the cave to feed along the slopes. Children and dogs swarmed over the canyon walls, making life miserable for squirrels and chipmunks. When the sun grew too warm, men left their fields and dozed or worked at crafts. Later, hunters returned with deer and mountain sheep.

At the elaborate evening meal, some version of corn bread baked on flat stone griddles was inevitable, with a thick stew perhaps, or green corn, or a pot of green beans. Venison roasted over coals was a delicacy. A fat prairie dog or a grouse brought happy exclamations from hungry men. Each family gathered in a tight little circle around its steaming pot. Fingers dipped in recklessly. It was a noisy meal—the better the food, the more finger-sucking and lip-smacking. After it was over, a deep, rumbling belch complimented the cook.

Near the end of the 13th century, nature turned against these Indians. Year after year crops failed, springs dwindled. Perhaps nomads plagued the famine-weakened farmers. Turning their backs on their homes, families drifted southward. Shortly, every pueblo, every cliff dwelling was silent. Only the wail of the coyote and the mournful call of the owl echoed through the empty canyons.

MELVILLE BELL GROSVENOR AND (LEFT) WILLIAM BELKNAP, JR.

Wetherill Mesa: Five-year dig by National Park Service-National Geographic team sheds new light on cliff dwellers

MESA VERDE'S TREASURES began to disappear soon after their discovery in the late 19th century. Archeologists collected artifacts for museums in this country and abroad. And local people invaded the ruins, searching for pots. In recent times, hundreds of thousands of tourists pouring through this popular national park each year threatened to trample to dust the fragile ruins of Chapin Mesa. Fortunately there were other cliff houses—silent, remote, seldom visited—on Wetherill Mesa, three miles to the west.

To learn more about the prehistoric builders of this lonely realm and eventually open it to the American people, the National Park Service, with grants totaling more than $300,000 from the National Geographic Society, conducted the Wetherill Mesa Archeological Project. It was one of the most thorough in the history of the United States. Beginning in 1958, a team of specialists led by Dr. Douglas Osborne spent five years excavating, restoring, and peering into prehistory through

In a sea of pottery found at Wetherill Mesa, Dr. Douglas Osborne (far left), chief archeologist of the project, studies a classic black-on-white bowl. Dr. Melville Bell Grosvenor, President and Editor of the National Geographic Society, inspects Mug House (left) during the early days of the dig. Several years later he took the photograph above of Long House after 700 tons of rock and dirt had been removed from it.

WILLIAM BELKNAP, JR.

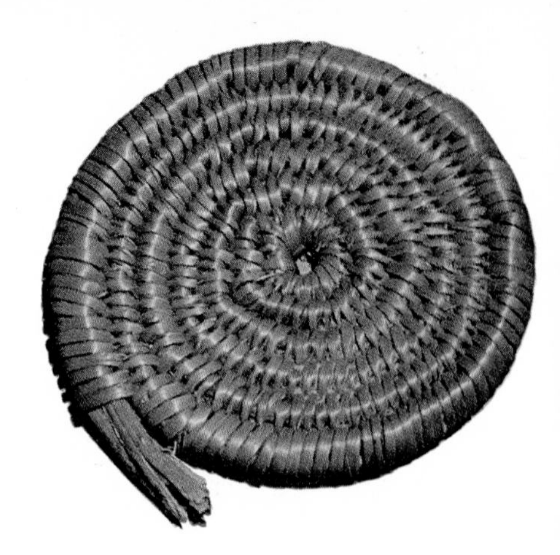

Mesa Verdean techniques live on among potters and weavers in today's pueblos

WHEN DROUGHT STRUCK in the 13th century and the cliff dwellers vanished from Colorado, where did they go? Artifacts uncovered at Wetherill Mesa bolstered the theory that they migrated to New Mexico and Arizona, where today's Pueblo people make strikingly similar tools and products.

Artisans of three New Mexican pueblos demonstrate the ancient skills. In Jemez, an Indian using core rods and wrapping material from a three-leaf sumac fashions a circular base for a coiled basket (left). He scrapes the bark off the rods, then splits other twigs and smooths them flat. For the designs, he normally uses synthetic dyes instead of the old vegetable stains which take too long to prepare. Otherwise his basket base closely resembles one found in the Mesa Verde ruins (above).

Before a crackling fire in her home at

Flaming-firing fixed the painting of a horned toad upon this vessel 700 years ago. Anasazi used wood to fire their pots; most Pueblo Indians today kindle slabs of dried dung.

Erosion and drought plagued the Mesa Verdeans on their dry tableland; they often hauled jugs to the mesatop to draw rainwater trapped in potholes. On Chapin Mesa, archeologists found traces of a canal network and a reservoir that irrigated fields and must have saved housewives many a weary step.

Santa Ana Pueblo, another Indian white-coats a jar before decorating it (right). She follows the methods of the prehistoric Coloradans who made the food bowl above.

And in an adobe house at Zia Pueblo, a belt-weaver keeps tension on the warp with a leather strap circling his waist (lower right). His wooden batten tightens the weft threads; his roller separates the warp threads. Almost identical batten and roller were found at Mesa Verde (below).

The progress of the Anasazi—a Navajo term meaning "Old Ones"—at Mesa Verde is written in their works. First reaching this region a couple of centuries after Christ, they lived in half-underground pit houses and showed great skill in basketry. As their culture steadily advanced, they built above-ground houses of stone and adobe, with wood beams. They became excellent potters, pinching together coiled ropes of clay and shaping the vessels without help of a potter's wheel. Eventually the Anasazi withdrew from their mesatop pueblos into the caves below the sandstone rim.

COLORADO STATE MUSEUM

the lenses of 28 different sciences. Boring down to ancient underlying soils, they discovered evidence of severe water (and possibly wind) erosion that might have resembled the disaster of our own Dust Bowl of the 1930's. They also uncovered a pile of hardened clay patties that the cliff dwellers prefabricated and used as mortar in building the mud-and-stone walls.

Analyzing fecal matter 700 years old, chemists found that these Indians consumed nearly anything that could be called food but—from the decreasing levels of phosphorus and manganese—may have had less and less to eat. Other experts put to use the dendrograph, a machine which measures otherwise imperceptible growth in a tree's diameter. They fixed dates ranging from A.D. 750 for several mesatop ruins to 1280 for the latest timber found in Long House, the grandest of all Wetherill Mesa sites.

Long House has 21 kivas, plus one great kiva, and some 150 rooms—one kiva to seven rooms, almost double the ratio in most cliff dwellings. This suggests that people from smaller surface houses crowded into the village; each group required its own kiva.

In Room 28 a digger cleared away two feet of dry soil and a fallen roof and wall. He glimpsed a bit of fabric. Gently he troweled deeper. There lay a mummy, that rarest of treasures in North American archeology. The bundle, wrapped tenderly in a feather blanket, was the 700-year-old remains of a baby girl. With her was a mummified turkey, perhaps food for the journey to the hereafter.

Excavators came upon 40 other burials among the garbage, potsherds, and discarded building materials of the trash slope which stretched away below the village. From the bones, scientists determined that the ancient inhabitants suffered greatly from poor teeth, rheumatism, and arthritis.

One mile north, Mug House clings to the rim of Rock Canyon like a swallow's nest. It yielded some 430 mugs, pots, bowls, and jars—far more artifacts than the much larger Long House.

And so the Wetherill Mesa story took shape as clue joined clue. The project workers did far more than dig; they preserved. They shored up and braced the ancient structures, providing firm foundations and protection from the elements. Target date for opening the Wetherill Mesa section to park visitors is 1968. If Mesa Verde National Park is to continue as one of the great outdoor museums of the world, the treasured remnants of its past must be prepared to survive long into the future.

A blanket of piñon and juniper atop the tableland inspired the Spanish name Mesa Verde—"Green Table." Park visitors drive a loop road, see the museums, or join a guided trip to a cliff ruin all year; they camp or stay at the lodge from May to late October. Motorists arrive on US 160 from Cortez or Durango, Colo.; bus service from Durango in summer.

WETHERILL MESA FROM THE AIR BY W. E. GARRETT, NATIONAL GEOGRAPHIC STAFF

Castlelike ruins lend a medieval look to Hovenweep (Deserted Valley), named by the Utes.

HOVENWEEP

FRIGHTENED FARMERS once lived here in the gaunt, erosion-gutted Four Corners region where Utah, Colorado, Arizona, and New Mexico meet. Their enemies: thirst and marauders. They built their pueblos on ledges and in open caves, clustered about springs at the heads of box canyons. On the rimrock above rose the symbols of their fear: square watchtowers with loopholes commanding the open mesa. Other forts protected homes, the terraced garden plots, the stored crops—and the precious water bubbling from the springs below.

Six such settlements make up Hovenweep National Monument, four in Colorado, two in Utah. Their distinctive stone towers—square, circular, D-shaped, or oval, conforming to natural foundation rock—have no counterpart in historic pueblo architecture. Each has one small door.

The Square Tower Group in Utah (left) comprises 19 buildings. The largest, Hovenweep Castle, has walls 60 feet long and 20 feet high and is a superb example of pre-Columbian masonry. When did the Hovenweep people abandon these structures? Probably around the end of the 13th century, when famine and raids also drove their cliff-dwelling relatives at nearby Mesa Verde toward the Rio Grande.

The unpaved access to Hovenweep sites gives the average motorist pause. Ask at Cortez, Colorado, or Blanding, Utah, about road conditions. There are picnic and camping areas with water near ranger headquarters at the Square Tower Group, but bring fuel and supplies.

AZTEC RUINS

THESE SPLENDID BUILDINGS have nothing to do with ancient Mexico's "Halls of Montezuma." To white settlers, any Southwest Indian ruin was apt to be "Aztec." These, in New Mexico's northwest corner, perpetuate the misnomer. Pueblo Indians flourished here, beside the cottonwood-shaded Animas River, influenced first by the culture of Chaco Canyon, then of Mesa Verde. Early in the 12th century they built their masterwork: a huge rectangular apartment village enclosing a plaza. It rises three stories at the north wall and contains some 500 rooms. Masonry is straight and even, as at Pueblo Bonito.

One huge circular kiva, built during the Chaco period, was restored to its former glory by Earl H. Morris of the American Museum of Natural History. From the central plaza, today's amateur archeologists descend into this 48-foot-wide room through an antechamber. Four square pillars support the peeled log roof beams. Rectangular masonry vaults in the floor may once have been covered with planks to serve as foot drums, stamped upon during ritual dances, while watchers lined the bench along the wall. Another raised rectangle was the fire box. Curiously, the sipapu, that small, mystical hole through which earth spirits emerged to commune with Indian celebrants, does not exist here.

JACK BREED

The easily reached 27-acre monument, open every day of the year, is 16 miles east of Farmington, which has travel facilities and accommodations. Thousands of motorists take a breather at Aztec Ruins and make a short tour that reveals more of the Southwest's vanished civilization than they might garner in days of scrambling among the scattered ruins of larger park areas.

RALPH GRAY, NATIONAL GEOGRAPHIC STAFF

Prehistoric picture window looks out on ruined Tyuonyi, once a fortress city.

BANDELIER NATIONAL MONUMENT

BANDELIER, in the upper Rio Grande Valley of New Mexico, is a beginning and an end. Here, along little Frijoles Canyon, that slices the wooded Pajarito Plateau, Southwestern archeology began. But here also the golden age of a gentle, master-building people came to an end. We find evidence of their once-great skill in the deserted ruins of site after site through the Southwest—monuments that strike awe and wonder in us today.

Here stands Tyuonyi, a 400-room fortified town, built in the form of a circle by Pueblo refugees from Chaco Canyon, Mesa Verde, and other drought-ridden and beleaguered areas. These farmers, builders of permanent homes, weavers of fine cloth, potters, and traders moved into already-settled Frijoles Canyon around the start of the 14th century. Soon its cliffs echoed the voices of masons, the crack of stone against stone as slabs were hand-split to fit Tyuonyi's even walls. Mud and pebbles served as mortar. Trees, felled with stone axes, supported flat roofs. With an eye to bands of marauders, Tyuonyi's builders put entrances in the roofs. Ladders took the place of doorsteps. Almost all ground-floor rooms were windowless; few connected with each other.

These Pueblos emerged on their ladders to greet the bright morning, shouldered their digging sticks, and made for the gardens watered by Rito de los Frijoles (Bean Creek). Wives swept out the dwellings that were their undisputed domain. Perhaps they replastered a wall, then settled down to plait sandals and baskets. Children romped with such toys as a feather on a string. Boys, trembling with excitement, were initiated into secret all-male lodges that met in circular underground kivas. The community elected its leaders. Pueblos did not tolerate strong men or hereditary chiefs.

Tyuonyi's dwellings piled up two and three stories high, with sheer, blank outer walls to keep attackers at bay. Nevertheless, raids and famine eventually drove the villagers away. By 1580 the fragrant smoke of their cooking fires no longer wreathed the canyon. But when the Swiss-American scholar Adolph Bandelier came upon the site in the late 19th century, the flavor of early life in Frijoles Canyon re-emerged in his notable novel *The Delight Makers.*

Pre-Columbian ruins in the southwestern United States were carelessly called "Aztec" or "Moqui" or dismissed as merely "Indian" until Bandelier lavished years of scientific study on them and added a fascinating chapter to American ethnology. He in turn is remembered here in the silent and empty ruins that so inspired him—for a national monument that preserves them bears his name.

Some Bandelier homebuilders hacked dwellings from cliffs of tuff, a cemented volcanic ash

Like cliff swallows, many Indians nested high above the central pueblo; others burrowed into the base of the cliff and built masonry additions in front—so-called talus houses. These cubicles, measuring about six by nine feet, may have housed arrivals who found Tyuonyi's 400 rooms already taken and established a suburb in the tuff.

The creek that slaked thirsts and watered crops still sparkles nearby. Monument guests can camp near it, or (May through September) bed and dine at Frijoles Canyon Lodge adjoining the visitor center and museum. Trails wind through the 46 square miles of wilderness south of the main ruins. A nine-square-mile detached section contains unexcavated sites. Motorists pass through it on the 46-mile drive from Santa Fe.

JUSTIN LOCKE

Keet Seel, Arizona's largest cliff dwelling, sprawls in a lonely cleft streaked by minerals

NAVAJO
NATIONAL MONUMENT

JOSEF MUENCH

and blackened by cooking fires that burned two centuries before Columbus discovered America.

SILENT, EMPTY, tucked away in northeastern Arizona's maze of wild and solitary canyons lie three magnificent cliff ruins, Keet Seel, Betatakin, and Inscription House. Their sightless windows brood over sun-washed canyon floors as if waiting for their owners to return after 700 years and pick up the fabric of their daily lives. Among Keet Seel's mellow walls, the visitor feels the centuries slip away. He stands removed in a desert wilderness,

CANYON DE CHELLY

By RALPH GRAY, National Geographic Staff

RALPH GRAY, NATIONAL GEOGRAPHIC STAFF

I HEARD CANYON DE CHELLY before I saw it. Approaching the rim one morning at daybreak, I listened to the faint falsetto song of a Navajo herdsman greeting the sunrise from the canyon floor. The curious sound directed my steps to the cliff's edge and I saw for the first time this breath-taking, red-walled slash in the northeastern Arizona plateau. The ground dropped away before me a sheer 500 feet to a sandy rift a quarter of a mile wide. A cottonwood grove lent shade to the hogan and corral of my singing Indian. From a cave in the opposite canyon wall the ghostly twin towers of White House Ruin peered up at me.

Hundreds of other cliff dwellings cling to crevices and alcoves along the jagged, 25-mile length of Canyon de Chelly (pronounced shay) and its branch canyons, del Muerto (Canyon of Death) and Monument. And here amid the gaunt reminders of a vanished civilization, Indians live today, tend their sheep and goats, plant their corn and peaches, build their hogans and corrals. Here, deep within their huge reservation, they have the right to remain forever.

For this is sacred ground to the Navajos. Here they have returned in time of peril —when Spanish soldiers and later the U. S. Army hunted down Navajo raiders. Fourteen of them were killed in this stronghold in 1864 by a cavalry detachment under frontiersman Kit Carson during a roundup of The People ordered by the Federal Government. Some 8,000 of them—from all parts of the Navajo country—were exiled to the hated Bosque Redondo reserve in New Mexico. The proud plateau dwellers languished and died from heat, humiliation, and homesickness.

Finally, in an act of humanity, the United States returned the remaining Navajos to their beloved canyon country where they have now become the largest Indian tribe in the land.

But long before the Navajos made Canyon de Chelly their own, it was home for other Indians. Mummy Cave Ruin (right), one of the best examples anywhere of the Great Pueblo Period (12th and 13th centuries), was itself a rank newcomer, being built on top of Basket Maker pit houses 2,000 years old. Early excavators of this 80-room village found lovely turquoise and shell jewelry, beaded cloth, as well as mummified remains.

Twenty centuries, however, is but a wink in the staggering scale of time that created Canyon de Chelly's stratified walls, and carved such monoliths as 800-foot-high Spider Rock. Here erosion has made one of the world's most

JOHN EDWIN HOGG

Going home the hard way. Some Indians climbed to their cliff dwellings by finger and toe holds. Most used ladders. With these pulled up at night, thresholds were secure from nomad raids. A three-story, cut-stone tower (right) guards Mummy Cave Ruin.

EDWARDS PARK, NATIONAL GEOGRAPHIC STAFF

This Navajo antelope has coursed the sandstone walls of Canyon del Muerto for 150 years. Other designs in the region are pre-Columbian.

stupendous treats for the eye. People journey to this remote, 131-square-mile national monument mostly to marvel at nature's handiwork. But they soon find that exploring the ruins of an ancient culture adds an archeological dividend. And the casual presence of the Navajos gives flavor to the entire scene.

Paved roads from north and south reach Chinle, Arizona, at the monument entrance. You can camp near headquarters at the canyon mouth; bring your own fuel. The Thunderbird Guest Ranch in Chinle offers meals and lodging (May 15—Oct. 15) and conducts canyon tours in specially equipped vehicles. A new visitor center and museum interpret the monument's varied features.

Ashen towers of White House huddle beneath a beetling, iron-stained cliff. This 150-person pueblo was begun in the 1060's, at the time the Normans conquered England.

RALPH GRAY AND (ABOVE) EDWARDS PARK, NATIONAL GEOGRAPHIC STAFF

SUNSET CRATER

By EDWARDS PARK
National Geographic Staff

THE young park ranger pushed back his hat. "To get an idea why Sunset Crater is a national monument you've got to put yourself in the year 1064. You're an Arizona Indian, living in a pit house, trying to farm these highlands east of the San Francisco peaks.

"You're worried by tremors and rumblings underfoot. So you pack up your family and take off. Soon your farm blows sky-high. The earth flames. Rocks soar skyward followed by a rain of cinders. Reddish lava oozes from cracks in your cornfield. When things cool off, you come back for a look. This is what you see—a newborn mountain, jet black."

I stared with new interest at Sunset Crater, a 1,000-foot cinder cone, its cratered crest stained red and orange as though tinted by the setting sun. Around its base stretch acres of somber earth, softened only by stubborn pines that have fought through the cinder blanket.

"Sunset Crater smothered many cornfields," the ranger continued. "But it also kicked off a land rush. Its ash, settling for miles beyond the lava, trapped rainfall. Returning Indians found new grass growing through cinders."

Eager to stake a claim in the black bonanza, Indians headed for Sunset Crater from all corners of the Southwest. Languages and customs mingled, dwellings

RALPH GRAY, NATIONAL GEOGRAPHIC STAFF

Like toothpaste from a tube, viscous lava squeezed up from volcanic fissures. It may still look soft, but clambering over Bonito Lava Flow can cut shoes to shreds.

Youngest of nearly 400 volcanoes around Flagstaff, Arizona, Sunset Crater spewed ash and cinders over some 800 square miles. Near the foot of this once-fiery cone a lava cave contains ice all year. Yellow pines straggle in sparse array up the inhospitable slopes.

EDWARDS PARK, NATIONAL GEOGRAPHIC STAFF

and great pueblos rose—like those preserved at Walnut Canyon and Wupatki nearby. But eventually winds stripped away the fertile, moisture-retaining blanket of ash. Crop failures drove families from the again-barren land.

Sunset Crater remains, hulking above its lava field amid fumaroles or small spatter cones. Bonito Lava Flow curves from its base like an inky glacier. Windblown cinders form contoured dunes. Knife-edged squeeze-ups show where cooling lava was forced out of cracks, then froze upright.

"We don't have any camping facilities in the five-square-mile monument," the ranger told me, "but we're only a half-hour drive from Flagstaff, a favorite stopover for travelers. However, we do welcome picnickers. It's my job to keep kids from breaking their necks tumbling down the cone and generally to talk their dads out of climbing it. For every step you make you slip back two."

I soon saw what he meant. Cinders gave way under me in rustling cascades as, short of breath because of the 8,000-foot elevation, I mounted the slope. But the crest was worth it. I circled the lip of the black, 400-foot-deep crater and examined yellow sulphurous rock and crimson-hued ash that explain the sunset coloring. To the west towered the San Franciscos, Arizona's highest peaks. Northeastward stretched the Painted Desert with its Navajo hogans and Hopi villages. The Hopis still look on Sunset Crater as the home of their Kana-a kachinas, friendly spirits who see to it that Indian storerooms are crammed with corn. In this other-world setting I found the legend easy to believe.

WILLIAM BELKNAP, JR.

Horned toads, living for centuries amid Sunset's cinders, have developed camouflage.

Rangers say it's quite possible to walk, not fly, down Sunset Crater's steep flank. But youth prefers soaring leaps over the rattling cinders.

WALNUT CANYON

PRESENT A MAN with a ready-made roof, floor, and rear wall, and he'll build a house. Walnut Canyon, a 400-foot gorge, proves the point. Stone Age Arizonans settled along the canyon's gray walls in deep-cut recesses between shelflike limestone ledges. They built front walls of masonry and partitioned off each one-room house from its neighbors. When newcomers flocked into the area after Sunset Crater's eruption, the cliffside town grew to more than 300 attached dwellings, as orderly as row houses.

Establishment of Walnut Canyon as a national monument stopped careless "pot-hunting" that had destroyed many dwellings. Now travelers stopping at nearby Flagstaff can drive in any day of the year and take a 50-minute hike around the village's "Main Street," 185 feet below the canyon rim. Along this path, 800 years ago, strode the homecoming hunter or farmer, sniffing the cooking odors and greeting children as they played outside their T-shaped doors. Far below on the canyon floor walnut trees shaded the creek.

WUPATKI NATIONAL MONUMENT

NESTLING BELOW A LAVA MESA, red-walled Wupatki marks the culmination of Arizona's 12th century land boom. Here Sunset Crater's soil-enriching cinders had their kindest effect. As settlers moved into the basin between the San Francisco Peaks and the Little Colorado River, Wupatki (Tall House) mushroomed to a three-story, 100-room pueblo

WILLIAM BELKNAP, JR.

beside its precious spring. Cultures from north, east, and west mingled with that of migrants from the south who built a masonry ball court on which to play their regional game.

A 40-mile drive from either Flagstaff or Cameron, where accommodations are available, brings visitors to Wupatki's sandstone walls. More than 800 other ruins dot the 56-square-mile monument, open all year. Two fortresses, the Citadel and Wukoki, command views of the Painted Desert. Navajos herd sheep outside silent Wupatki, abandoned by drought-stricken farmers 700 years ago.

MONTEZUMA CASTLE

TO REFUGEES from the parched plateau country to the north, the green irrigated fields along central Arizona's Verde River were salvation. And here amid the vestiges of a southern pit-dweller culture they built their high-perched masonry apartment houses. Montezuma Castle, standing high and dry in a limestone cave during some 550 years of neglect, remains 90 percent intact. Ceiling timbers in the five-story, 20-room pueblo are as sound as ever. The original earth mortar still seals the walls. Plaster on the inside retains the handprints of the 13th century Indians who patted it smooth.

Montezuma, the Aztec emperor, had nothing to do with this structure. But it is well-named a castle. Its inhabitants, who farmed along Beaver Creek, scaled ladders to reach the only entrance. Protected passageways lead to other floors. The topmost level suggests a penthouse. Its walled terrace, commanding a view of distant peaks, must have served as a battlement for ancient warriors.

The national monument, some 60 miles from Flagstaff or Prescott, includes a detached area, Montezuma Well, where cliff dwellings flank a deep pool that watered irrigation ditches. Picnickers and passing motorists find cotton textiles and other well-preserved relics in the two museums, open all year.

TUZIGOOT NATIONAL MONUMENT

IT STANDS AGAINST THE SKY, an oblong citadel capping a limestone ridge in the Verde River Valley. Around it sprawls a maze of weathered walls. Archeologists dubbed it Tuzigoot, "Crooked Water," Apache name of a nearby lake. Who knows what the pueblo was called by its people seven centuries ago!

Like their neighbors at Montezuma Castle, 27 miles away, Tuzigoot's builders sought a defensible site. Since no cliff offered shelter, they chose the highest point they could find. As dry farmers moved into the irrigated valley, the hilltop village grew 500 feet long with 110 rooms. Each family lived in a chamber averaging 12 by 18 feet. Returning from the fields, the father swung down a ladder from a hatchway in the roof. His wife had food ready in red pottery she had made. She wore deer-bone hairpins and perhaps a bracelet of sea shells traded from the Gulf of California. While he repaired his farming tools, the youngsters played with carved toys and figurines.

These items lie on display all year in Tuzigoot's museum, one of the Southwest's largest. A mining company owning the ruin safeguarded it from "pothunters" until excavation in 1933-34. To see its treasures and recapture the life that throbbed on the hilltop until overpopulation, famine, disease, and interpueblo strife ended the valley's heyday, travelers need only swing off US 89A.

A pocket-size edition of Mesa Verde's Cliff Palace, Montezuma Castle rates as one of the Nation's best preserved cliff dwellings. Inaccessible to visitors, it shares the pockmarked cliff with other prehistoric homes.

J. BAYLOR ROBERTS, NATIONAL GEOGRAPHIC STAFF

WESTERN WAYS BY RAY MANLEY

White man's steel canopy protects adobe Casa Grande tower, "America's first skyscraper."

CASA GRANDE RUINS

THIS 40-FOOT RELIC juts like a burned-out beacon from the desert floor of Arizona's Gila River Valley, dominating the cactus and mesquite as it once did villages clustered about it. Crumbling walls are all that remain of houses in the national monument. Only traces of a widespread irrigation system are etched on the sunburned flats. But the four-story watchtower that kept vigil over prehistoric farms now attracts thousands each year. Visitors drive from Phoenix or Tucson to the site two miles north of Coolidge and hear rangers explain the 600-year-old landmark and the two cultures it represents.

Settling here in the first century A.D., the Hohokam (Ancient Ones) built houses of brush and mud, similar to modern Pima and Papago homes. They made red-on-buff pottery, cremated their dead, and turned parched lands green with watered crops of maize, beans, and cotton. In the 13th and 14th centuries Indians from the north settled among them, possibly as traders. These Pueblo people built straight wall houses of adobe, painted their pottery black, white, and red, and buried their dead. They may have shared the Hohokam's amazing irrigation works—some canals, 25 feet wide and 15 deep, extended 26 miles. Both peoples may also have joined in the use of the Casa Grande, its four-foot-thick walls fashioned by the Pueblos from wet caliche, a limy clay.

When Father Kino, a Spanish missionary, named the tower in 1694, he noted its smooth walls. Later pioneers, cowboys, and settlers scratched names and dates, accounting for its present indentations.

Open all year, the monument offers picnic facilities and guided tours.

TONTO NATIONAL MONUMENT

THE SUN, rising above Arizona's Salt River Valley, shines into two caves in a serene side canyon, warming the walls of the Tonto Cliff dwellings. Six centuries ago, it signaled Salado Indians to tend crops or hunt deer among the junipers on the canyon rim while women gathered mesquite beans and saguaro fruit on the talus slopes. Now the two-story pueblos where ancient potters, cotton weavers, and yucca sandalmakers plied their skills slumber while visitors snap pictures and picnic.

A trail climbs to Lower Ruin where some 20 families lived behind a protective wall. Upper Ruin, half a mile away and 300 feet higher, is twice its neighbor's size. It commands a view of Roosevelt Dam's huge reservoir, which drowns the plots irrigated by Tonto's builders. The two-square-mile monument, 100 miles east of Phoenix, is open all year.

GILA CLIFF DWELLINGS

DEEP in southwestern New Mexico's Mogollon Mountains stands a yellow volcanic cliff with five caves, three of them linked by natural archways. Well-preserved dwellings crowd these cavities, high above a trickling stream on the canyon floor. Those who drive the scenic but winding 50 miles to this once remote national monument find more than ruins to reward them. Stark wilderness beauty awaits—and the haunting mystery of a people who lived here, then vanished, leaving their fingermarks in the adobe walls. Gila Hot Springs Ranch offers accommodations and transportation from Silver City.

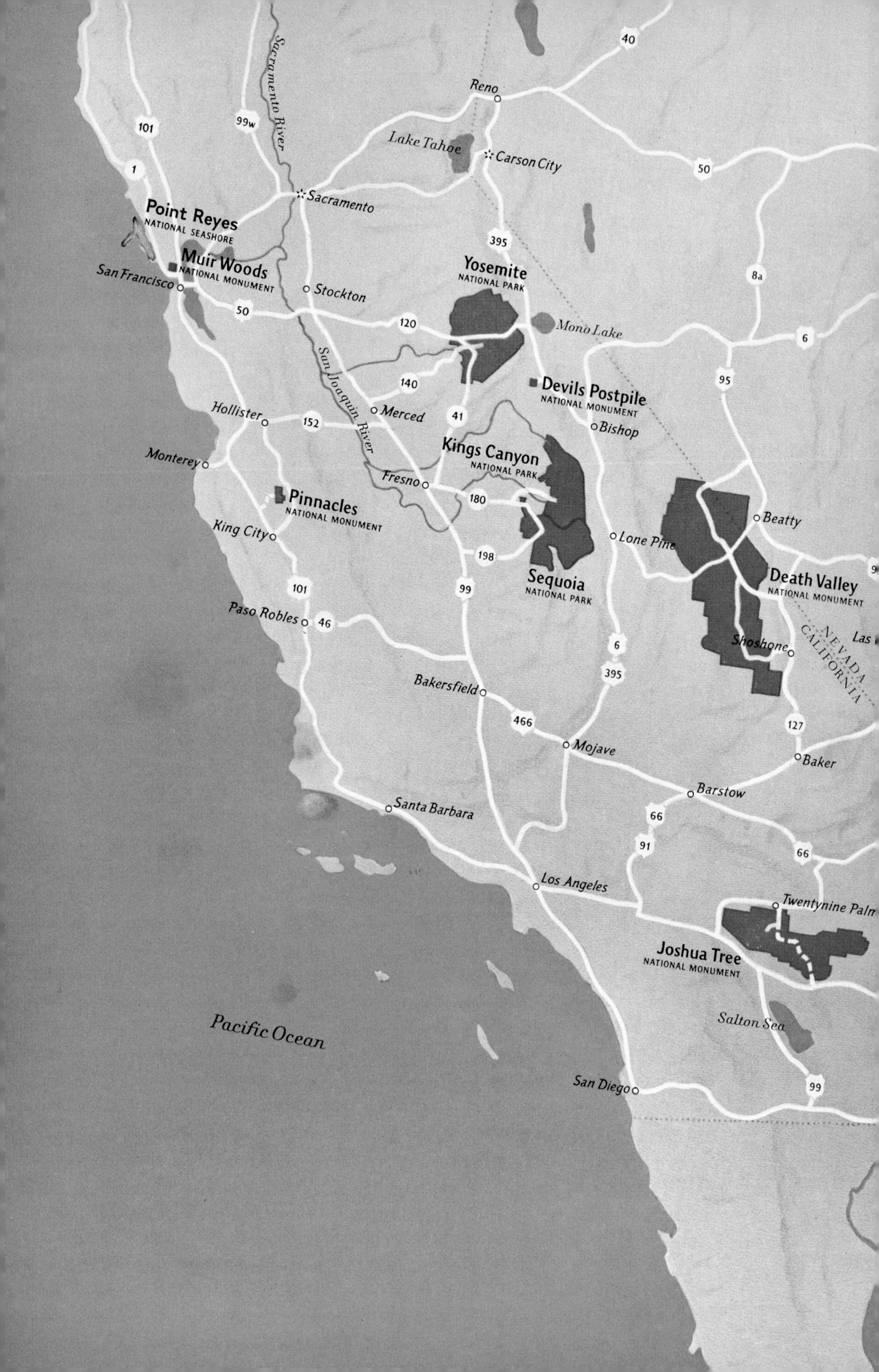

Point Reyes
NATIONAL SEASHORE
Muir Woods
NATIONAL MONUMENT
Yosemite
NATIONAL PARK
Devils Postpile
NATIONAL MONUMENT
Kings Canyon
NATIONAL PARK
Pinnacles
NATIONAL MONUMENT
Sequoia
NATIONAL PARK
Death Valley
NATIONAL MONUMENT
Joshua Tree
NATIONAL MONUMENT

Reno
Carson City
Lake Tahoe
Sacramento River
Sacramento
San Francisco
Stockton
Mono Lake
San Joaquin River
Merced
Hollister
Monterey
Fresno
Bishop
King City
Lone Pine
Beatty
Paso Robles
Shoshone
NEVADA
CALIFORNIA
Las
Bakersfield
Mojave
Baker
Barstow
Santa Barbara
Los Angeles
Twentynine Palm
Salton Sea
San Diego
Pacific Ocean

40 · 101 · 99w · 1 · 50 · 395 · 8a · 120 · 6 · 140 · 95 · 41 · 152 · 180 · 198 · 99 · 101 · 46 · 6 · 395 · 466 · 127 · 66 · 91 · 66 · 99

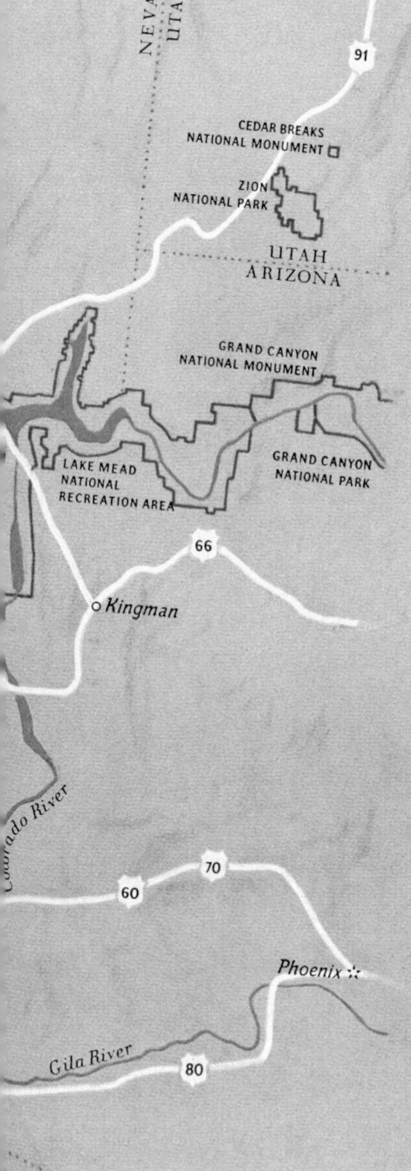

PART FOUR

THE GOLDEN WEST

WAGON MASTERS filed their trains through South Pass, tossed a final gibe at wisecracking Fort Hall trappers, and headed down the California Emigrant Trail. If you asked the dust-chewing drivers where they were bound, like as not they'd answer, "To see the elephant!"

The elephant meant anything that stretched belief. It meant gold for the taking . . . or going bust. It meant free land, new grandeur . . . or only disillusion.

These pioneers crossed the Great Basin, a saline, sagebrush desert. They cursed through towering ranges of snow-scarfed peaks. They threaded awesome forests and meadows of hip-deep grass. They skirted lakes and streams filled with eager fish, and whole mountainsides of wildflowers.

They saw the elephant, all right! Some even found gold. And they fell in love with California, where nature not only sustained the body, but nourished the spirit.

Today the phrase is dead, but the urge to go west still lives. With ease and pleasure, travelers explore Death Valley, the Sequoia groves, the clear vistas of the Sierras. And they see things most forty-niners never saw: the waterfalls, the granite walls, the luxuriant floor of Yosemite, the Incomparable Valley.

Jacob's ladder aims for the sun as it scales Half Dome's granite scalp nearly a mile above the valley. California's Yosemite National Park, vacation paradise for more than 1½ million each year, lies on the Sierra's western slopes about 150 miles from San Francisco.

PHOTOGRAPH BY THE AUTHOR

YOSEMITE

By PAUL JENSEN

THE LAST 600-foot stretch was the hardest. Half Dome's shoulder humped before me, rock rising starkly to the summit of Yosemite's celebrated landmark. I had hiked eight miles from the valley floor. Here at 8,350 feet I felt the muscle rust of months in the office.

I gripped the hand cables that point the way up the sharpest pitch. Fifteen feet, then rest and blow.... Fifteen feet... I hauled myself straight into the eye of the two o'clock August sun. Fifteen feet.... At last the grade eased off and I walked out on an 11-acre stone desert hanging in the sky.

Curved slabs of granite shingled the summit like cabbage leaves. These slabs jut into space to form a visor over Half Dome's fractured face, so I crawled the last few feet on hands and knees. I took a firm hold on the outermost rock, swallowed, and peered down.

The cliff cut back 80 feet under me, then dropped sheer as a skyscraper wall for 2,200 feet, half again the height of the Empire State Building. From there, bare rock plunged at an angle some 2,500 feet more. I was perched above one of the world's most awesome drops and I plead guilty to vertigo. But the immensity of the sight that spread before me soon drove away my qualms.

Yosemite Falls leap in spring flood, shaking the earth with the force of their combined 2,425-foot plunge—North America's highest. August drought reduces the falls to a gossamer spray, fades red snow plants atop Glacier Point.

JOSEF MUENCH

Dark Wawona Tunnel leads to this dazzling vista: cliffbound Yosemite Valley

Stern El Capitan (left), rising 3,600 feet above the pine- and fir-clad floor, contains enough granite for three Gibraltars. Bridalveil Fall's

B. ANTHONY STEWART, NATIONAL GEOGRAPHIC PHOTOGRAPHER

plume of mist seems to drop out of a lost world. The 620-foot cataract, strongest during May's thaws, wears a triple crown: Cathedral Rocks. Its sparkling waters feed the Merced River, which flows through the seven-mile valley. Half Dome projects on the distant skyline.

1 **Twenty-five million years ago,** Yosemite Valley was a lush lowland flanked by gentle hills. Half Dome's ancestor (center) rose only 1,500 feet above the sluggish, winding Merced River. Rains drenched the subtropical vegetation.

How Yosemite Valley was formed

2 **Gradual uplift of the entire region,** some 12 million years later, caused the Merced to cut a V-shaped valley. Cooler climate fostered hardwoods and evergreens like the first sequoias. Yosemite's landmarks began to take shape.

 Paintings by EUGENE KINGMAN

Mirror Lake glittered like quicksilver nearly a mile straight below, and to the left Yosemite Valley spread its evergreen carpet. At least 20,000 people must have been in the valley, nucleus of the great national park. But the only signs of life were cars—tiny beads strung along threadlike roads.

I raised my eyes to a sea of domes, ridges, forests, and snow-patched peaks that filled the eastern horizon: the Sierras rising in magnificent tiers. Closer to my right, Mount Watkins hulked above Tenaya Canyon. Behind me, past 18 miles of pines and firs, I could picture Mariposa Grove's immense sequoias. Fifteen miles ahead I could make out peaks flanking the Grand Canyon of the Tuolumne. Between the valley and that great granite gash sprawled the wild high country of Tuolumne Meadows where the Tioga Road cuts across the park. Sierra Club members, particularly, seek out this wilderness tract. And here I would soon go—to see the spectacular canyon; to roam the lofty meadows with their canvas cabins spaced a day's hike apart; to examine the glacial polish that so entranced naturalist John Muir, granite expanses that still glisten from the buffing of ancient ice. Besides, I had appointments with impatient trout in half a dozen lakes and streams.

All this was Yosemite. What an array of riches! I gazed at Glacier Point, still imposing even though it was now 1,600 feet below me. How it had towered above when I arrived in the valley the evening before! Driving in from the South Entrance, I emerged from Wawona Tunnel and pulled up as everyone

3 **A final shrug of earth's shoulders** hoisted the Sierra Nevada to snow-capped eminence, while the rushing Merced chiseled out its bed in the rising rocks. El Capitan (left) faces Cathedral Rocks. Evergreens cloak the slopes.

4 **A frozen sea smothered the valley** as glaciers pushed in from the east. Rock-shod ice carried away one side of Half Dome, obliterated the Merced River's sharp bends, widened the valley floor, and created hanging glens.

does at the sight of the immense natural portal that frames Yosemite Valley's forested floor—El Capitan's overwhelming brow glowering at the leaning spires of Cathedral Rocks, where earlier in the summer Bridalveil Fall wavers in the valley breeze. Farther up the valley, Upper and Lower Yosemite Falls seem to shake the ground then with their combined drop of some half mile, one of the world's greatest. At times, half a dozen waterfalls lace the seven-mile valley.

That evening, gloom had pervaded the valley. A boy, trying a short cut from Glacier Point, had gotten trapped on a shelf inches wide, 1,500 feet up the cliff. Darkness fell and prevented rescue, so rangers talked to him all night with a loudspeaker to keep him awake. Moral: stay on the trails!

SITTING serenely now on Half Dome's noble crest, I felt proud and elated at my climbing feat. A chipmunk scurried out from under a slab, came flirting over, and started eating my cracker crumbs as tame as you please. Suddenly I felt foolish. Why, people came up here every day—this was one of the best-fed chipmunks in the park!

Coasting back down the trail, I passed through thickly forested slopes to Little Yosemite Valley. This hanging glen ends abruptly where the Merced River, swinging past Liberty Cap, spills from the spout of a giant's pitcher. After a pulsing, thunderous 594-foot drop at Nevada Fall, the river charges to a final

5 **Glaciers returned twice more,** deepening the U-shaped valley and polishing the granite monoliths ice had sculptured. The last advance, extending just past El Capitan, left it, Half Dome, and Cathedral Rocks much like today.

6 **Lake Yosemite,** impounded by glacial debris, reflected the grandeur of its walls for several centuries. Its shallow basin gradually silted up, and today evergreen forest clothes the bottomland, center of park activities.

Campers ring a fire on Tuolumne Meadows in the High Sierra country. "Camp out among the

317-foot plunge down Vernal Fall, then boils along its gorge past Happy Isles.

When I reached the valley floor, it felt good to soak my feet in the tingling, ice-melt water of the Merced as it swept past the hotel, lodge, and campgrounds of the Yosemite Valley community. Crowded? Yes. But Yosemite, like our other splendid parks, brings out the best in people. Utter strangers, relaxing to-

CHARLES E. MOHR

grass and gentians of glacier meadows," wrote John Muir. "Cares will drop like autumn leaves."

gether after dinner, swap yarns and share the day's experiences like old friends.

"It's like that in winter, too," a young Fresno couple told me as we sipped instant coffee around their cheery campfire. "That's when the skiers come."

Heavy snows and light winds, I learned, draw throngs of skiers to Badger Pass, a ski center on the Glacier Point road. Tows, trails, a ski school with special

B. ANTHONY STEWART, NATIONAL GEOGRAPHIC PHOTOGRAPHER, AND (OPPOSITE) TED SPIEGEL

classes for children, even a baby-sitter service await the thousands of experts and tyros who come from mid-December to mid-April, bantering and singing as they drive to the ski house in cars shod with snow tires and antlered with skis.

Skiers lodge at Wawona or Yosemite Valley. Some find ample thrill in the valley, where towering cliffs shade the skating rink and toboggan slide. Often, following snowstorms, avalanches plunge down the granite walls, throwing off clouds of snow. Their dull rumble, swelling to a roar, can be heard for miles.

My new friends told how cold winter nights turn Upper Yosemite Fall's spray into crystal icing on the rocks. Dislodged, tons of ice thunder to the middle ledge, where spray and cold weld the chunks into an icy cone hundreds of feet high.

As the evening wore on, the magic bond among thousands of tanned, tired visitors strengthened spectacularly. Tents, cabins, and hotel emptied just before nine o'clock. We gathered outside, eyes trained at the dark overhang of Glacier Point. Suddenly there was a stir—a soft whispered exclamation—as far above a leisurely finger of glowing coals pointed down, seemed to hesitate, then fused into a shimmering, incandescent stream: the firefall. It made my day complete.

Oh yes, the boy on the ledge. Certainly the park rangers got him down—with 500 feet of rope and that brand of skill and courage that has become routine.

Wawona Tree's living tunnel, in Mariposa Grove, was cut in 1881 for stagecoach traffic

Yosemite's Big Trees were discovered by Joseph R. Walker's expedition to California in 1833. Coast redwoods were found by Spaniards in 1769.

In 1852 an English botanist named the Sierra tree *Wellingtonia* in honor of the British general. But patriots, eager for an American name, rejoiced when scientists decided the Big Tree belonged to the coast redwood's genus, named *Sequoia* for the Cherokee who gave his tribe an alphabet.

Sequoia gigantea's fissured bark grows up to 24 inches thick. Asbestos-like, it resists fire. The tree's heart is dead. Only inner bark and outer rings, or sapwood, live to carry water and food through the trunk. The majestic sequoias are the champion heavyweights of the plant world.

Soldiers of California's Mariposa Battalion entered the valley in 1851 and named it for the Indian tribe they were sent to subdue—Uzumati, meaning grizzly bear. With a different spelling, the name stuck to the valley and the national park, established in 1890. Yosemite has no grizzlies left but black bears are common. Nearly 300 kinds of birds and mammals inhabit the park.

Mule deer browse in the high country, wandering up from the valleys in spring when the bucks' budding antlers are clothed in velvet (above right). Lizards, squirrels, and chipmunks find a living even on the bald summit of Half Dome, hulking in the distance (right) as weary sightseers freshen up with a splash in the chilly Merced River.

J. BAYLOR ROBERTS AND (RIGHT) B. ANTHONY STEWART, NATIONAL GEOGRAPHIC STAFF

A fiery cascade tumbles nightly from Glacier Point

In the 1870's a settler pushed hot coals off the cliff, starting the tradition of the firefall. Others tried flaming gunny sacks, fireworks, even bombs to heighten the spectacle. Today's fire-builder uses fir bark, burned down to embers.

Every summer evening a call floats up from the valley, "Let the fire fall!" A long-handled rake does the rest. Most coals burn out by the end of the 900-foot fall.

In the valley, Camp Curry bustles with tenters. Evergreens and wood smoke scent the air. Mom's cooking, served on enamelware from a crate cupboard, never tasted better.

YOSEMITE NATIONAL PARK *Central California, 1,189 sq. mi.*

Features: Glacier-sculptured Sierra wilderness. Leaping waterfalls, sheer-walled Yosemite Valley, Grand Canyon of the Tuolumne. Three groves of giant sequoias; nearly 300 bird and mammal species.
Activities: Visitor center, Yosemite Village; Happy Isles nature center. 216 mi. of scenic roads; 751 mi. of trails. High Sierra pack and hiking trips. Horses at valley, Wawona, Tuolumne Meadows. Boating, fishing (Calif. license). Nature walks, campfire programs, junior rangers (ages 7-13), firefall in summer. Skiing winter.
Weather: Summer days pleasant, nights cool. (Valley elev. 4,000 ft.)
How to get there: From west, Calif. 140. South, Calif. 41. East, Calif. 120 (over Tioga Pass, 9,941 ft.; closed winter). See map at back of book. Southern Pacific, Santa Fe Ry., United Airlines to Fresno or Merced, Calif.; TWA to Fresno; bus to park.
Accommodations: Hotels and lodges (three open all year), cabins, tents. Write Yosemite Park and Curry Co., at park. Camp and trailer grounds crowded mid-June–Sept.; first come, first served.

For further information write Supt., Yosemite National Park, Calif.

POINT REYES

IT REARS out of the Pacific mist like some mysterious island, a land apart. And in fact Point Reyes peninsula, an hour's drive north of San Francisco, is a geologic orphan. Adjoining the mainland along the San Andreas Fault, it has crept northward for 80 million years. Today it moves about two inches annually—an "island in time."

A national seashore since 1962, the 53,000-acre triangle preserves a wild, haunting beauty. Sea lions bark from surf-bashed rocks at its blunt apex. Seabirds dance with surging waves along solitary beaches. Wind and water whip dunes into ever-changing shapes. Inland, cows graze on downs that roll away to Inverness Ridge, haunt of deer and bobcat.

Trails from park headquarters near Olema lead to lichen-draped Douglas firs in foggy forests. Hazardous combers rake Point Reyes Beach, but bathers frolic safely at sheltered Drakes Bay. Here, some scholars say, under white cliffs that resemble those of Dover, Francis Drake careened the *Golden Hind* in 1579 and claimed "New Albion" for England.

Humpbacked tip of Point Reyes thrusts a ragged rock wall against Pacific breakers. Fog often shrouds the headland; to warn ships a lighthouse, built in 1870, stands at land's end.

HAL ROTH

Centuries ago Miwok Indians built driftwood tepees on the rolling uplands, speared fish around Drakes Bay in the distance, and trod the dunes as visitors do today (opposite). The friendly, peaceful tribe welcomed early explorers, including the Spaniard Sebastián Vizcaíno who anchored near the promontory in 1603 and gave it its regal name.

MUIR WOODS

"COME TO THE WOODS, for here is rest," said John Muir, and what better place than this lovely haven north of the Golden Gate. Superlatives are not for Muir Woods; its 502 acres preclude camping or long hikes; its trees are not as tall as some. But they grow almost in the shadow of San Francisco—a virgin stand of coast redwoods, *Sequoia sempervirens*.

Like *Sequoia gigantea* of the Sierras, the coastal species has rosy wood, but its bark is chocolate, not cinnamon. The craggy giant of Yosemite and Sequoia bulks like a lighthouse—the world's most massive tree. The slimmer coast redwood towers like a mast to a world record 367.8 feet.

John Muir loved them both, as he did all wild things. Landing in San Francisco in 1868, the young Scot set out afoot to explore the wilderness. He'd sleep in hollow logs or on pine needles. Caught by a blizzard, he'd burrow in the snow. During a windstorm, he climbed a great pine to exult in its wild thrashing.

Muir could not bear to see man wipe out in a day what nature took millenniums to produce. No doubt, he said at his soft-spoken, sarcastic best, the sequoias "would make good lumber after passing through a sawmill, as George Washington after passing through the hands of a French cook would have made good food." His writings crystallized public sentiment in favor of saving our natural heritage.

Vigorous to the end, Muir died in 1914 at 76. To recall him there is the 226-mile John Muir Trail in the Sierras and Muir Glacier in Alaska. But perhaps his most fitting memorial is Muir Woods. Half a million people come here each year, to walk quietly among the great trees and to remember that our parkland riches are the legacy of men who fought hard for an ideal. Men like John Muir.

PAUL A. ZAHL AND (OPPOSITE) B. ANTHONY STEWART, NATIONAL GEOGRAPHIC STAFF

A sun-dappled aisle weaves through a sylvan sanctuary

"Majestic brothers," as Walt Whitman called these redwoods, surround fire-scarred elders from whose broad roots they sprouted. How long ago? Determining the ages of uncut titans poses a problem: rain, drought, and crowding vary yearly growth; corings prove difficult to interpret. Annual rings of a dead giant (right) at the national monument show that the tree was 583 years old when Columbus found America. The oldest known redwood lived 2,200 years.

DEVILS POSTPILE

GOLD-HUNTING PROSPECTORS and restless pioneers were first to take note of this 900-foot-long colonnade of basalt rising 200 feet out of the eastern California forest. To them, the sight was other-worldly; they called it Devils Postpile. Naturalist John Muir wondered at its origin, and so do visitors today, as they arrive via US 395.

Geologists say that a Sierra volcano spewed lava here perhaps 150,000 years ago. The deep river of liquid rock cooled too quickly; like a hot dish set on ice it cracked. Later a great glacier laid bare the edge of this freak formation and polished the upper ends of the packed posts. Sightseers mounting the easy trail remark that the top looks like a huge mosaic or tile inlay.

Once part of Yosemite and still under that park's superintendent, this national monument, 7,600 feet above the sea, offers surprising variety in its 798 acres. Here in summer you can picnic, fish and swim in Middle Fork of the San Joaquin River, hire horses nearby, and hike to Rainbow Fall, where the river takes one sheer leap to a green pool 140 feet below. The monument even has hot and cold running springs. The Soda Springs bubble with naturally charged water, the makings for free soda pop. Reds Meadows Lodge and store are close by.

PINNACLES NATIONAL MONUMENT

BURIED TREASURE awaits its finder among the weird peaks of Pinnacles National Monument—or so say hopeful romantics in the Coast Ranges of central California. The notorious bandit Tiburicio Vasquez supposedly hid stagecoach loot in a gulch hereabouts. Many a visitor has searched for Vasquez' cache, but each has settled for the scenic treasure that enriches all who explore these extraordinary formations.

In summer, a park naturalist tells the story of the Pinnacles' creation: how slow-flowing lava welled up through a fissure and formed a dome-shaped mountain. Violent eruptions piled the dome high with rubble. Then—during 30 million years—erosion chewed this volcanic mass into grotesque crags and 1,000-foot spires where golden eagles, turkey vultures, and many other birds now nest. Green even in winter (high point is 3,305 feet), the preserve is open all year. Hiking trails thread its 23 square miles; two pass through canyons so narrow that falling rocks have wedged, forming cave roofs. Prudent campers provision at nearby Hollister or King City and bring their own fuel to the tent or trailer sites; the mantle of brush produces no wood to spare.

Climbing a stairway to the sky, a hiker surveys the rugged Sierra scene in Devils Postpile National Monument. The splinters of basalt, about two feet thick and 40 to 60 feet high, cluster like great organ pipes.

FRED G. HINES

SEQUOIA AND KINGS CANYON

By JOHN M. KAUFFMANN
National Park Service

THE HIGHWAY writhed up the Sierra Nevada ramparts. Behind, drenched in June sunshine, lay California's San Joaquin Valley; ahead beckoned the hazy ridges of Sequoia National Park.

Up this canyon, a century before, Indians led a rancher along dim trails to see an incredible wonder—the giant sequoia trees, largest of living things. Now, thanks to highway engineering, more than a million visitors each year drive these heights.

I rounded a bend and caught my breath. Before me stood the Guardsmen: four sequoias like pillars of a city gate. Cinnamon-red trunks rose massively amid the green. I parked and walked over to a group of trees. An auto paused, its driver grinned: "You look like a midget!"

He was right. In the Giant Forest we are all Gullivers in a Brobdingnagian world. I found the Sentinel Tree watching over hundreds of other Gullivers eagerly buying film and camping supplies. "Relax, youngsters," the old trees seemed to say. "Your lives are short enough. Enjoy them!"

A wary doe takes to the High Sierra Trail in this giant twin-park wilderness of silent forests, savage canyons, and granite peaks, an easy day's drive from Los Angeles or San Francisco.

B. ANTHONY STEWART, NATIONAL GEOGRAPHIC PHOTOGRAPHER

I raised my tent between two sequoias where the long light of sunset would filter through the boughs to make the trunks glow. I unpacked my gear. Then the welcoming committee arrived: inquisitive robin, bumptious chipmunk, and truculent jay, panhandlers all. The jay hopped onto my table, scolding for food.

At suppertime the forest filled with fragrant wood smoke, children's laughter, faint notes of a guitar. Families gathered, each united in primeval comfort around its evening fire. Birds began to sing, flute answering tiny flute in trilling antiphony—elfin music sung to giants.

Crash! I recognized what rangers call the "Trash Can Symphony." Bears were busy tipping over receptacles in search of tidbits. A mother bear and her cub shuffled by. I knew they would not harm me if I did not molest or feed them, so I settled back against a tree to read by lantern light.

A coyote chorus was my dawn alarm clock, and a delegation of deer trotted by to see I was making the most of the morning. I joined the stream of human ants circling the base of the General Sherman, most massive and one of the oldest of living things. I wondered how many tons of tree towered here, high as the Capitol dome in Washington, D. C. Some say 2,000, with enough wood to build 40 five-room houses. The 272-foot trunk is nearly 37 feet in diameter.

"I feel so . . . infinitesimal," murmured a young woman as she gazed upward.

"I feel like a youngster," replied a white-haired grandmother with a twinkle.

Egypt was conquering an empire when the Sherman sprouted. The tree was a thriving adult when Greece flowered into its Golden Age. And on a winter's night when a great star blazed over Bethlehem, this tree stood straight and tall, already more than 1,500 years old.

Next to the Giant Forest, Grant Grove is the best known and most accessible of the parks' 24 groves of *Sequoia gigantea*. The General Grant Tree, which is second in size to the General Sherman and thought by many to be even more impressive, is widely known as the Nation's Christmas Tree. In addition, Congress designated it a national shrine honoring America's war dead.

"CLIMB the mountains and get their good tidings!" Alta Peak, rising northeast of the Giant Forest 11,204 feet above sea level, seemed to echo John Muir's exhortation. A friend and I shouldered knapsacks one morning and plunged into red-fir forest. Above the timber line we panted onto Alta's snow-splotched summit to gaze upon an endless world of mountains. From north to south the Great Western Divide sawed the sky. One summit far beyond must be 14,495-foot Mount Whitney, high point of the Sierra Nevada—the Snowy Range.

Since most of the snow melts away in summer, Muir, I thought, had a better name: The Range of Light. Dawn turns its peaks into pinnacles of pearl. The midday sun shimmers across the pale rocks with blinding intensity. The light mellows as afternoon wanes, and at sunset the cliffs blaze with alpenglow.

Sequoias of Giant Forest tower over pygmy campers. The two parks protect thousands of these ancient Big Trees, native to a 4,000–8,000-foot zone in western Sierras. Trunk tapers little, hence tree's enormous mass.

B. ANTHONY STEWART, NATIONAL GEOGRAPHIC PHOTOGRAPHER

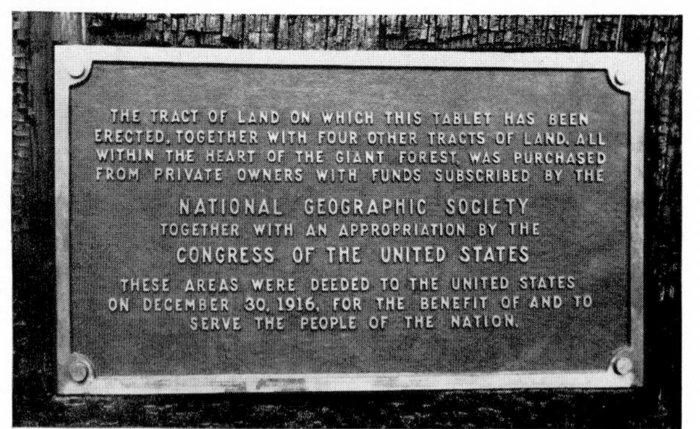

LINDLEY EDDY

A grove says thanks to those who saved it. The Society's contributions helped stay the saw.

Earth's biggest living thing: the General Sherman Tree

High as a 25-story building, this 3,500-year-old conifer sprang from a winged seed no larger than a rolled-oats flake—a tiny package for such a mighty life.

Sequoia roots are shallow; should erosion unbalance it, a great tree could topple while still in its prime.

J. BAYLOR ROBERTS
NATIONAL GEOGRAPHIC STAFF

Sequoia and Kings Canyon National Parks are so large that one can hike or ride for days. I explored the High Sierra Trail, high road to Hamilton Lakes, Kaweah Gap, and down the Big Arroyo toward the mile-deep canyon of the Kern. The more I ventured, the more I longed to push deeper into the Sierra fastness. For "there is a love of wild nature in everybody," John Muir wrote, "an ancient mother love ever showing itself whether recognized or no, and however covered by cares and duties." Nearly 40,000 people each summer pack into this back country.

I encountered scores of outdoorsmen and women—even campers so young they were carried papoose-fashion. One pigtailed six-year-old strode proudly down the trail carrying her own hefty little knapsack. There were Scouts, too, and rock climbers and fishermen. At Wanda Lake an angler showed me a fine catch of golden trout, the most sublime

Campers' moving day: fun for the family, work for the burros.

B. ANTHONY STEWART, NATIONAL GEOGRAPHIC PHOTOGRAPHER

FOLD OUT, DO NOT TEAR

SEQUOIA AND KINGS CANYON

By JOHN M. KAUFFMANN
National Park Service

THE HIGHWAY writhed up the Sierra Nevada ramparts. Behind, drenched in June sunshine, lay California's San Joaquin Valley; ahead beckoned the hazy ridges of Sequoia National Park.

Up this canyon, a century before, Indians led a rancher along dim trails to see an incredible wonder—the giant sequoia trees, largest of living things. Now, thanks to highway engineering, more than a million visitors each year drive these heights.

I rounded a bend and caught my breath. Before me stood the Guardsmen: four sequoias like pillars of a city gate. Cinnamon-red trunks rose massively amid the green. I parked and walked over to a group of trees. An auto paused, its driver grinned: "You look like a midget!"

He was right. In the Giant Forest we are all Gullivers in a Brobdingnagian world. I found the Sentinel Tree watching over hundreds of other Gullivers eagerly buying film and camping supplies. "Relax, youngsters," the old trees seemed to say. "Your lives are short enough. Enjoy them!"

A wary doe takes to the High Sierra Trail in this giant twin-park wilderness of silent forests, savage canyons, and granite peaks, an easy day's drive from Los Angeles or San Francisco.

B. ANTHONY STEWART, NATIONAL GEOGRAPHIC PHOTOGRAPHER

I raised my tent between two sequoias where the long light of sunset would filter through the boughs to make the trunks glow. I unpacked my gear. Then the welcoming committee arrived: inquisitive robin, bumptious chipmunk, and truculent jay, panhandlers all. The jay hopped onto my table, scolding for food.

At suppertime the forest filled with fragrant wood smoke, children's laughter, faint notes of a guitar. Families gathered, each united in primeval comfort around its evening fire. Birds began to sing, flute answering tiny flute in trilling antiphony—elfin music sung to giants.

Crash! I recognized what rangers call the "Trash Can Symphony." Bears were busy tipping over receptacles in search of tidbits. A mother bear and her cub shuffled by. I knew they would not harm me if I did not molest or feed them, so I settled back against a tree to read by lantern light.

A coyote chorus was my dawn alarm clock, and a delegation of deer trotted by to see I was making the most of the morning. I joined the stream of human ants circling the base of the General Sherman, most massive and one of the oldest of living things. I wondered how many tons of tree towered here, high as the Capitol dome in Washington, D. C. Some say 2,000, with enough wood to build 40 five-room houses. The 272-foot trunk is nearly 37 feet in diameter.

"I feel so . . . infinitesimal," murmured a young woman as she gazed upward.

"I feel like a youngster," replied a white-haired grandmother with a twinkle.

Egypt was conquering an empire when the Sherman sprouted. The tree was a thriving adult when Greece flowered into its Golden Age. And on a winter's night when a great star blazed over Bethlehem, this tree stood straight and tall, already more than 1,500 years old.

Next to the Giant Forest, Grant Grove is the best known and most accessible of the parks' 24 groves of *Sequoia gigantea*. The General Grant Tree, which is second in size to the General Sherman and thought by many to be even more impressive, is widely known as the Nation's Christmas Tree. In addition, Congress designated it a national shrine honoring America's war dead.

"CLIMB the mountains and get their good tidings!" Alta Peak, rising northeast of the Giant Forest 11,204 feet above sea level, seemed to echo John Muir's exhortation. A friend and I shouldered knapsacks one morning and plunged into red-fir forest. Above the timber line we panted onto Alta's snow-splotched summit to gaze upon an endless world of mountains. From north to south the Great Western Divide sawed the sky. One summit far beyond must be 14,495-foot Mount Whitney, high point of the Sierra Nevada—the Snowy Range.

Since most of the snow melts away in summer, Muir, I thought, had a better name: The Range of Light. Dawn turns its peaks into pinnacles of pearl. The midday sun shimmers across the pale rocks with blinding intensity. The light mellows as afternoon wanes, and at sunset the cliffs blaze with alpenglow.

Sequoias of Giant Forest tower over pygmy campers. The two parks protect thousands of these ancient Big Trees, native to a 4,000–8,000-foot zone in western Sierras. Trunk tapers little, hence tree's enormous mass.

B. ANTHONY STEWART, NATIONAL GEOGRAPHIC PHOTOGRAPHER

FOLD OUT, DO NOT TEAR

JOHN M. KAUFFMANN

In a world of golden eagle and fighting trout, nature entertains Boy Scouts at glacier-carved Hamilton Lakes, two days' hike from the road. Angel's Wings jut above.

Dancing flames warm campers at Bearpaw Meadow tent camp, a mile and a half high. Alpenglow and full moon bathe California's roof at twilight.

of fish, the Sierra's own native glory. Long ago the waters must have trapped the reflections of a sunset and transformed them into living things.

This is stupendous country, incredible country, where superlatives seem inadequate—Le Conte Canyon, Black Giant, Dusy Basin, Grouse Meadows, Lake of the Fallen Moon, and finally Kings Canyon, plunging more than 8,000 feet from mountaintop to river bed. So measured, it's the deepest in North America.

SEQUOIA and KINGS CANYON NATIONAL PARKS *Central California. 1,322 sq. mi.*

Features: Spectacular High Sierra setting for world's most massive trees, continent's deepest canyon, state's highest mountain. **Activities:** Visitor centers at Giant Forest, Grant Grove. Scenic roads into both parks. Hiking, riding trails. Wilderness camping, fishing (Calif. license). Guided tours, nature walks, campfire programs; skiing in winter. **Season:** Parks open all year. Most activities June–Sept. (nearly rainless days, cool nights). Elevation at Giant Forest 6,400 ft. **How to get there:** Calif. 180 or 198 from US 99. See map at back of book. So. Pacific, Santa Fe Ry., United Airlines to Fresno or Visalia, Calif., TWA to Fresno; bus to park in summer. Trails to high country from Owens Valley, east of Sierra, on US 6-395. **Accommodations:** Lodge, cabins among sequoias; tent chalet on High Sierra Trail. Camp Kaweah all year. Write Sequoia and Kings Canyon Nat'l Parks Co. at park or (Oct.–May) Visalia. Camp, trailer sites. **Services:** Coffee shops, supplies, gas. Garage, church in summer. Ski gear rental.

For further information write the parks' Superintendent, Three Rivers, California

An awesome inferno unfolds beneath Dantes View: waves of salt and sand rub wounds where earth's crust sank

Gold-seekers, struggling to break out of this fiery trench, had little eye for the scenic riches more than one-third million visitors enjoy each year.

Eastern California's Death Valley extends 140 miles from north of Ubehebe Crater, where an eruption shook the ground early in the Christian era, to south of Saratoga Springs, one of many water sources desperate forty-niners failed to find. Some 550 square miles lie below sea level. In the salt-rimmed depression at far left is the Western Hemisphere's lowest spot—minus 282 feet. From Dantes View, the visitor can look beyond it at 14,495-foot Mount Whitney (not shown), California's highest peak.

Thunderstorms may rage in the mountains, but most rainfall and run-off evaporates or is absorbed before reaching the valley floor. Despite aridity, more than 600 kinds of plants thrive, among them desert holly, salt-bush, cacti of a dozen kinds, mariposas, lupines, and dahlias. Sunflowers turn to their god. Primroses and poppies splash color in the vast basin.

Visitors (below) are intrigued by Death Valley's "riddle of the sands." What causes large rocks to move and leave tracks on the level clay floor?

JOSEF MUENCH

J. BAYLOR ROBERTS, NATIONAL GEOGRAPHIC STAFF

DEATH VALLEY

By EDWARDS PARK, National Geographic Staff

TOMESHA, the Panamint Indians called it: "Ground Afire." And in the height of summer there is no better name for this sun-tortured trench between blistered ranges. But when a group of forty-niners blundered into it, they renamed it Death Valley.

Drive in from the east through Death Valley Junction to get an inkling of how those emigrants felt. Short-cutting to the gold fields, they had crossed a weary succession of deserts and hills. At last they came to this range, seemingly topped by a peak flying a banner of snow. Surely these must be the Sierras! They flung themselves at the bald mountains, wrenched their groaning wagons through the washes and gullies, then stared in numb despair at the trick nature had played.

Fringe-toed lizard hugs its sand dune haven. Burrowing with special toes (below), shy *Uma notata* "swims" into loose sand to avoid enemies or blazing sun. Valley folks say when lizards blow on feet to cool them, it's hot!

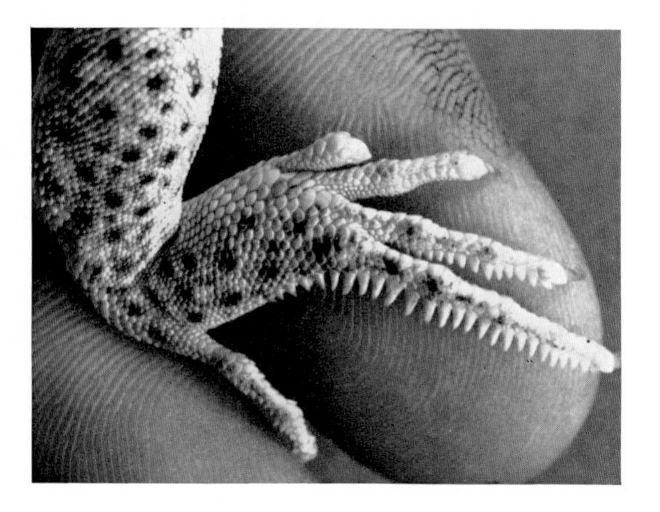

ROY S. PENCE

Spiny lizard, sporting a prickly collar, hunts insects in the shade, hibernates in winter. A 7-inch tail is half his length.

Miles yet from the Sierras, they stood amid the Amargosa Range. Between them and the peak whose snow had lured them—11,049-foot Telescope Peak, high point of the forbidding Panamint Range—spread a desolate sink, four to 16 miles wide, mostly below sea level. Rather than turn back, the half-starved forty-niners decided to cross the salt-crusted, lava-smeared plain.

Thus the trap snapped on them.

In your car today you can drive freely and comfortably along the valley floor

Death Valley's 20-mule team pulls again—for TV.

and spend the night at Furnace Creek with its irrigated date palms, its inn and ranch, its tennis courts and swimming pool. Here the Jayhawkers, one of the emigrant parties, scrabbled frantically for water. You may park beside the Devils Golf Course, that strange rubble of crystalline salt pinnacles and gravels that stretches down the valley 40 miles and is 1,000 feet deep. This bed of an Ice Age inland sea blocked the Bennett-Arcane party when they sought escape to the south. Your road skirts close under the brooding Panamints where those slow-dying men and women finally turned west and clawed their way out of the valley, then looked back on it and cursed it with a lasting name.

Death Valley—a bitter name, and hardly a just one, for life abounds here. The kit fox, desert coyote, and Bailey bobcat pad across the desert floor at night. Rabbits and ground squirrels scurry through the mesquite. Only sand dunes and salt beds are bare of plants—and the pale green pickleweed, resistant to salt and alkali, braves the very edge of the Devils Golf Course. Water flows sweet in many subsurface veins. Gardens flourish. Except in summer, when temperatures have hoisted to a poleaxing 134°, Death Valley's climate smiles on man by day and treats him to technicolor sunsets as lowering rays play on the eroded, mineral-stained hills. Nights are often cool.

It took the ubiquitous prospector to discover that the place was livable. One of the lost forty-niners, searching for the gunsight he had accidentally knocked from his rifle, found a chunk of rich silver ore. His story brought miners with their burros. Though no one ever located the Lost Gunsight Mine, other strikes were made. Boom towns sprouted along the mountains, howled on Saturday nights, then withered away, leaving slag heaps of broken bottles. In 1880 a destitute couple, trying to scrape a desert living, learned of valuable borax and how its deposits look. Aaron Winters felt he might have seen some of that stuff in the valley. He went and looked, and for years the 20-mule teams hauled 36½-ton loads of borax from the works at Harmony.

J. BAYLOR ROBERTS, NATIONAL GEOGRAPHIC STAFF

Two generations ago mules hauled borax on the grueling 10-day, 165-mile desert trek to Mojave.

DEATH VALLEY NATIONAL MONUMENT *California-Nevada. 2,981 sq. mi.*

Features: Desert showplace in "North America's basement"; lowest point in hemisphere. **Activities:** Visitor center at Furnace Creek; illustrated talks. Roads lead to Dantes View, Panamint overlooks, dunes, borax works, Ubehebe Crater, Scotty's Castle. Trail up Telescope Peak. Horses at Furnace Creek. **Season:** Most activities Oct. 15–May 1 (weather is pleasant). Roads open all year. **What to bring:** Jacket for cool evenings. Sunglasses, binoculars, camera, light meter. **How to get there:** Highways through monument intersect US 95, 91, 395. By rail or air to Las Vegas, Nev., where cars can be rented. Airstrips in monument for private planes. **Accommodations:** *October–May.* Furnace Creek Inn, Ranch, Stove Pipe Wells Hotel; write Death Valley, Cal. *All year.* Scotty's Castle (Goldfield, Nev.); cabins at Wild Rose Station (Trona, Cal.). Camp, trailer grounds.

For further information write Superintendent, Death Valley, California

Death Valley Scotty lived in Alhambran splendor in this castle but kept the secret of his easy-going wealth

A former trick rider in Buffalo Bill's Wild West Show, Walter Scott hit the 1905 headlines when he emerged from Death Valley with padlocked sacks of gold, scattered bills like confetti on Los Angeles streets, and hired a train for a record run to Chicago. For years he fostered the legend that a hidden gold mine kept his pockets jingling. Actually, a millionaire friend set up Scotty just for laughs.

The pair built this $2,000,000 mirage in concrete, with its imported tiles, hand-carved woodwork, and crenelated towers, in the 1920's. It perches 3,000 feet high in Grapevine Canyon at the valley's northern end. The "desert rat's" fabulous home, now a hotel and museum, opens to hourly tours.

J. BAYLOR ROBERTS, NATIONAL GEOGRAPHIC STAFF

GEORGE A. GRANT

"He went thataway!" gesture the tufted Joshua trees of Lost Horse Valley.

JOSHUA TREE NATIONAL MONUMENT

BY MOONLIGHT they raise grotesque arms as if supplicating a pagan goddess. By day these outstretched arms, seeming to point to a promised land, reminded westward-trekking Mormons of Joshua at prayer—hence the name Joshua tree. Ranging up to 40 feet high and 14 feet around, this overgrown member of the lily family lives—who knows?—perhaps 500 years. It produces no telltale rings.

In southern California, where the Colorado and Mojave Deserts meet at the Little San Bernardino Mountains, 872 square miles bear this shaggy plant's name. From monument headquarters at Twentynine Palms the road follows a gently rising plateau. Scarlet-tipped ocotillos and cholla cacti give way to Mojave yuccas; Joshua trees take hold around 3,000 feet. Suddenly at Salton View, 5,185 feet in the sky, the land tumbles away to reveal distant Salton Sea, 235 feet below the ocean, and San Gorgonio Mountain, 11,502 feet above. Beneath lies San Andreas Fault, the great earthquake-making rift. Campgrounds await all year. Bring water, firewood, warm clothes—even summer nights may be nippy.

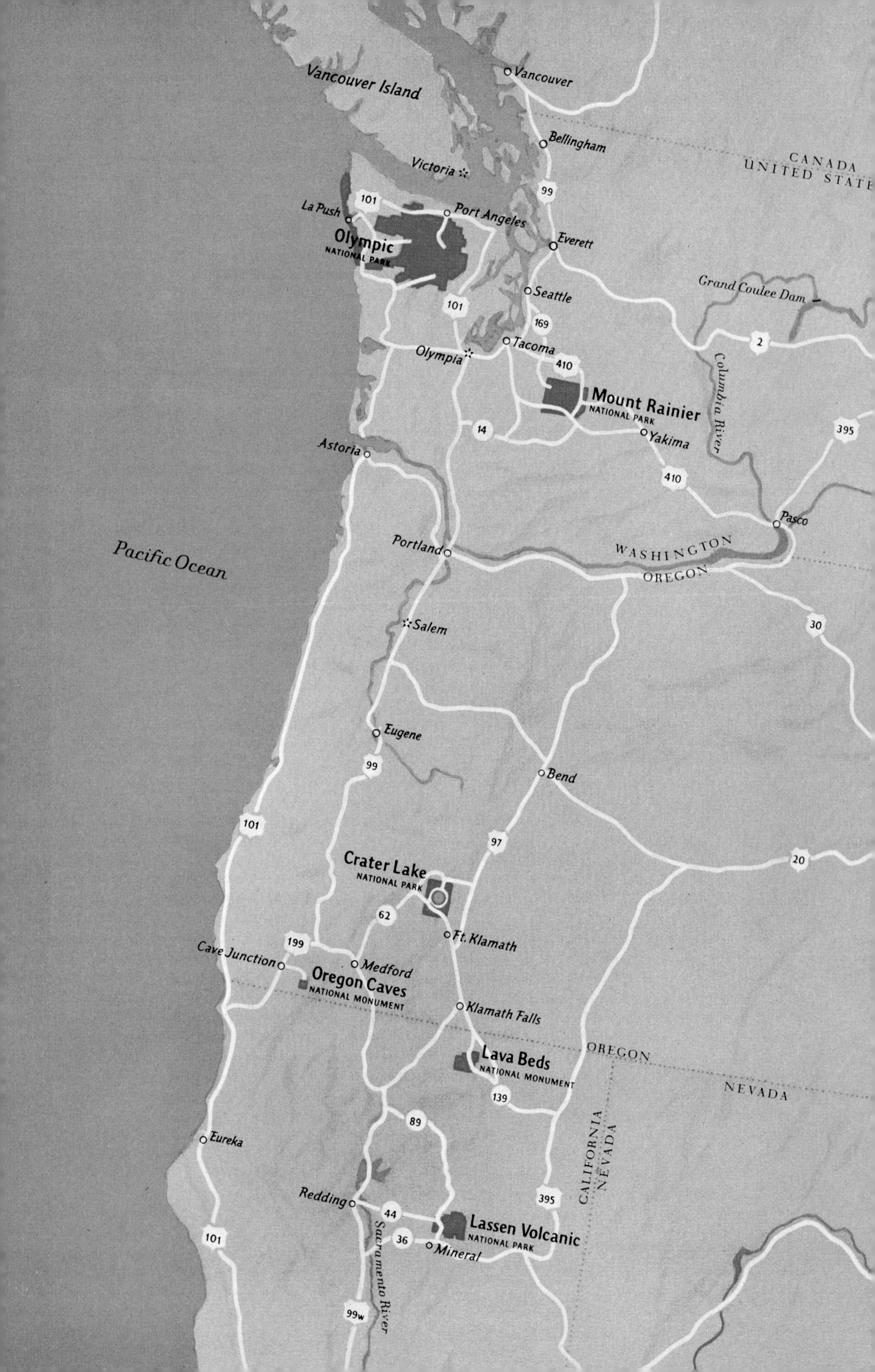

Vancouver Island
Vancouver
Bellingham
CANADA
UNITED STATES
Victoria
99
101
La Push
Port Angeles
Olympic
NATIONAL PARK
Everett
Grand Coulee Dam
Seattle
101
169
Tacoma
2
Olympia
410
Columbia River
Mount Rainier
NATIONAL PARK
14
Yakima
395
Astoria
410
Pasco
Pacific Ocean
Portland
WASHINGTON
OREGON
30
Salem
Eugene
99
Bend
101
97
Crater Lake
NATIONAL PARK
20
62
Ft. Klamath
199
Cave Junction
Medford
Oregon Caves
NATIONAL MONUMENT
Klamath Falls
OREGON
Lava Beds
NATIONAL MONUMENT
NEVADA
139
89
CALIFORNIA
NEVADA
Eureka
395
Redding
44
Lassen Volcanic
NATIONAL PARK
36
Mineral
101
Sacramento River
99w

PART FIVE

THE PACIFIC NORTHWEST

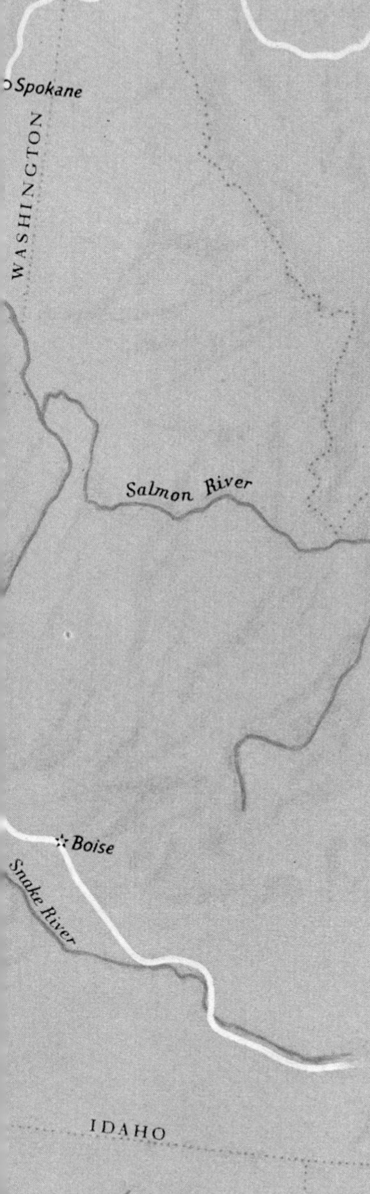

THIS IS THE BIG WILDERNESS—a land of fire and ice gentled by a cloak of green and washed by Pacific swells. Its trees are big, its mountains big, its spirit as big as all outdoors.

Cataclysmic eruptions shook this region in the yesterday of geologic time. Molten lava seared its signature on earth's face; volcanic surges heaved up noble Rainier, Lassen, and long-gone Mazama, in whose flooded basement now lies Crater Lake.

Today the fires are banked and ice grips the Cascade peaks. And in the shadow of Olympic glaciers where summer is a fleeting thing lie ocean beaches and the green growing miracle of the rain forest.

Lewis and Clark staked a claim to the Northwest in 1805, but prairie schooners were slow to follow on the Oregon Trail. Returning today, pioneers would find much of the young land's solitude unchanged. As park visitors do, they could hike for weeks in dense evergreen forests, flowered alpine meadows, an untamed realm of rock and snow. They'd rest by fish-filled streams now roaring, now muted to a trailside chuckle, and top off the day with campfire yarns as leaping flames sent sparks to join the stars.

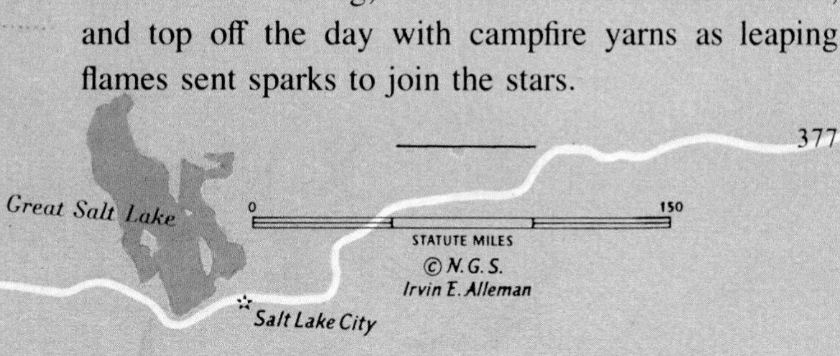

A New York family explores a wilderness of rain forests, glaciers, and flowered alpine meadows in western Washington

OLYMPIC
NATIONAL PARK

By PAUL A. ZAHL, National Geographic Staff
Photographs by the author

A SNOWBALL whizzed past me, followed by a peal of laughter. "Happy Fourth of July, Daddy!" What a strange Independence Day! That morning my wife and I and our two small children, Eda and Paul, had left our cabin in the Elwha Valley and driven up mile-high Hurricane Ridge—into a sky-touching world of dazzling snow.

Below lay steep, densely forested ravines. Beyond, an arc of snow-capped peaks saw-toothed across the horizon, topped by the crags and glaciers of Mount Olympus, 7,965-foot high point of Washington's Olympic Peninsula. Northward the landscape tumbled abruptly toward Pacific waters fingering through the Strait of Juan de Fuca to produce Puget Sound. There, above a blue haze, we could distinguish Vancouver Island, Canada.

Two weeks earlier we had left our New York apartment and set out in search of a wilderness. Here, in the 1,400 square miles of Olympic National Park, an up-and-down world of wonders, we found it. Spurning the elegance of Lake Crescent Lodge and other hotels, we settled for nearly three months in a one-room log cabin. Living centered around a wood-burning stove, with papa responsible for chopping wood, children for filling the woodbox, and mamma for stoking the fire and preparing meals. Radiating from this base, we could ex-

In cathedral-like rain forests of the Olympic lowlands, giant conifers struggle sunward from the matted floor where life and death keep pace. On the snow-chilled heights bloom wildflowers like the bluebell above.

MERLE SEVERY, NATIONAL GEOGRAPHIC STAFF

Lookouts scan for telltale smoke among Olympic's treasured trees. If fire breaks out in remote areas, planes drop equipment to fire fighters.

plore hot mineral springs, inky-blue Lake Crescent with its sentinel Storm King mountain, miles of rain forest laced with plunging streams and cascading rivers, and the high country with its peaks, jewel-like lakes, and scouring glaciers. There was Enchanted Valley and the long, narrow strip of park land along the Pacific. There were Roosevelt elk, deer, marmot, mountain beaver, and bear.

We had made this day's ascent to seek wildflower meadows that should by now have set Hurricane Ridge aglow. But the only glow came from snow. Rangers had warned that this was a late spring, "but a few days of warm weather and flowers will pop as if they had springs under them."

Well, we had those few days of warmth. So where were the wildflowers?

Crowning the park wilderness, these majestic ranges are visible far at sea. Sighting them in 1788, English navigator John Meares named the highest peak Mount Olympus—home of the gods.

My wife resolved the dilemma. I heard shouts and saw her point down the mountainside to a sprinkling of golden dots around a snow patch. We skidded down into the midst of thousands of glacier lilies nodding yellow heads close to the melt-soaked turf, some pushing boldly through the snow—our first sign of spring in the Olympic high country.

The Olympic Peninsula is as unusual in climate as it is geographically and botanically. Moisture-laden Pacific winds are deflected upward by Olympic peaks. The resulting rainfall on the western slopes reaches 140 inches a year, and around Mount Olympus precipitation is an amazing 200 inches. Yet by the time these winds cross the peninsula they are nearly dry. Thus, while the west side is the wettest region in the continental United States, an area 50 miles to the east, in the Olympic "rain shadow," approaches aridity.

The downfall on the western slopes has produced one of the most luxuriant temperate-zone rain forests in the world. From temporary quarters in the lower Hoh Valley we would drive day after day to the end of the spur road, then

set out on foot up the trail. Papa had to carry junior a good part of the way, and once had to fish Eda out of a stream; but aside from such minor hazards the going was easy. Yet, pressing in on the trail is a forest as wild and primeval as any in the world. Up the Hoh Valley, a large Sitka spruce boasts a circumference at chest height of 41 feet 8 inches. Near the valley mouth, the world's largest western red cedar has a girth of 66 feet 1 inch. In the Queets River Valley is the largest Douglas fir (45 feet 5 inches around), and on the east fork of the Quinault River, the record western hemlock (27 feet 2 inches).

Though many big trees towered 200 feet beside the trail, what dominated the scene was the profusion of smaller species—understories of big-leaf maples, vine maples, ferns, lichens, fungi, Oregon oxalis, and the smaller life of this prodigious tangle. Club mosses hung from nearly every branch, covered nearly every surface in trailing strands and great sweeping tufts like the magnified beards of invisible elves and hobgoblins. We felt we had entered a nether world—mysterious, almost palpably quiet.

Clouds hung low on our first visit to Hoh Valley's rain forest. Then the sun came out and a brilliant yellow-green light replaced the somber shadows. Like pale mist it filtered through the vegetation, reflected by a billion chlorophylled surfaces, bathing us in a soft yet all-pervading glow.

This great rain forest has been standing relatively undisturbed for centuries. With much of it in the climax state (a climax forest is one that has developed to its maximum extent), profuse growth continues, but the overall mass barely changes. Creative and destructive processes have reached equilibrium.

When an old tree crashes, a hundred seedlings, stimulated by the light, leap up to fill the space, though only one or two reach full growth. Meanwhile, lichens, fungi, bacteria, ants, termites, and beetles set upon the fallen giant and convert it into humus. Seeds from living conifers light upon it, and soon a virtual nursery of new evergreens sprouts and grows, often in straight colonnades, from the decayed trunk. Their roots may loop around the side of the fallen log; trees on stilts are not uncommon. Finally the disruption caused by the crash is corrected, and the forest regains its balance.

Animals, too, inhabit this moss-draped world, but the visitor is hardly aware of them. Now and then an invisible bird sings high in the trees, a black beetle scurries across the trail, or a chipmunk performs briefly on a log.

Not Hänsel and Gretel, but Paul and Eda Zahl sit in the hushed stillness of a moss-draped fairyland. Only bird notes from atop 200-foot Douglas firs break the eerie silence. Park roads lead to rain forests of the Hoh, Queets, and Quinault Valleys. Trails continue through green-lit worlds where beetles (right) explore their own forests of matchstick lichens.

Life teems on the rain forest's floor; a new world opens for Eda.

DURING the summer my family and I made no fewer than two dozen trips to Hurricane Ridge. Packing a substantial lunch and other necessities for keeping two small children tranquil, we would leave the cabin early and spend the day in meadows of wildflowers.

Vegetation on the heights has a dramatically brief life cycle; blossoms must be developed quickly and seeds matured and hurriedly disseminated. We could sense an element of biological urgency in these alpine meadows. The great

UPPER LEFT: Bright spore capsules wave atop a moss plant. Winds will scatter reproductive cells as they sift from pods. (Enlarged 3 times.)

LOWER LEFT: *Nidula*, a common fungus, cradles spore masses like a clutch of eggs. The closed pouches have not yet matured. (Enlarged 3 times.)

Among these tiny plants live frogs, salamanders, slugs, shrews, and mice—but no venomous snakes.

woolly-coated bumblebees seemed to fly more energetically and hum more purposefully than those in the valley.

We would find space among the flowers to spread our blanket. We would glance toward the crags of Mount Olympus, half hidden in clouds, and down at flowered meadows running steeply into a thick border of evergreens, standing prim and clean. I would wander off looking for a particularly rich field of purple-blue lupine; and then great swirls of mist might roll in, sometimes so

UPPER RIGHT: Scarlet-crested *Cladonia,* coral-like lichen, carpets sunlit earth and rocks. Brilliant tips cast spores to the wind. (Enlarged 3 times.)

LOWER RIGHT: *Stemonitis,* a mold on the border between plants and animals, slides its matchlike spore cases over rotting logs. (Enlarged 3 times.)

Lupine and white buckwheat mantle Hurricane Ridge,

UPPER LEFT: Piper bellflower, *Campanula piperi,* nestles amid lichen-splotched rocks.
LEFT: Grass widow, *Sisyrinchium douglasii,* is not a grass, but a relative of the iris. Blossoms often last only a day. (Enlarged 1½ times.)
LOWER LEFT: *Phacelia sericea* clusters its flowers at tip of foot-long stem, thrusts antennalike stamens from the blooms. (Enlarged 1½ times.)

a mile above the sea, during the brief alpine summer.

BELOW, CENTER: Indian paintbrush, *Castilleja,* reverses usual flower pattern. Tiny green blooms peek between bright orange-red leaves and bracts. It cloaks many far-western valleys.
BELOW: Delicate *Anemone hudsoniana* wears a coat of silky hairs. A member of the buttercup family, it thrives on high meadows and rocky slopes. (Enlarged $1\frac{1}{2}$ times.)

dense that we would have to return to the car or seek shelter in the modern ski lodge perched high on a scenic clearing.

One day in this mountainous Eden we might find a particular stretch of meadow yellow with buttercups; a week later, blue with larkspur, white with phlox, or orange with columbine. Our joyous adventures among these delights were marred only once by anxiety.

We had been photographing columbine near where the clearing dropped perilously into a 200-foot ravine. My wife suddenly looked up, her voice shaky. "Where's Eda?"

Little Paul was sitting in a nearby patch of wallflowers, engrossed with a nectar-seeking bee. My eyes swept the area, including the precipice rim. I shouted, "Eda! Eda!" No reply.

I ran to the edge of the ravine, but the sight I feared was not to be seen, and I thanked God. In enlarging circles I searched wherever flowers were high enough to conceal a child.

Then I heard a whisper: "Daddy, *please* stop making all that noise. Do you want to scare the marmot?"

Too relieved to be angry, I saw Eda behind a rock, intent on a large, woodchuck-like rodent. Just then it let out a blasting whistle and scrambled into its hole. I listened silently to a lecture from Eda on disturbing animals in a national park. When it was my turn, Eda got a return lecture on hazards of mountain travel for unaccompanied first-graders.

Once when the fog came up thickly during our picnic lunch, we saw a figure materialize. "Hello," I shouted. No answer. What we had thought human was a handsome doe. To the children's delight, she went straight to my leather camera case,

Elk stroll a slope deep in Enchanted Valley. The park protects the largest remaining

sniffed, then began chewing with alarming vigor. Before I could point out that it is against park regulations to feed animals, Eda presented the deer with a peanut-butter sandwich. The animal accepted gratefully, turned, and fled into the mist.

At the park superintendent's suggestion I joined three of his staff for a trip into Enchanted Valley, now a popular objective for hikers. A day's drive from park headquarters at Port Angeles took us to the park's south side. After another long day on horseback we forded the east fork of the Quinault River and entered the valley itself.

Down an unbelievably high escarpment poured a series of waterfalls, some leaping from ledge to ledge 500 feet at a time, some sweeping down in great bridal veils, others zigzagging like fragments of frayed thread. In the rosy light

Blacktail buck on Hurricane Ridge spurns Eda's friendship. More than 50 different mammals, including bear and cougar, inhabit the park. "Whistler," the marmot (below), digs his den between rocks.

herds of Roosevelt or Olympic elk.

of evening the valley's northeast wall seemed to be bleeding in a hundred places. Each waterfall disappeared into a glistening, echoing ice cavern.

That night around the fire in a log chalet Coleman Newman, the park's elk specialist, mentioned that the park's four or five thousand famed Roosevelt or Olympic elk are shy and thinly spread in summer. But he agreed to scout the upper valley with me. Early in the morning we moved into a clearing near the river. Newman ducked. I followed his example as a group of elk moved cautiously out of the woods. Against the snow we

counted some 90 great elk—cows and calves, but no antlered bulls—carefully making their way across the sloping side of a huge cone of snow.

Weeks later on a trip to Bogachiel Peak, on High Divide, Newman and I spied more elk through our binoculars, this time magnificently antlered bulls. We watched 1,000-pound behemoths streamline their antlers back against their shoulders and batter through what seemed impenetrable forest growth.

I wanted my wife to join me on a trip to the glaciers of Mount Olympus, but with the children, that was out. So I chopped a week's firewood and left the cabin to my family, by now used to the deer, squirrels, chipmunks, and even bear that were their neighbors.

From the Hoh Valley, ranger Hugh Bozarth and I headed up the rain-forest trail on saddled mounts. Climbing and camping, we finally reached the glassy surface of Blue Glacier, close beside the cloud-mantled pinnacles of Mount Olympus. We rigged crampons and ropes and hiked over the ice to peer into yawning blue crevasses and explore vertical knife edges at the glacier's melting front. Between the craggy summits of Olympus a domed field of ice cracks off under the weight of new snow to feed six great glaciers. One icefall stood a quarter of a mile away, a crumbling cliff 500 feet high, with fallen blocks below. The 50 or so Olympic glaciers are only remnants of what they were. Blue Glacier, where we stood, shortened by more than 800 feet in only 15 years.

ON THE Olympic Peninsula, rain or overcast in one valley or on one peak does not necessarily mean that the same prevails elsewhere. "What's for today?" Eda would ask as our cabin stirred to life in the morning. I would glance at the ridge. "Looks clear as a bell. It's Hurricane Ridge for us." Or maybe: "Ceiling too low. How about the Soleduck forest, or Lake Crescent, or Blue Mountain, or the Ocean Strip?"

The national park's mile-wide Ocean Strip runs for about 50 miles along the peninsula's western coast and includes three Indian reservations. You reach it on US Highway 101, the road that circles the park's main mountain mass with spur roads poking inland through valley openings.

One day we headed for the strip—first, to view a whale that had washed ashore a few miles south of Ruby Beach; second, to visit the coastal village of La Push and show the children some real American Indians. You have to see this Olympic coastline, added to the park in 1953, to believe it: great needles of bare, occasionally tree-studded rock rising straight out of the surf; sculptured caves and rock bridges; sheer shore cliffs; heaps of white drift logs; glistening beaches; tidepools teeming with life; and sea birds everywhere.

The whale, of course, had no business being there. Its carcass might have fascinated tourists a month earlier, but now, after one whiff, we turned and ran. Climbing back up the sea-cliff trail, we headed north toward La Push.

Tracking a fugitive flower to its rocky lair, the Zahls discover Piper bellflower (page 386), one of eight flowering plants that grow only in the Olympics. Beyond tower the 7,000-foot Needles.

 Tree-studded isles flank the rocky coast where the Olympic Mountains meet the Pacific. Sea

birds skim creamy surf; seals bask on warm ledges; deer and bears share beaches with families like the Zahls.

In this picturesque fishing village, Eda found her Indians, some in outboard-propelled dugouts, smelt-fishing in the bay. She noted that neither their garments nor speech differed from our own.

One September morning, lumber jackets and heavy underwear gave way to city clothes as we prepared for the homeward trip. I knew that bull elk, coats sleek and antlers sharp, were clearing throats for autumn's mating calls; that bears were fattening on late-season berries, getting ready for the big sleep; that wildflowers were withering and winds gathering force.

Soon winter would whiten this mountain land, turning it from a paradise for summer naturalists, campers, and hikers into one for skiers. But the summoning of school bells back East saved us from the temptation of staying longer.

Park visitors and Indians fish side by side on Ruby Beach along the park's Pacific coast strip. Early explorers avoided this section of the coast after Indians slew two landing parties. Nearby Destruction Island derives its name from the seamen's deaths. Today city folk and tribesmen from the Hoh Reservation net surf smelt, which ride in on the tides to lay eggs in the sand. Hooks will not do; the fish spurn bait in any form.

B. ANTHONY STEWART, NATIONAL GEOGRAPHIC PHOTOGRAPHER

Coastal Indians once harpooned whales from huge dugouts. Adept carvers, they recorded their legends in wood. This Makah wears the symbolic headdress of the Wolf clan.

OLYMPIC NATIONAL PARK *Area 1,400 sq. mi.*

Features: Only park embracing snow-capped peaks and ocean beaches, rain forests and alpine flowers. Olympic elk.
Activities: Visitor center at Port Angeles. US 101 nearly circles park; spur roads to key areas. 600 mi. of trails. Horses, guides at Sol Duc Hot Springs, Elwha River. Hiking. Trout, salmon fishing. Nature walks, campfire programs. Skiing at Hurricane Ridge weekends Dec.–Mar.
Season: Park open all year. Best weather summer and early fall. Deep snow at high elevations Nov.–June or July.
What to bring: Rough-it clothing, warm jacket, rain gear.
How to get there: US 101. See map at back of book. Also ferry across Puget Sound and Hood Canal. To Port Angeles by air or bus from Seattle, by ferry from Victoria, B. C.
Accommodations: Lodges, inns, cabins; write Olympic Peninsula Hotel and Resort Assn., Coleman Ferry Terminal, Seattle. Campgrounds high and low, some accessible to trailers.
Regulations: Don't disturb nature. Fires on trail trips or beach hikes by permit. No pets on trails.

Write Supt., Olympic National Park, Port Angeles, Wash.

MOUNT RAINIER

By MERLE SEVERY, National Geographic Staff

MERLE SEVERY, NATIONAL GEOGRAPHIC STAFF

THE GREAT MOUNTAIN played coy with us as we approached it over Chinook Pass from Yakima on the east. We caught only tantalizing glimpses through clouds clambering over its shoulders of rock and ice. We wound through somber forests of fir and hemlock, past glacial moraines and waterfalls. Fallen timber streaked the slopes where avalanches

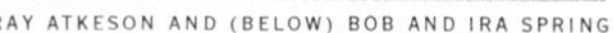
RAY ATKESON AND (BELOW) BOB AND IRA SPRING

Exploding snow pursues a skier leaping a hummock in Paradise Valley. Drifts nearly bury Paradise Inn (below), sometimes even reach the chimney tops; one season 83 feet of snow fell. Rainier's white mantle lingers to greet summer riders; volcanic cone of Mount St. Helens, 50 miles distant, rises beyond the Tatoosh Range.

B. ANTHONY STEWART, NATIONAL GEOGRAPHIC PHOTOGRAPHER

had thundered down. Arriving amid the swirling mists at Sunrise, 6,400 feet high on a northeastern spur, we found families of little firs huddling together, like jagged islands in a foggy sea.

"Guess we won't see Rainier today," said my wife Pat as she spread lunch. Squirrels and chipmunks came to greet us. Birds flew in to share our picnic.

Then the surging fog parted and Rainier filled the sudden blue sky. Blinding sun danced on fresh snow. Enormous glaciers seemed poised over our heads. Here, close up, we beheld the "round snowy mountain" seen from afar by Capt. George Vancouver of the British Royal Navy as he explored Puget Sound in 1792. He named the distant peak in honor of his friend Rear Adm. Peter Rainier.

Indians called this dormant volcano Tacoma, "The Mountain," and feared a demon who waited at the top to cast all trespassers into a fiery lake. But white men pushed up its slopes, and in 1870 Hazard Stevens and P. B. Van Trump struggled to the summit. For 11 hours they had clawed over rock and ice, only to stagger into a numbing gale on the crest. Lacking shelter, they faced a frigid death as

Wind and water hollowed this fairyland grotto in Paradise Ice Caves. Filtered sunlight tints the walls a luminous blue. Mount Rainier's flanks support more glaciers than any other U. S. peak outside Alaska.

RAY ATKESON

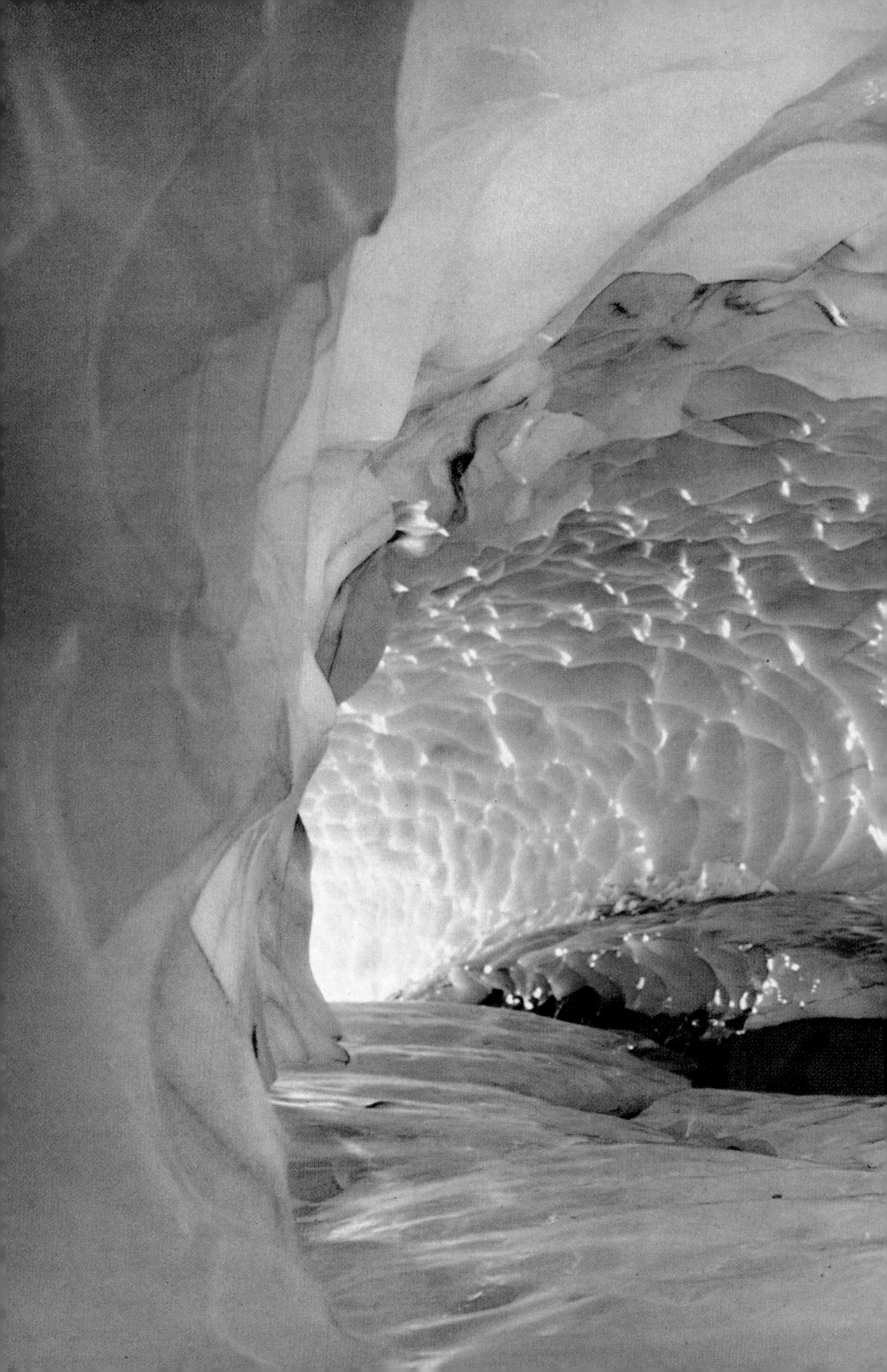

darkness closed in. Then on the crater rim they found an ice cave formed by a steam jet. There they huddled through the night, "freezing on one side," Stevens wrote, "and in a hot steam-sulphur-bath on the other."

I pictured them hurrying down the mountainside the following day—but again mists billowed in, erasing the image. Behind the swirls loomed a mystic mountain in a surrealist painting. An eerie chill enveloped us and we hastened on.

NEXT MORNING, outside our window at Longmire the 14,410-foot white giant stood majestically alone in a cloudless sky. We drove up to Paradise Valley, 5,500 feet high on Rainier's south shoulder, and there roamed parklands ablaze with autumn reds and mounted slopes dotted with dark green spires.

We surveyed blue-green crevasses and seracs on Nisqually Glacier and heard the rumble of ice crashing into the milky stream that snakes below its debris-littered snout. In the crisp distance snow-crowned Mount Adams and Mount St. Helens poked above the sawtoothed Tatoosh Range. Loping up mountain trails through sun-splashed alpine meadows, we felt a million miles from anyone, in a lofty, timeless realm. "Reminds me of *Heidi,*" Pat said.

Later, stopping along Stevens Canyon Road, carved out of Rainier's broad southern flank, we hiked over granite ledges polished in gentle swells and troughs by ancient glaciers, and peered into a breath-taking chasm at glacial melt frothing over rocks 180 feet below. At afternoon's end the wind died; no ripple blemished Rainier's mirror image in Reflection Lake. The sun's failing rays climbed the icy summit as we returned to Paradise, and the Nisqually valley flamed from wall to wall. The evening star had risen above the silhouetted Tatoosh peaks when we rode down off the mountain.

"Want to see how Paradise looks in winter?" the park superintendent and his wife asked us that evening in their Longmire home. "The snow was 30 feet deep, with drifts of 40 and 50 feet." A color slide flashed on the basement screen. Just the chimneys of Paradise Inn showed above the curving dunes of snow. "Altogether we measured 992 inches of snowfall there last year!"

We heard the back screen door slam, then again impatiently. "Raccoons," smiled the soft-spoken superintendent. "They say they're hungry. Wild animals seem instinctively to know they are protected in our national parks."

Mount Rainier National Park's 378 square miles have something for everybody. Each summer a million or more visitors, lured by the Cascades landmark so convenient to Seattle and Tacoma, delight in the alpine flowers that garland it to glacier's edge. Campgrounds serve the outdoorsman, and some 300 miles of trails probe the wilderness. Pat and I found autumn peace on the quiet slopes, before winter's breath turned them into a skier's playground. But perhaps Rainier's special appeal is to the climber, whose adventures the next pages record.

In training for Everest, climbers strike for Rainier's summit in 1962. The following spring American Mount Everest Expedition members carried Old Glory and National Geographic's banner to the top of the world's mightiest mountain. Among Pacific Northwest peaks, Rainier is a favorite of seasoned mountaineer and beginner alike. For information write the park superintendent, Longmire, Wash.

W. E. GARRETT, NATIONAL GEOGRAPHIC STAFF

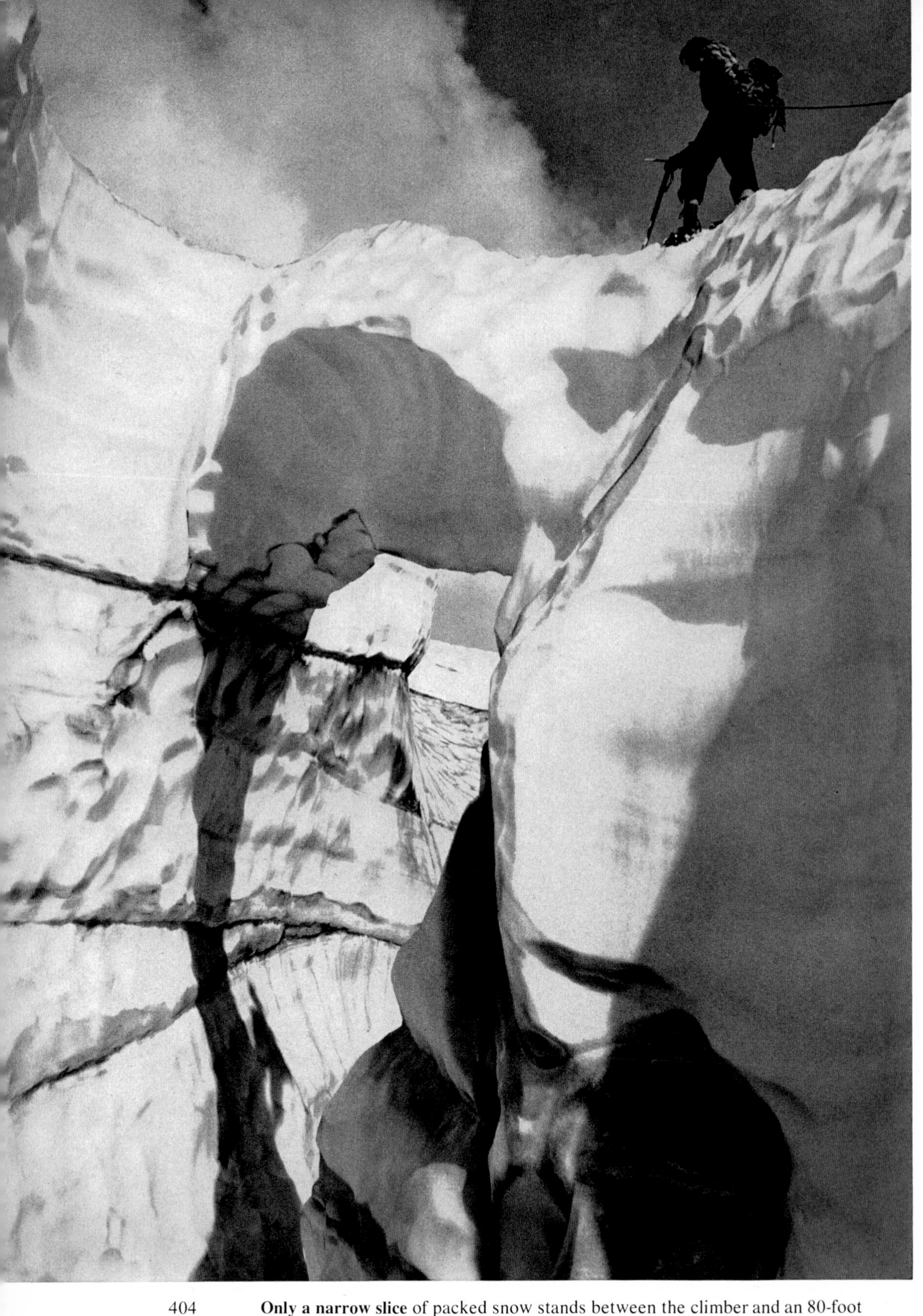

Only a narrow slice of packed snow stands between the climber and an 80-foot plunge. Horizontal lines mark Nisqually Glacier's yearly accumulation of ice.

Alpinist safeguards a teammate's crossings by snubbing his climbing rope around anchored ice ax used to chop frosty footholds on steep slopes. He secures the rope's other end around waist and shoulder with a bowline on a bight (right). Later he may loop it into a sliding sling to rappel down cliffs. Spike-studded crampons (below), strapped to climbing boots, give firm footing.

BOB AND IRA SPRING

High-altitude adventurers thread a maze of chasms

Climbing season, June to Labor Day, brings hundreds of enthusiasts to Mount Rainier. From lofty campsites climbers look down on lakes, rivers, and roads spread out as on a huge relief map. At night they watch the twinkling lights of distant cities.

Parties trying for the summit must register with a ranger and show they are physically fit, properly equipped, and experienced. Teams check every inch of nylon rope, cram lightweight foods in waterproof containers into compact packs. Most start from Paradise Valley after lunch, reach Camp Muir at 10,000 feet, and lay over until midnight. They try to get to the top and back to Muir by afternoon before intense sun brings rock and icefall dangers. They return to Paradise that day.

Crossing a glacier, two to four rope together. Their rhythmic "rest step" is geared to thin air. Between steps they pause three seconds, time for a full breath. Reflected sunrays can cause bad burns in half an hour. Climbers quench thirst with oranges, canned juice, and candy drops dissolved in melted snow.

Twenty-six major glaciers cling to Rainier; ages ago some may have reached Puget Sound. As brittle flows hump over rocks, huge cracks open. Some could swallow a hotel. Crevasse floors provide shelter in extreme cold because glacier interiors stay around 32°. On the summit, caverns melted out by volcanic steam offer refuge.

These men cross a snow bridge on Winthrop Glacier, one of six ice rivers originating at Rainier's summit. They head for distant Steamboat Prow.

BOB AND IRA SPRING

A gigantic gem of incredible blue, set among volcanic scars, crowns a great national park

CRATER LAKE

By WALTER MEAYERS EDWARDS, National Geographic Staff
Photographs by the author

PALE-BUFF, POWDERY PUMICE swirled around our feet at every step, filled our shoes, filtered into our clothes. For a quarter of a mile we had toiled uphill, clambering over fallen trees and banks of snow that lingered on into summer. My wife Mary, a step or two ahead, brushed between the drooping branches of two hemlocks and disappeared. Scrambling on, I found her gazing out over the edge of a cliff. Before us stretched Crater Lake —an enchanting vision of some other world. It was a full minute before Mary broke the silence.

"That blue," she said. "Can you believe it?" Varicolored rocks and stately evergreens enhanced the effect of the lake—just as a jeweler's setting points up the brilliance of a gem.

At first this Oregon lake did not seem large. Then we began to comprehend its size. The tiny island below us, called the Phantom Ship, was as high as Niagara Falls. What looked like two water bugs were 30-foot launches—floating on a lake with an abyss of 1,932 feet, the deepest in the United States. On our right, a cliff rose almost 2,000 feet above the water. From our overlook at Sun Notch, the opposite rim, more than five miles away, seemed a third as far.

I reflected on those terrible days some 6,500 years ago when Mount Mazama erupted with a titanic roar. Fiery magma poured out to form avalanches, some spreading 35 miles. Then the 12,000-foot peak collapsed. It was a spectacle that man must have witnessed. Mount Mazama pumice has been found on Indian cultural remains in Oregon caves, and Klamath Indian legends tell of a war between two gods, Llao on Mazama and Skell on Mount Shasta. Explosions and smoke from burning forests darkened the sky for a week as the mountains flamed. At the height of battle, Llao's throne tumbled down.

When we drove through the South Entrance of 250-square-mile Crater Lake National Park in early July, maintenance crews were clearing the last of winter's snow from Rim Drive. Most tours of that breath-taking 35-mile circuit begin at Rim Village on the southwest side of the lake. With its lodge, cafeteria, community building, and campground, it is the busiest part of the park.

Walking along the rim one afternoon, we came to the spot where John Wesley Hillman discovered Crater Lake on June 12, 1853. In a scrapbook at park head-

PAINTING BY PAUL ROCKWOOD, UNDER DIRECTION OF GEOLOGIST HOWEL WILLIAMS, UNIVERSITY OF CALIFORNIA

DIAGRAMS BY J. E. BARRETT, NATIONAL GEOGRAPHIC STAFF

Wracked by violent eruptions, Mount Mazama loses a mile of its height and gives birth to 20-square-mile Crater Lake

Steam condensed into billowing thunderheads as the volcano belched molten rock down glacier-sheathed slopes. Magma also drained away in underground channels, creating a void within the mountain. Then, with a roar of 10,000 locomotives, the summit collapsed, leaving a caldera six miles wide and 4,000 feet deep. Carbon-14 tests on charred trunks in the area fixed the date around 4600 B.C.

Rain and snow have filled the crater to about half its depth. Why is the lake so incomparably blue? Sunlight, scattering in water of such exceptional depth and purity, has all its colors absorbed except blue.

The lodge and cabins at Rim Village (left, foreground) are closed in winter and the campgrounds buried under snow, but roads from Medford and Klamath Falls stay open for winter sports enthusiasts, who find skiing in the park superb. In summer, buses connect with trains and planes.

quarters, I read the reminiscences of prospector Hillman. He and his companions, he wrote, were riding up a long, sloping mountain looking for a rumored lost mine and "did not expect to see any lakes. . . .

"Not until my mule stopped within a few feet of the rim of Crater Lake did I look down, and if I had been riding a blind mule I firmly believe I would have ridden over the ledge to death. . . ."

Less than two miles north of Discovery Point stands Hillman Peak, 8,156 feet above sea level and highest point on the rim. Nearby a saddle offers one of Rim Drive's best spots for a view of Wizard Island, a volcano within a volcano and so named because it resembles a wizard's hat. We visited the island and climbed to the top of the cinder cone, 763 feet above the water. In and around the 100-yard-wide crater grew a few stunted, straggly pines. When we returned to the island's shore, I resisted the temptation to swim in the chill waters—about 55° in summer. Next day we cruised around the lake, exploring the caldera walls. We seemed quite alone in this vast and incomparable setting. People on the rim were too small to be seen without binoculars, but sometimes, when the breeze died, their voices floated to us across the stillness.

I landed two rainbow trout. We could watch the fish, deep down, trail the spinners, then strike. The water is so clear that moss has been found 425 feet down.

"Fossil" fumaroles stab the sky along Wheeler Creek southeast of the lake. Mazama's eruption choked the valley with pumice; when hot gases forced vents to the surface, they hardened the passages. Wind and water then carved these Pinnacles. At Sinnott Memorial Overlook (left), a naturalist uses a relief map to dramatize Mazama's story.

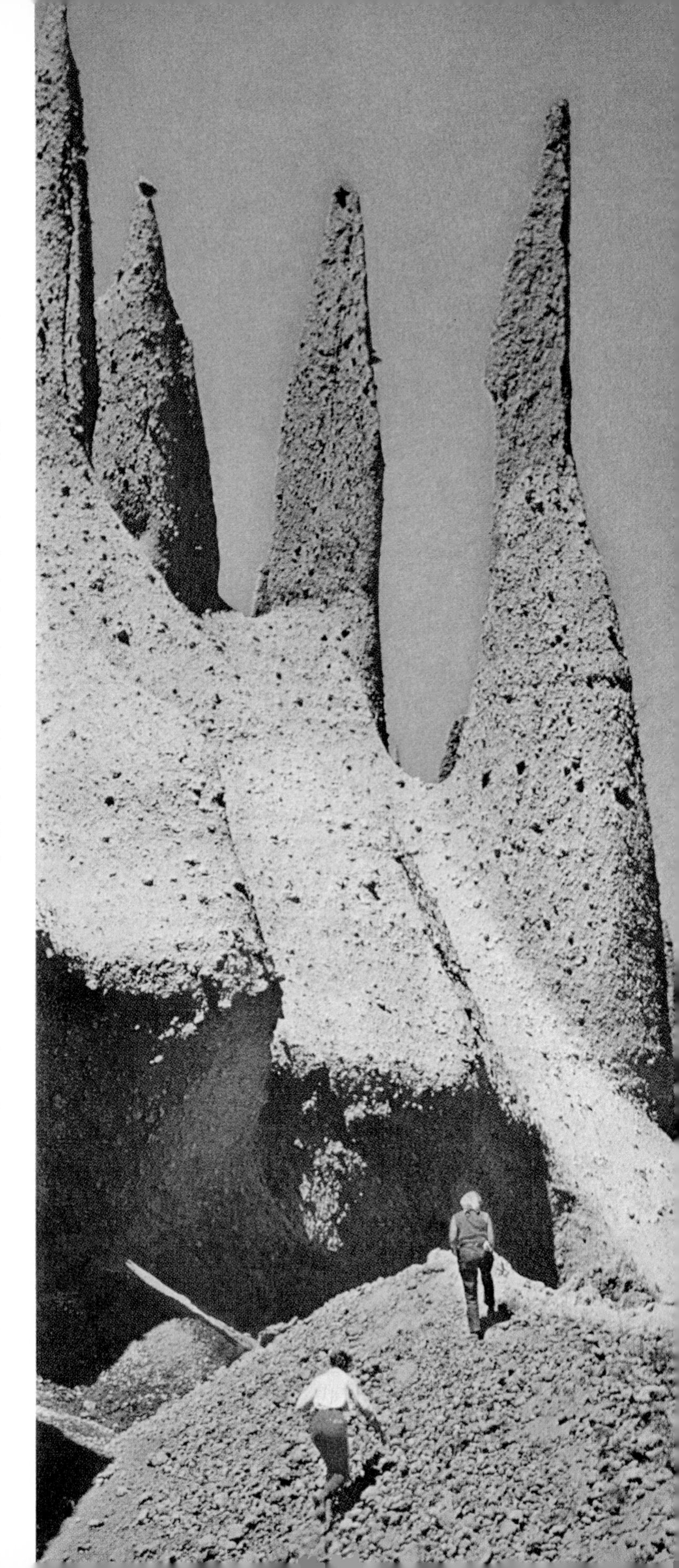

Moss needs sunlight, and the kind found here lives no deeper than 120 feet in most lakes.

Back from our Wizard Island digression, we wandered through Castle Crest Wildflower Garden near park headquarters. Here flowers and shrubs and trees abound in glorious variety. The garden's beauty is at its peak in August when rufous hummingbirds dart among the monkey flowers and lupine. The blooming season is short; by mid-September the snow begins to fall.

"It doesn't get really cold," said the maintenance foreman. "It's seldom down to zero. But you should see the snow. More than 50 feet falls in a year, and some years we've had more than 70. We keep the South and West Entrance roads open as far as the lodge. Snow gets 20 feet deep up on the rim, and the drifts nearly cover the lodge."

He paused, then added in homage to this magnificent marvel, "But the lake sure is beautiful in the snow."

OREGON CAVES

A LUCKY MAN was Elijah Davidson. With his old muzzle-loading rifle he wounded a bear and chased it down a hole. The story does not go on to say whether he retrieved his bear, but lighting a pitch torch, he found himself in a weird underworld of winding passages and decorated chambers. And if Elijah was fortunate in discovery that August day in 1874, so have been the many thousands who have followed his trail into Oregon Caves.

One of these was Joaquin Miller, the Poet of the Sierra, who often sang the praises of "The Marble Halls of Oregon." Chandeliers, columns, miniature waterfalls, even bric-a-brac, all rendered by the relentless seepage of water bearing dissolved limestone, embellish these cool, silent rooms. Coveralls and rubber shoes, available near the entrance, are a good idea when taking the mile-and-a-quarter guided trip, for the electrically lighted caves are damp.

Near the California line, Oregon Caves National Monument opens its mountain chateau and cabins in summer. You can picnic within these 480 acres, but Greyback Campground is eight miles away. A nursery tends children while parents explore; you must be over six to enter these lovely, fragile chambers.

LAVA BEDS NATIONAL MONUMENT

VIOLENCE KEYNOTES this northern California scene. Here volcanoes flamed in centuries long past. Lava spewed from 17 cones, cooling into porous chunks. Rivers of fire flowed from fractures and crept into gullies. There, hardening on the outside while the molten interior drained off, they formed lava tubes and caves; when roofs collapsed these became trenches and chasms, sometimes 100 feet deep. Fumaroles belched and hissed gas, then left dead chimney shafts probing far underground.

Into this black labyrinth in 1872 came a band of Modoc Indians who had broken free of the reservation they unwillingly shared with the Klamaths, their traditional foes. Defeating a cavalry force, the ill-armed Modocs, encumbered by women and children, took to the lava and fought the United States Army to a standstill five months. Their leader, "Captain Jack," deployed his warriors, never more than 71, through the serpentlike trenches. He stood off odds of 15 to one, dodged artillery fire, rearmed his braves with captured rifles. In one pitched battle he wiped out two-thirds of the attacking bluecoats, killing four out of five top officers.

Rock forts and foxholes still stand. Bleached bones of horses lie underfoot, and you almost expect to hear the crack of an Indian rifle. But campers and picnickers can safely explore the lava bridges and statuary, the Indian inscriptions, and many of the caves with "lavacicles"—stalactites of once-molten rock.

CHARLES E. MOHR

A riot of green in Fern Cave contrasts with Lava Beds' dry landscape overhead.

On the ice floor of Skull Cave, Indians refrigerated bighorn and pronghorn meat. The bighorn are gone, but mule deer winter in the monument's 72 square miles. In spring, wildflowers burst into bloom among the lava flows—a new and less violent eruption, ever pleasing to the eye.

LASSEN VOLCANIC NATIONAL PARK

WAGON TRAINS heading for the Sacramento gold fields found Lassen Peak a welcome landmark. An old volcano, probably as extinct as most of its sister peaks in the Cascades, northern California settlers judged it. Only a few saw signs of life. In 1865 a backwoods hunter named Bumpass reported steam vents hissing and mud pots bubbling and spitting beside the mountain.

They say Bumpass led a newspaper feller to the display, cautioned him to watch his step, then himself broke through the crust and dunked a leg in boiling mud. He was so mad he clean forgot to cuss. As if to make up for that lapse, the thermal basin is today called Bumpass Hell.

In May, 1914, Lassen awoke. For a year it belched ash and cinders in more than 150 explosions. Then red tongues of lava lapped from the crater and seared the mountain's flank. Deep snow melted in a rush, sending a torrent of

mud and 20-ton boulders plunging five miles into the valleys. A mighty, low-angle blast mowed down trees on Raker Peak three miles away, neatly peeled the bark, and drove sand an inch into them. A column of vapor and ash rose more than five miles above the crater.

Lassen's eruptions died away in 1921, and out of the chaos emerged a wild and beautiful national park. Cones, crags, the scarred Devastated Area, the seething Bumpass Hell and Sulphur Works—all recall Lassen's violent past. But forests and lakes make this a hiker's and camper's park, with eight campgrounds and 100 miles of trails, some passing trout-stocked waters. Visitors follow a self-guiding motor tour to lava flows and wildflower meadows alike; a 2½-mile summit trail gives hikers a view of Lassen's lava-plugged throat. At Manzanita Lake, hub of summer activities, a lodge and cabins await.

Timber-free slopes and long winters attract skiers. In spring they follow the receding snow line up the mountain; some years they find patches of snow above 8,500 feet as late as August. Cross-country routes, most popular in spring and early summer, radiate from the ski area near the park's southwest entrance. Here tows operate for novices and experts until mid-April. Skaters enjoy a limited season on frozen lakes before snow covers the ice.

Named for Peter Lassen, an early California emigrant guide, the 10,457-foot peak 200 miles northeast of San Francisco, is still a landmark for tourists. A nice old volcano, people think. Extinct, of course.

More likely, Lassen is just dozing.

CHARLES E. MOHR. OPPOSITE: CHUCK ABBOTT, RAPHO GUILLUMETTE

Lichens spread gold on the bark of firs and pines in Lassen's evergreen forests. Stands of aspen, cottonwood, and willow add autumnal hues to the 167-square-mile park, and wildflowers paint mountain meadows from June to September.

Sulphurous vapors cloud Bumpass Hell (opposite), a colorful thermal area where oxides tinge the lava yellow. A self-guiding nature trail skirts steaming fumaroles, hot springs, and boiling mud pots; visitors stay on the path to avoid a scalding. A bus links Redding and park in summer. Superintendent's address is Mineral, Calif.

CANADA
UNITED STATES
MONT.
N. DAK.
Missouri River
S. DAK.
WYO.
Rapid City
WIND CAVE NATIONAL PARK
BADLANDS NATIONAL MONUMENT
Isle Royale
NATIONAL PARK
Grand Portage
FERRY
Houghton
Duluth
MINN.
MICH.
WIS.
Pipestone
NATIONAL MONUMENT
Luverne
Effigy Mounds
NATIONAL MONUMENT
Detroit
IOWA
NEBR.
Omaha
Chicago
Cleveland
Mississippi River
ROCKY MOUNTAIN NATIONAL PARK
Denver
COLO.
OHIO
ILL.
IND.
Columbus
Indianapolis
Mound City Group
NATIONAL MONUMENT
Topeka
Kansas City
KANS.
St. Louis
MO.
Louisville
GREAT SAND DUNES NATIONAL MONUMENT
KY.
Mammoth Cave
NATIONAL PARK
Santa Fe
OKLA.
Great Smoky Mountains
NATIONAL PARK
TENN.
Bryson City
Oklahoma City
N. MEX.
ARK.
Russell Cave
NATIONAL MONUMENT
Chattanooga
Little Rock
CARLSBAD CAVERNS NATIONAL PARK
MISS.
ALA.
GA.
Dallas
Ocmulgee
NATIONAL MONUMENT
TEXAS
LA.
Rio Grande
BIG BEND NATIONAL PARK
New Orleans
Houston
UNITED STATES
MEXICO
Padre Island
NATIONAL SEASHORE
Gulf of Mexico
2
61
27
41
16
18
12
85
75
66
40
23
25
31w
11
67
285
80
90

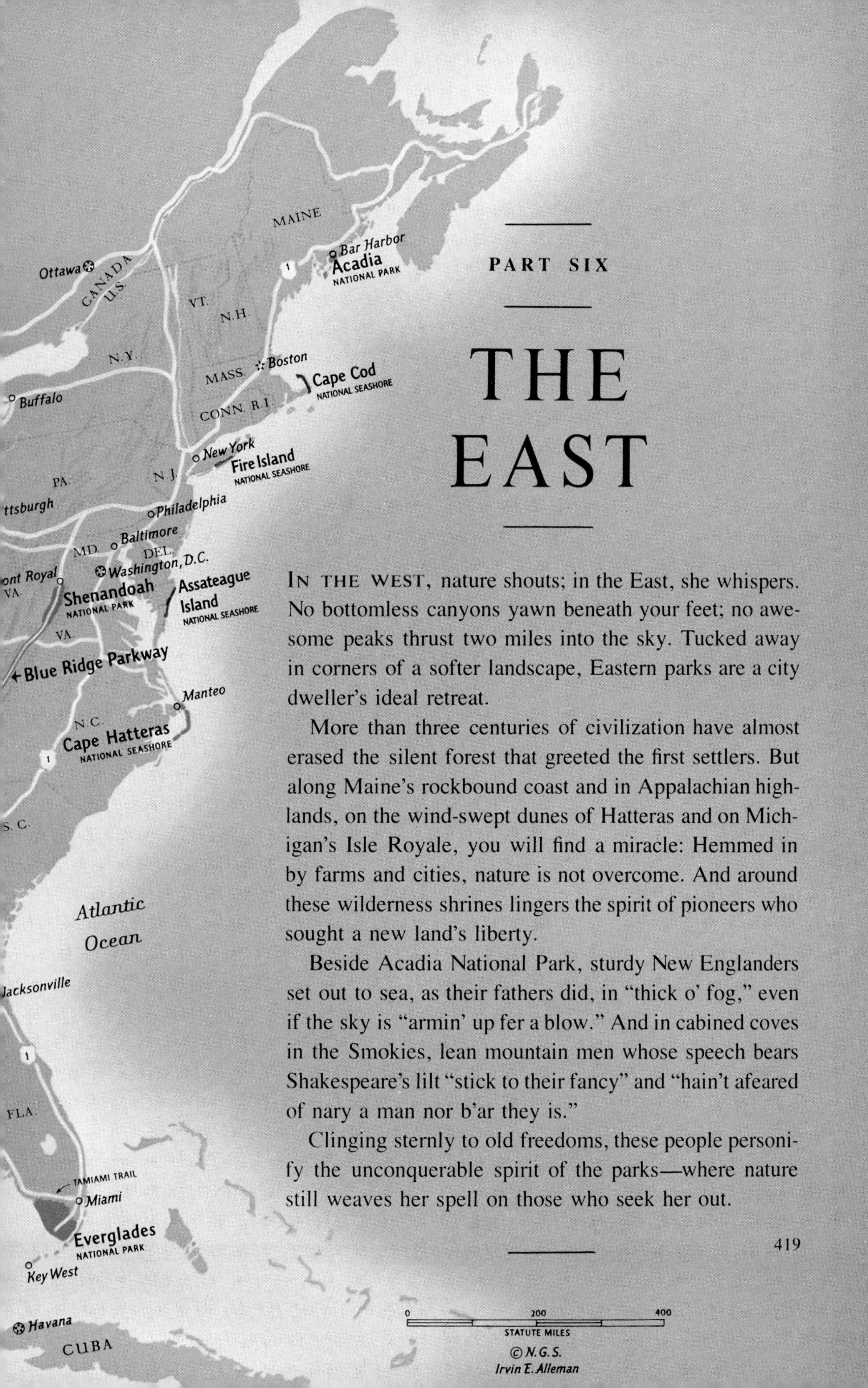

PART SIX

THE EAST

IN THE WEST, nature shouts; in the East, she whispers. No bottomless canyons yawn beneath your feet; no awesome peaks thrust two miles into the sky. Tucked away in corners of a softer landscape, Eastern parks are a city dweller's ideal retreat.

More than three centuries of civilization have almost erased the silent forest that greeted the first settlers. But along Maine's rockbound coast and in Appalachian highlands, on the wind-swept dunes of Hatteras and on Michigan's Isle Royale, you will find a miracle: Hemmed in by farms and cities, nature is not overcome. And around these wilderness shrines lingers the spirit of pioneers who sought a new land's liberty.

Beside Acadia National Park, sturdy New Englanders set out to sea, as their fathers did, in "thick o' fog," even if the sky is "armin' up fer a blow." And in cabined coves in the Smokies, lean mountain men whose speech bears Shakespeare's lilt "stick to their fancy" and "hain't afeared of nary a man nor b'ar they is."

Clinging sternly to old freedoms, these people personify the unconquerable spirit of the parks—where nature still weaves her spell on those who seek her out.

EVERGLADES

By DANIEL B. BEARD, former Superintendent, Everglades National Park

Florida dawn turns the Everglades mists to gold and rouses a common egret from its treetop perch. This huge national park offers bird watchers a year-round kaleidoscope of beautiful subtropical species.

OTIS IMBODEN, NATIONAL GEOGRAPHIC PHOTOGRAPHER

THE DENSE CANOPY of red mangrove trees bordering Squawk Creek gave way to the open vastness of the Florida Everglades. All morning, National Geographic artist and naturalist Walter A. Weber and I had worked our way through uncharted waters from our camp at Little Banana Patch, historic campsite of the Seminole Indians and perhaps the ancient Calusas before them. Walt, armed with cameras, binoculars, and sketch pads, wanted to record firsthand some of the spectacular birds and animals that make subtropical Everglades unique among our national parks.

Every bend of the stream looked the same—thickets of spraddle-rooted mangroves along the swampy shore. As our outboard churned up the sepia waters

TOBY MASSEY AND (OPPOSITE) JAMES P. BLAIR, NATIONAL GEOGRAPHIC PHOTOGRAPHER

Airboat skims through the Everglades at 70 miles an hour. Driven by airplane propellers, these light scows with high bows can run over sawgrass flats—permitting park rangers to round up wildlife poachers in marshes beyond the reach of roads.

and weeds, a procession of yellow-crowned and black-crowned night herons pumped their way out of the trees and flew ahead of us. The squawks of these birds gave the creek its name. The stream shoaled and we began to pole our skiff. On this hot winter afternoon, a flock of white ibis circling far off was the only sign of life. Hammocks, the Everglades' tree islands, dotted the landscape.

A fallen cabbage palm log blocked our boat. A nearby hammock, dominated by a large mahogany tree, beckoned. As we struggled toward it, knee-deep marl sucked at our feet, sawgrass tore into our clothing. Breaking through cocoplum bushes into the hammock, we paused. It was like stepping from a sunlit street into a darkened movie theater. Oaks, reddish-limbed gumbo limbo trees, tamarinds with their lacy leaflets, wild coffee bushes, and vines almost blotted out the sun. The sing of attacking mosquitoes was the only sound.

In the vast Everglades, a zoo without cages nearly on Miami's doorstep, ibis, egrets, herons, and other birds have gathered since time immemorial to nest and rear their young. Squalling, pushing, fighting, chattering birds by the thousands—

Wakes cleave the Shark River, which slips between mangrove thickets stretching to the horizon. Called a "continent in the making" because these amazingly flat lands emerged from the ocean in geologically recent times, the Everglades at their highest rise barely 12 feet above the sea.

Clomp! An alligator's gleaming ivories get a grip on a gar. He'll swallow the fish headfirst.

here is more excitement, more doing, than at Coney Island on the Fourth of July. Flights of adult birds are continually coming in with food or to give nest relief to their mates. Other flights are going out, while high overhead the swing shift, perhaps, is taking its recreation in lazy, soaring circles.

The first arrivals, the wood ibis, come in December. These huge storks, commonly called "flintheads," present a wonderful show, their white bodies glistening in contrast to their jet black wing tips. Then come common egrets, snowy egrets, Louisiana herons, and others. Last to arrive are white ibis. By the end of February the rookeries are filled; by late June they are about empty.

The nesters choose sites by instinct—near their food supply, yet protected from raccoons, bobcats, and other foes. The birds feed on freshwater crayfish, minnows, snails, frogs, and maybe even a baby alligator now and then. This great annual spectacle is vastly different in years when drought and diversion cut the supply of fresh water. Aquatic fare runs low; the rookeries fail to form, or the birds come to nest but cannot raise their young successfully.

WINFIELD PARKS, NATIONAL GEOGRAPHIC PHOTOGRAPHER

"Look there!" A ranger points out a vignette of Everglades life along the Anhinga Trail.

On one trip to East River Rookery, we passed a manatee and her calf in a shallow bay. This sea cow, a mammal that has adapted to a marine environment, "grazes" on the grasses of bay bottoms. Still rare, it is hard to observe except when it pokes its nose up for air. We got between the cow and her calf. Frantic, she hurled her bulk clear of the water—not in the graceful curve of a porpoise, but in a tremendous "bellywhopper" that made one scientist aboard ask nervously, "Do they ever jump into the boat?"

"Sure, lots of times," fibbed our boatman spinning the wheel hard aport. "We take 'em home and milk 'em."

The long, swinging arm of the Florida Keys protects the shoal expanse of Florida Bay. In summer, the bay mirrors the statuesque cumulus clouds parading over the distant 'Glades. Sometimes it is lashed by the merciless fury of a hurricane still unabated by crossing any land mass. In winter, when a "norther" strikes, the surface churns into a milky froth as waves wash the marl bottom.

Some of the rarest and most beautiful birds in the United States adorn this

FREDERICK KENT TRUSLOW

Flamingo, once a collection of weather-beaten shacks, now offers motel lodgings, a campground, marina, museum, and restaurant. At the visitor center a park naturalist (below) shows a touring group where reddish egrets fish along Florida Bay. Lucky birders may spot bald eagles (above); on the decline elsewhere, they still nest successfully in the park.

WINFIELD PARKS AND (RIGHT) JAMES P. BLAIR, NATIONAL GEOGRAPHIC PHOTOGRAPHERS

bay. Here breed the roseate spoonbill, a pink bird with crimson splashes, and the reddish egret, quickly identified by its unheronlike habit of chasing down its killifish prey. Another famous Florida Bay bird is the pugnacious great white heron, which displays a seven-foot wingspread.

Crocodiles also inhabit the bay and the mainland's south shore. Years of persecution by man have made the saucy reptiles timid, but there's still something sinister—and majestic—about these last of U. S. crocodiles.

How do you tell one from an alligator? "Don't worry," I often reply. "If you see a croc, you'll know it." Actually, the croc has a long, slim snout; the gator's is stubbier. Crocs stick to the salt water; gators to fresh water.

Along this Gulf of Mexico coast lie the sparkling beaches of Cape Sable. Giant loggerhead turtles—some of them six feet long and weighing half a ton—offer a memorable sight on a moonlit night when they crawl onto the sand, deposit their eggs in shallow holes, and plod clumsily back to sea. Behind the coconut palms

stretch a mangrove swamp, a lake, and a series of salt marshes and ponds where white pelicans, roseate spoonbills, and many other birds rest and feed.

Farther up the coast is Ponce de Leon Bay, the mouth of Shark River and boatway to Whitewater Bay. Mangrove trees—red, white, and black—grow tall here, perhaps taller than anywhere else in the Western Hemisphere. Brown pelicans raise spray as they dive into a school of fish; frigatebirds soar effortlessly above, swooping occasionally to pick up a fish on the wing.

Gradually the shore line breaks into mangrove keys, the Ten Thousand Islands. Here white ibis roost in summer. Their high, circling flights are a wonderful sight —the bright flash of red feet and red bill against snow-white body.

Beyond, the winding Barron River leads to the picturesque little town of Everglades, where President Truman dedicated Everglades National Park in 1947. For decades, conservationists watched helplessly while ruthless hunters decimated the area's unique wildlife. Now America's families can see these splendid creatures "at home" in a great wilderness preserve.

Going – going – gone! Anhinga gigs and gulps a dinner of fish

Impaling a bream, the snakebird (opposite) heads for shore, shakes her catch violently, flips it off the skewers, and swallows.

Food for much of the wildlife in Everglades National Park grows in fresh water. In the mid-1960's irrigation and flood control projects north of the Tamiami Trail and sustained drought in the Everglades severely curtailed the park's vital water supply. Great rookeries produced no young. Alligators thrashed in caking muck; dead fish littered receding ponds. Alarmed, park officials planned measures to relieve the water shortage and insure the future of this irreplaceable sanctuary.

Whitetail doe pokes her head shyly through the foliage—a reminder that the park is not just an aviary. Bobcat, raccoon, opossum, otter, and puma dwell here, as do burly black bears and chattering squirrels.

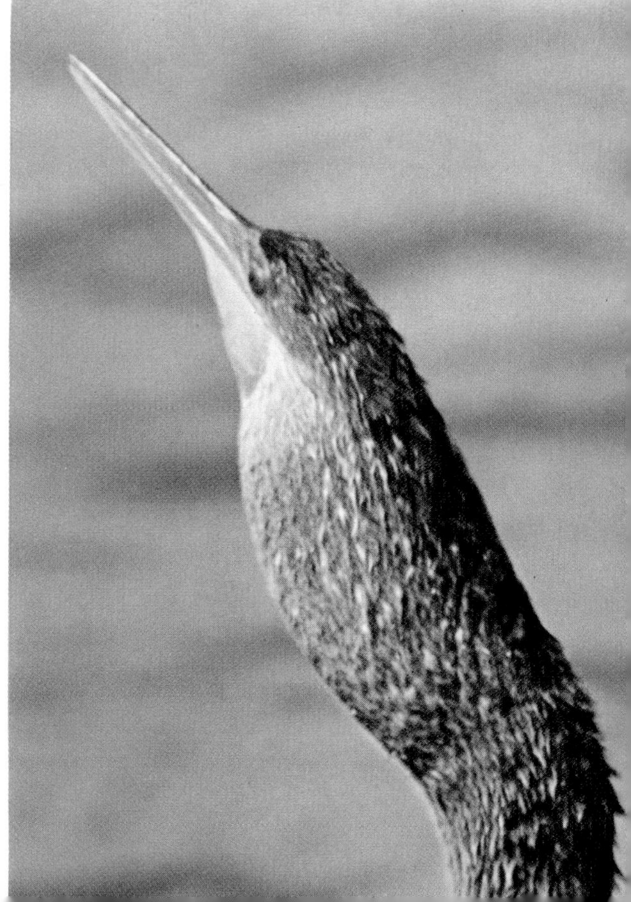

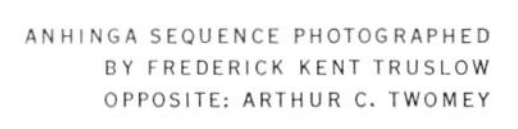

ANHINGA SEQUENCE PHOTOGRAPHED
BY FREDERICK KENT TRUSLOW
OPPOSITE: ARTHUR C. TWOMEY

EVERGLADES NATIONAL PARK *Southern Florida. 2,188 sq. mi.*

Features: Largest subtropical wilderness in U. S., teeming with wildlife. Marshy prairies, mangrove, cypress swamps fringed with tidal rivers, lakes, bays, and beaches.

Activities: Visitor centers at park entrance, Flamingo, Royal Palm Station. Nature talks, guided walks. Gumbo Limbo Trail: air plants, ferns, orchids. Anhinga Trail: fish, alligators, birds. Pa-Hay-Okee Overlook: "River of Grass," main watercourse of Everglades, untracked area of sawgrass, bald cypress. Mahogany Hammock: island with largest mahogany trees in continental U. S. Mangrove Trail: boardwalk through weather-beaten mangrove jungle. Cuthbert Lake Rookery: nesting site of water birds. One-way loop road to tower overlooking Shark River Basin wilderness. Tarpon, marlin fishing offshore; boating tours.

Season: Park open all year. Most birds nest in winter; temp. usually 60-80°, skies clear, little rain, waters may become rough for boating. Summers hot and humid; brief torrential showers, waters calmer.

What to bring: Cottons, visor cap, light jacket, insect repellent, sunglasses, binoculars, telephoto lens.

How to get there: US 1, 41, Fla. 27. Air, rail to Miami (40 mi.); car rentals at Miami, Homestead. By cruiser on inland waterways.

Accommodations: In park: motel at Flamingo (write Everglades Park Co., 3660 Coral Way, Miami); camp and trailer grounds at Flamingo, Long Pine Key. Motels in Miami, Homestead, Everglades, Key Largo.

Services: Restaurant, stores, gas, marina, charter boats at Flamingo. Hospital and churches in Homestead.

Regulations: Back-country camping by permit; campfires only in designated areas; no smoking on nature trails. No teasing alligators. Boaters must practice rules of water safety; charts of park waters available at Flamingo. Fla. fishing license in fresh water.

For further information write Superintendent, Box 279, Homestead, Florida

OTIS IMBODEN AND (BELOW) B. ANTHONY STEWART, NATIONAL GEOGRAPHIC PHOTOGRAPHERS

Before pitching tents, campers at Flamingo stake their claim to a site at a self-registry board. After breaking camp (opposite), they drop by the board to check out. Nearby marina stocks staples; at Long Pine Key campground, six miles from park entrance, only water is available.

NATURE'S CHILDREN spring to life on the canvas of National Geographic artist-naturalist Walter A. Weber. Before he set up his easel, he spent weeks boating and hiking the great Everglades preserve, studying his subjects in their habitat. His skilled brush drew inspiration from on-the-spot sketches, notes, color motion pictures and slides. He checked the fidelity of engraver's proofs.

The result: not mere likenesses, but unbelievably accurate re-creations in action of the exotic birds, mammals, and reptiles that make Everglades National Park unique.

A portfolio of Everglades wildlife paintings by Walter A. Weber

Snowy Egret

To put "a bird on Nellie's hat," shooters destroyed whole rookeries, almost wiped out these dainty egrets by 1910. Today they safely parade their courtship plumage in Everglades National Park.

Wood Ibis North America's only stork, the "flinthead" soars above East River Rookery, where thousands winter amid a labyrinth of islands. The wary flocks post sentinels when feeding.

White Ibis

Evening sees black-tipped squadrons
winging from Everglades marshes
to roosts on nearby keys.
Audubon watched a crafty white ibis
drop mud into a crayfish hole,
then gobble the little crustacean as
it came up to remove the plug.
Impatient mothers often lay eggs
in unfinished nests.

Black Skimmer

Wearing formal dress, this bird skims low over the sea, scooping up fish and shrimp in its flat lower mandible, day or night. Its petulant cry sounds like a puppy's bark.

Black-necked Stilt

This shrill comedian's antics lead searchers away from its nest. If rising waters threaten, it pushes twigs under its eggs, jacking them up as high as eight inches.

WALTER A. WEBER

White Pelican After a slow take-off, these heavy northerners wintering at Cape Sable spiral out of sight. Horny growth on bills forecasts breeding season. If disturbed, white pelicans may desert nest and young.

Brown Pelican

Neck forward, wings back, this ungainly bird plunges into the water after its prey. Unlike its white cousin, it is sociable and does not fear man. Forked tail identifies a frigatebird.

Squawk Creek is named for these raucous dwellers along its red-mangrove banks. Yellow-crowned (perching) and black-crowned (flying) night herons fish off their doorsteps.

Night Heron

Reddish Egret

When excited, reddish egrets ruffle their long plumage and change their look. Some, belying their name, are chalk white. These members of the heron tribe hunt killifish in the shallows.

In spring, gobblers are often too busy strutting before their hens to eat; fat reserves sustain them. They seldom fly except to roosts, but can run like a streak through grass and scrub.

Wild Turkey

Anhinga Swimming, this spear fisherman submerges all but its serpentine neck, whence the name snakebird. Many call it the water turkey. Young birds hiss if alarmed. The neighbors are wood ibis.

Great White Heron

It has the wings of an angel, but sometimes devours young birds. When fishing, it stands like a statue, waiting for prey to swim to it. Hunters used to salt down great whites as food.

Common Egret In breeding season, this majestic white bird trails filmy aigrettes up to 21 inches long. Here it joins the little blue and Louisiana herons in flight.

Pileated Woodpecker

A jaunty red plume distinguishes this crow-size woodpecker, which dwells in Everglades trees. Strong neck muscles power its triphammer beak.

Crocodile Ruddy turnstones scatter before a crocodile, who asks no favors and grants none. Now protected, this long-victimized denizen of salt water grows to 14 feet. Color and pointed snout tell croc from gator.

Alligator

Limpkins (left) and gallinules ignore an alligator daydreaming in a cypress pool. Seminoles eat his tail flesh. Hide hunters, firing at torch-reflecting eyes, almost exterminated him. Teeth alone brought $5 a pound.

Manatee

Everglades lagoons pasture underwater livestock, Florida's air-breathing, grass-eating manatee. Seemingly put together from nature's spare parts—seal head, whale flippers, cow flesh—this sluggish mermaid suckles her young.

Raccoon

Three masked henchmen join mamma on a stream-border raid. Their plunder: mussels, crayfish, frogs, turtles, birds, eggs. Mainly nocturnal, coons dwell in trees. They often dunk food before eating. Marsh rabbit is the innocent bystander.

Puma Everglades National Park shelters some of the last pumas east of the Mississippi. On silent pads, the big cat stalks its prey remorselessly, then springs and hurls it to the ground. Its mating call in the night is a wild, unearthly shriek.

Otter An otter pounces; his sharp teeth dispatch a watersnake. Artist Weber reconstructed this Everglades drama from signs of the battle. To the sleek, web-footed otter, the snake was an appetizer. Fish is his favorite fare.

GREAT SMOKY MOUNTAINS

By VAL HART

ABOUT THAT GROUNDHOG you saw yesterday," Sam said. "Tell you how we cook them. First you get yourself a nice fat young groundhog, dress it, and boil it." Sam paused to throw a log on the fire. "Now, if you're out in the woods, you get sassafras or spicewood for season; then you take the meat out of the water and bake it." He smacked his lips. "Wonderful flavor. Couldn't tell the difference if it was coon or bear."

This introduction to mountain cooking made my kitchen and the gray routine of housekeeping in Washington, D. C., seem far away. We were on a pack trip

M. WOODBRIDGE WILLIAMS

through Great Smoky Mountains National Park. I glanced at the friendly faces lit by the fire and thought how odd it was that only a few days before we had been strangers: Ruby Bere, Wisconsin bacteriologist; Genevieve Bass, Florida housewife; Elizabeth Yates, a writer from New Hampshire; Bob Sisson, National Geographic photographer; and I. We had met at Tom Alexander's Cataloochee Ranch near Waynesville, North Carolina. Tom was our outfitter and guide. In his very quietness at that moment he seemed a part of the mood of the hills. So did Glenn Messer, Tom's helper, and Sam Woody, our camp cook.

"COME ON, you cowpunchers, let's get going!" Tom yelled early the first day as he led out from the ranch toward Hemphill Bald, the first steep climb. Ruby and I glanced at each other. Both inexperienced riders, we were pleased that our horses took their place in line and moved at all.

Entering the park, we headed northeast along the crest of Cataloochee Divide. In the distance clouds drifted low, merging with the blue haze which gives the Great Smokies their name. This highest section of the Appalachian Mountains straddles the North Carolina-Tennessee border. Sixteen peaks top 6,000 feet.

Our trail narrowed through a jungle of rhododendron intertwined with dense masses of dog hobble, then emerged from the quiet darkness into a sun-drenched meadow where butterflies flitted among the goldenrod and sunflowers.

Leaving the crest of Cataloochee Divide, we made the sharpest descent of the trip—2,000 feet in one hour. The lead horses seemed terrifyingly far below. I hung on grimly, praying that my horse wouldn't go over the side.

In the quiet valley of Caldwell Fork, where mountain men had once lived, the only sign of life was the clawed-off bark of apple trees whose fruit had tempted bears. Off somewhere a ruffed grouse drummed in the loneliness. We moved on and made camp in an old homestead clearing on Rough Fork of Cataloochee Creek.

Bob Sisson, an experienced camper, gave us good tips: Put on top of your duffel bag the things you'll need in the morning, pick a good spot for your sleeping bag, and blow up your air mattress before dark. This sound advice we all ignored. Liz and Ruby, bird and flower books in hand, disappeared around the bend of an inviting path, while the rest of us lazed about. Later, warmed by a fire, we sang ballads. Then, by flashlight, Genevieve and I struggled to blow up our air mattresses and rummage through duffel bags for soap and toothbrushes. Gen couldn't find her blanket, so we pulled close to the fire and tried to sleep.

But sleep outdoors does not come easily to one used to four walls and a ceiling. We watched a gypsying mist envelop a moonlit trail and listened to night sounds—the splash of a stream, whinnying of our horses, crackles of the dying fire. "About bears," Gen whispered. No one had mentioned bears. "Banging tin plates scares them off and wakes everybody to help." Fine idea, I agreed, and we tiptoed to the "kitchen." With tin plates by our sides, we finally dropped off to sleep.

Hundreds of black bears range the Smokies sanctuary. Next morning Tom

ROBERT F. SISSON, NATIONAL GEOGRAPHIC PHOTOGRAPHER

Laurel brightens a trail through lush forest that never feels an ax's bite. Nearly as many tree varieties as in all Europe mantle the park, visited by more than five million persons a year.

showed us their tracks, and from high on Trail Ridge he pointed out dense laurel thickets where bears like to live. The colorful patches, called "slicks" by some mountain people, brightened the side of Spruce Mountain in the distance. The vastness was overwhelming. The park embraces half a million acres of forest. In a few hours' climb riders pass through sweet gums, umbrella magnolias, and short-leaf pines common in the South; maples, oaks, and hemlocks of the North; and finally into red spruce, fir, and mountain ash atop the highest peaks.

Temperatures often changed suddenly. Riding along the crest of Balsam Moun-

Stripped for action, small fry try for whoppers in Laurel Creek

Anglers of all ages enjoy the action in Great Smoky's crystal waters. Six hundred miles of streams, many harboring trout and some bordering campsites, course the half-million-acre highland wilderness. In the more remote corners, campers rough it with park permission.

Playful black bears (opposite) charm tourists, beg along roads, sometimes swat the hands that feed them. Foxes, raccoons, and noisy red squirrels called boomers share the forested domain.

THOMAS NEBBIA, NATIONAL GEOGRAPHIC PHOTOGRAPHER (ALSO RIGHT)

B. ANTHONY STEWART, NATIONAL GEOGRAPHIC PHOTOGRAPHER

tain, in the shadow of oaks, beech, and basswood, we kept our jackets on. But we quickly took them off when we came out into the hot sun on Ledge Bald.

Why are so many Smokies bald? Some scientists say excessive evaporation, caused by winds and altitude, killed the trees. Cherokee Indians believed their ancestors cleared the tops as lookouts for a monster that was carrying away their children; the Great Spirit sent thunder and lightning against the marauder, and forever after the mountains remained bald. But Tom is convinced that men cut them to pasture cattle and the balds eventually will grow back into forest.

It was raining when we halted, but the weather cleared and the moon came out before we went to sleep. During the night a mouselike shrew ran across my face. I never knew whether it got into my sleeping bag because right then I set some kind of Smoky Mountain record for busting out of that tightly zipped pouch.

Two days later we rode through a low gap to Raven Fork of the Oconaluftee.

THOMAS NEBBIA AND (BELOW) OTIS IMBODEN, NATIONAL GEOGRAPHIC PHOTOGRAPHERS

Cades Cove cups a rustic remnant of pioneer America

Rimmed by mountains and ridges, this idyllic valley in the park's western reaches recalls a frontier way of life little changed for more than a century. Here settlers found wooded hollows rich in bear, deer, nuts, and berries. Clearing the land, they pooled their labor in "corn shuckin'," "hay thrashin'," and "house raisin'."

They fashioned nails and door hinges of wood, tanned leather for homemade shoes, and spun flax for "britches that'd last a man longer than those boughten pants."

Social life centered in the churches; in their graveyards rest many who never left the Cove. Seclusion from the outside world preserved a way of speaking that harks back to Elizabethan England: "Can I borry a race of ginger?" may still be heard among the few remaining families.

Reminders of the past await visitors along a loop road: log houses, a blacksmith shop, smokehouse, and gristmill. An information shelter (below) tells the Cades Cove story.

"Over to your right," Tom said as we forded the stream, "is the most beautiful part of the Smokies—the real wilderness area of the park. Trails that used to lead in there have been closed off for years and no horses are allowed. People can go in, of course, if they can get in."

"Nobody asked my opinion," Glenn said, "but was somebody to ask me, I'd say it's a place for roughnecks, not city slickers. Especially women city slickers."

Our next overnight stop was at a junction 5,700 feet high on the Appalachian Trail. From there our route led into a spruce and balsam forest called Paul Bunyan's Toothpicks. Under the quiet spell of these high, dark forests with their soft, mossy floors the ancient Cherokee belief in *Yunwi Tsunsdi*—Little People—seems credible. These kindly dwarfs, with hair falling below their knees, danced, beat tiny drums, and always led lost Indian children home.

Rail fence zigzags to the post-Civil War Becky Cable House, first frame dwelling in Cades Cove.

We had been warned about The Sawteeth, where sharp mountain crests drop off thousands of feet on both sides. No one talked much on this stretch. We were too busy holding reins and watching our horses' footing—up almost perpendicular sides. Later Tom told us we were approaching the Boulevard and advised us to stay well off the road because the horses were unused to fast-moving traffic. Of course the Boulevard sign turned out to be a bear-clawed marker pointing up a steep, narrow trail to Mount Le Conte, nearly five miles away. We rode in silence through dense fog, scarcely able to see the switching tail of the horse ahead.

"Camp" for the night was a lodge on Mount Le Conte, its cabins inviting with comfortable beds and roaring fires. With sudden enthusiasm to watch the sunset, we climbed to the vantage point of Cliff Top. A white churning sea of clouds hid the valley below, and in the distance sunset flamed on the clouds above 6,642-

Becky, who "could do a man's work in the fields and a woman's work in the house," lived to 96.

THOMAS NEBBIA, NATIONAL GEOGRAPHIC PHOTOGRAPHER

foot Clingmans Dome, second highest mountain in the eastern United States.

We camped four more nights before the final day's ride through virgin forest. Back at Tom's ranch we were welcomed with an old-fashioned "hoot-e-nanny gathering." People came from miles around and a mountain fiddler sang for us.

Then there were wilderness hikes and the ranch to enjoy—and the fair on the Cherokee Indian Reservation adjoining the park. Besides the midway exhibits, I was fascinated by the singing contests: singers' faces and lips were strangely motionless, for in the Cherokee language the lips never close.

Mainly a farmer, the modern Cherokee has found another "cash crop": posing in feathers and war paint in front of roadside souvenir shops. "We lost one of our best Sunday School superintendents all last summer because he started 'chiefing,'" one official told us. "Sunday is the busy tourist day."

If only more of these Sunday tourists would leave the park's paved roads and get out into this beautiful American wilderness! It was an experience this city slicker will never forget.

OTIS IMBODEN AND (OPPOSITE) THOMAS NEBBIA, NATIONAL GEOGRAPHIC PHOTOGRAPHERS

An 1868 gristmill, powered by an overshot water wheel, grinds corn into meal for Cades Cove visitors each summer. Across the park at the Cherokee Reservation, Indians twirl in tribal dances (above), demonstrate traditional crafts, and relive their past in the drama "Unto These Hills."

GREAT SMOKY MOUNTAINS NATIONAL PARK *Area 800 sq. mi.*

Features: Roof of eastern America astride Tenn.-No. Carolina border, cloaked in virgin forest. Some 1,300 varieties of trees, shrubs, herbs; 50 fur bearers; 200 birds.

Activities: Pioneer Museum at Oconaluftee Visitor Center. Gristmill, log houses, drive-through barn at Cades Cove. 109 mi. of roads; one-way, slow-traffic wilderness motor trail near Gatlinburg; Clingmans Dome Highway rises to 6,311 ft. 653 mi. of horse and foot trails (70 mi. of Maine-to-Georgia Appalachian Trail in park with trailside shelters and campsites). Trout fishing in 600 mi. of streams; state license required. Nature hikes, wilderness camping; illustrated talks May–Oct.

Season: Park open all year. Lowlands warm in summer, mild in winter; summits always cooler. Autumn has least fog and rain.

What to bring: Hiking shoes, rough-it clothing, rainproof jacket, camera, light meter, binoculars.

How to get there: See map at back of book. US 441 from Knoxville, Tenn., to Asheville, N.C., crosses park. Air, rail, bus via the two cities; Smoky Mountain Tours in summer.

Accommodations: 8 camp and trailer grounds. Le Conte Lodge (6,400 ft.) by foot or horseback; write Le Conte Lodge, Gatlinburg, Tenn. Hotels, motels in nearby towns.

Park regulations: Do not feed or approach bears. Camping, fires outside campgrounds by permit only. Keep pets on leash.

For further information write park Superintendent, Gatlinburg, Tennessee

BLUE RIDGE PARKWAY

Mile-high Craggy Pinnacle rewards two who climbed it with a panorama of winding highway and tree-robed North Carolina mountains. Pinnacle Gap Overlook, one of scores of turnouts along the crest-hugging Blue Ridge Parkway, entices motorists with its dazzling view.

B. ANTHONY STEWART, NATIONAL GEOGRAPHIC PHOTOGRAPHER

THEY SHOULD put up a sign: "Slow, next 469 miles. Look out for gentle curves, heart-stopping views, and sudden plunges into the 19th century."

An elongated park of its own, the Blue Ridge Parkway threads the Appalachian crests from Shenandoah National Park in Virginia to Great Smoky Mountains National Park in North Carolina and Tennessee. "Detroit-style" hikers enjoy a cool, quiet otherworld of gristmill and log cabin, fawn and fern. Once our western frontier, these ancient hills still cradle the homesteads of mountain folk whose forefathers shunned the settled valleys to wrest a living from the highlands and hollows.

At Mabry Mill, water powers a creaking wheel and a smithy's hammer clangs in the clear air. Caldrons of apple butter bubble in the autumn chill.

A few miles south stands the Puckett Cabin, where Mrs. Orlean Hawks Puckett lived from 1865 to her death in 1939 at 102. Local folk say she was midwife to more than a thousand babies, yet all of her own 24 died in infancy.

The Appalachian Trail parallels the parkway in the north; Daniel Boone's Wilderness Road meets it in the south. Deer often graze on its shoulders, birds in great variety enliven forest and meadow, and lucky visitors sometimes glimpse bobcats, elk, and black bears.

Visitor centers, trails, campsites, and craft centers wait discreetly along the way. An inn at Mount Pisgah, lodges at Doughton Park and Peaks of Otter, and cabins at Rocky Knob welcome travelers from spring to fall.

Giant gardens flaming in the sky greet the Blue Ridge visitor in June

"Ride awhile, stop awhile." The parkway's main purpose is not to take you somewhere—once in the highland fastness, you are there. No neon and billboard jungles assault your senses; no stoplights, no goading horns. If it suits your fancy, you can side-trip to 6,684-foot Mount

W. E. GARRETT, NATIONAL GEOGRAPHIC STAFF

Mitchell, high point east of the Mississippi, or rhododendron-covered Roan Mountain in North Carolina (above). Spring's bloom of dogwood, azalea, and rhododendron gives way to autumn's reds and golds as Mother Nature, unable to decide on a color pattern, empties her paintpots playfully over the mountainsides. Overlooks offer scenic balconies where motorists stretch and watch the show.

Snow or ice may close parts of the parkway during winter months. For information, write the superintendent, Box 1710, Roanoke, Va.

SHENANDOAH

By ROBERT T. COCHRAN, JR.

Where Indians once tracked deer, today's car-borne vacationist stops at Baldface Mountain

A DAY'S DRIVE from New York or Pittsburgh, two hours from Washington, Shenandoah spreads its gentle slopes and cool, shady coves like a wrinkled picnic blanket. This slender national park in Virginia's Blue Ridge Mountains provides a handy oasis for Eastern city dwellers when the urge comes to get away from it all. It's one of the most visited of U. S. national parks. Hundreds of thousands come in spring, when new leaves hang like

Overlook to view forested ranges repeating to infinity. Constant haze gave Blue Ridge its name.

B. ANTHONY STEWART, NATIONAL GEOGRAPHIC PHOTOGRAPHER

green mist over the forested mountains, and in fall, when the leaves take a riotous, color-splashed curtain call. But seasons do not limit Shenandoah's charm. Skyline Drive winds south from Front Royal 105 miles through the park to Rockfish Gap, where it joins Blue Ridge Parkway. Overlooks, 75 in all, flare outward from the lofty highway. To the east, Virginia's rolling Piedmont flattens as it becomes the distant Tidewater. To the west, the trim farms and apple orchards of historic Shenandoah Valley stretch like a hazy checkerboard around Massanutten Mountain to the Allegheny Mountains beyond.

Many visitors see Shenandoah on a longish Sunday drive. Others camp, or sample the 207 miles of woodland trails. Alpinists might smile at the easy grades, but weekend hikers enjoy puffing to Hawksbill's 4,049-foot summit, highest in the park. Some rent horses at Skyland or Big Meadows and ride to hidden hollows and trout streams where a deer flicks its white flag and bounds away, a gray squirrel scuttles up a tree, and a wood thrush sings.

Quickly forgetting the nearness of great cities, you half expect to meet a painted Indian, a silent buckskinned hunter with his long rifle, or even John Lederer who was first to explore here in 1669. But don't expect the noisy Knights of the Golden Horseshoe, who, booted and plumed, accompanied Virginia's Governor Alexander Spotswood to Swift Run Gap in 1716. This gay band "drank the King's Health in Champagne, and fired a volley; and the Princess's in Burgundy, and fired a volley; and all the rest of the Royal Family in Claret, and fired a volley." Things are calmer now in this 330-square-mile preserve where the wild and quiet beauty of America's first frontier endures.

Soft mist swirls through autumn's gold in Shenandoah woodlands

Motorists sometimes drive above the clouds on Skyline Drive, rising to 3,680 feet. Except when fog, ice, or snow briefly closes the road, the park remains open all year.

April through October finds gift shops, restaurants, and service stations open. Fishermen break out their tackle, and hikers bunk in shelters along the Appalachian Trail. Summer fills campgrounds with colorful tents and trailers; cool highland air whets appetites (right). Visitors fill the picnic areas, throng the nature programs. To reserve lodgings at Skyland, Big Meadows, or Lewis Mountain, write Virginia Sky-Line Co., Luray, Va.

A bus traverses park in summer, and buses serve nearby Front Royal, Luray, Waynesboro (see map in back).

RICHARD S. DURRANCE. OPPOSITE: B. ANTHONY STEWART, NATIONAL GEOGRAPHIC PHOTOGRAPHER

J. BAYLOR ROBERTS AND (BELOW) B. ANTHONY STEWART, NATIONAL GEOGRAPHIC STAFF

CAPE HATTERAS

Hurl towering waves, whipped to a boil by Atlantic gales, against a slender barrier of lonely, wind-swept sand; add pirates and shipwrecks. From these ingredients, nature brews a magic tonic: Cape Hatteras. Words may describe but cannot fully explain the lure of the sea at North Carolina's Outer Banks. Just dig your toes in the clean beach sand and face the endless, crashing surf. And you'll know why people come back to Cape Hatteras National Seashore.

Winds and the mighty Gulf Stream's colliding with cold Atlantic currents shape this 70-mile stretch of America's stormiest coast, from Nags Head south to Ocracoke Inlet. Dune grass, wildflowers, loblolly pine, and weathered oak pin down the golden grains in places, but there is little permanence in this shifting world of sand and sky, wind and wave.

Hatteras remembers a host of turbulent yesterdays. A summer pageant, "The Lost Colony," portrays England's first North American colony, which vanished

Uncrowded beaches and the white roar of boisterous seas lure a growing number of vacationists to the Outer Banks. Cape Hatteras Light, highest in the United States, warns ships of dread Diamond Shoals. A few miles north of the national seashore, a soaring stone pylon on Kill Devil Hill (far left) honors the Wright brothers' first flight.

Hatteras Island's belt of sand guards Pamlico Sound (right) from the churning Atlantic. Tourists find lodgings, stores, and restaurants in villages like Hatteras in the distance; campers come equipped with long stakes and awnings for wind-swept, shadeless sites (inset).

FRANC SHOR, NATIONAL GEOGRAPHIC STAFF, AND (INSET) LARRY FRIED, PIX

Spin rigs slap the surf as anglers cast for bluefish. Channel bass, mackerel, tuna, dolphin, sailfish,

with scarcely a trace from Roanoke Island in the 1580's. Swashbuckling pirate Edward Teach (Blackbeard) fell before the slashing cutlass of a young Royal Navy lieutenant off Ocracoke Island in 1718. Months after her historic clash with the *Merrimac,* the Union ironclad *Monitor* foundered during a wintry storm in 1862 and sank a few miles off the Cape. Called the "Graveyard of the Atlantic," the Hatteras region has claimed some 2,200 ships in 400 years.

At Kitty Hawk, Wilbur and Orville Wright soared into immortality in 1903

B. ANTHONY STEWART, NATIONAL GEOGRAPHIC PHOTOGRAPHER

amberjack, and marlin also lure sport fishermen to Hatteras waters from April to November.

when their flimsy airplane skimmed the dunes in man's first power-driven flight. In World War II, Coast Guard stations at seven-mile intervals along the Cape ministered to Allied seamen blasted by submarines at "Torpedo Junction."

Today's visitors enjoy sunny dunes and surf warmed by the Gulf Stream, bird-watch at Pea Island Refuge, camp, boat, and fish—even hunt waterfowl in certain areas. For beachcombers, Hatteras abounds in driftwood and wreckage: small change from the price paid by those who gambled with the sea and lost.

FIRE ISLAND

FROM THE HECTIC CANYONS of Manhattan, New Yorkers by the hundreds hurry every summer weekend to this fabled retreat bounded, someone said, by Great South Bay, the Atlantic Ocean, Friday, and Monday. They spill from ferries onto the slender sandbar off Long Island's south shore—writers and advertising men, the beat and the offbeat, and just plain people who glory in the uncrowded beaches, the fresh sea air. Join them and you step into a relaxed world of quaint villages with weather-beaten old houses and stilted walkways. A world, too, free of traffic jams. From historic Kismet on the west, through lively Ocean Beach and its night-life, to quiet Davis Park on the east, the dune-top towns ban private cars.

The Government intends to keep traffic curtailed in the national seashore. No highway traverses the 26-mile-long park authorized in 1964, though bridges from Long Island bring motorists close to its boundaries. In the heart of the Seashore visitors can explore the tangle of sassafras and holly trees in Sunken Forest, or breast the wild breakers, or watch for waterfowl and white-tailed deer.

PADRE ISLAND

HIGH-FLYING white pelicans soar and swoop, glittering in the sun. Gulls and terns patrol the shore, looking for a meal. Below them ghost crabs side-step scurrying shorebirds, while beyond the grass-tufted dunes coyotes and jack rabbits play deadly games of tag. This wildlife paradise is Padre Island, a crescent-shaped strip that hugs the southern coast of Texas. No human inhabits the 80-mile stretch set aside as a national seashore in 1962. Visitors reach the island on causeways; at low tide they drive along hard-packed sand to swim or picnic or fish for sea-trout and black drum in the Gulf of Mexico. The island owes its name to Padre Nicolas Balli, whose cattle once grazed on it.

ASSATEAGUE ISLAND

"NO BUILDINGS, nothing but water, sand, marsh weeds . . . and the sky above. . . . Absolutely nothing of value that I can see." That's what Assateague looked like to a Baltimore observer in the early 1950's. Times change. As the concrete tentacles of Megalopolis spread over the eastern seaboard, an unspoiled sliver of seacoast suddenly became priceless. "Clear water, warm sandy beaches are a nation's real treasure," declared President Lyndon Johnson on the day in 1965 he signed the bill creating Assateague Island National Seashore.

This 33-mile-long barrier reef lies off the coast of Maryland and Virginia 140 miles southeast of Washington, D. C. Two bridges tie it to the mainland. Visitor facilities and roads will come in due time, but the real treasure is already there—gleaming dunes, frothing surf, a sky as big as all outdoors.

Assateague's famed wild ponies swim to Chincoteague, Virginia, during the roundup and auction held each summer. Southern end of the national seashore, comprising the Chincoteague National Wildlife Refuge, will remain a sanctuary for the ponies, as well as for waterfowl and shorebirds.

PATRICIA CAULFIELD, PHOTO RESEARCHERS, AND (BELOW) THOMAS J. ABERCROMBIE, NATIONAL GEOGRAPHIC STAFF

Beach buffs battle it out in a favorite Fire Island sport—volleyball. Recreational facilities at major areas connected by bicycle and foot trails are planned for swimmers and boaters, campers and picnickers.

Sun-dappled dunes and broad beaches bait New England's fishhook in the Atlantic—Cape Cod. Wind and wave constantly reshape Great Beach, the bold and lonely ocean side of the Massachusetts peninsula. Here the end of the Cape crooks a protective arm around Provincetown (center). Ships seeking sassafras, a folk medicine, visited these shores soon after 1600.

CAPE COD

By *NATHANIEL T. KENNEY*
National Geographic Staff

SPOUTING WHALES cruised past the Great Beach. They were hard by in a guzzle, a little channel between a sandbar and the gleaming shore. Above them shrieking terns rode the wind of the sea and tiny silvery sand launces frizzled the green water.

"Heavens!" said my wife Fran, staring at the whales. "Is that where we swim?"

"Happens they're humpbacks, which

don't bite people," said Charlie Rollins, owner of the weather-silvered cottage we had rented.

It was our first day on the beach and our daughter Janice remembers the beach days as the best of those golden days on Cape Cod. And one of the best of the beach outings started early in the morning when the quail were whistling in the fields and John Anthony blew his beach-buggy horn outside our door.

"Tide's out and the beach is right!" shouted Anthony, retired postmaster of Orleans. "Let's go!"

We piled in. Along a trail lined with wild beach plum —which Cape Codders transform into luscious preserves—John drove down the tilting face of the bluffs to the sun deck of sand below. Soft, fat tires bit into the drifts, and soon we purred along through the world of the Great Beach. Crabs scuttled to their burrows; shorebirds stilted at the edge of the yeasty surf.

Besides the sand and sea and salt and shells and fishes and special creatures that all ocean beaches have, the Great Beach has a geographical quirk: a gentle curve landward, so that you cannot see as far up and down the sands as you can on most beaches. This gave us a sense of isolation, even when we knew a thousand people were frolicking at a public beach a mile or two away.

Known to Cape folks as the "backside," the Great Beach faces the Atlantic and lies entirely within the Cape Cod National Seashore. Authorized in 1961, the Seashore runs some 42 miles from the southern tip of Nauset Beach to Long Point Light at the entrance to Provincetown Harbor. It crosses the Cape near Truro and Wellfleet to pick up ten miles of shore on Cape Cod Bay, favored by many bathers because it is warmer and calmer than the ocean side.

You could hardly make a national seashore on the Cape between its elbow and the shoulder where it joins the Massachusetts mainland, so heavily is the land developed. Motels and stores line the highway on the Nantucket Sound side, where summer traffic clogs well-groomed villages and posh resort towns.

Skeleton of the schooner *Montclair,* wrecked in 1927, saddles a dune on Nauset Beach. Nearly 4,000 ships have perished off the Cape; *Mayflower* almost ran aground in 1620. Restless sands may bury a wreck, expose it years later.

DEAN CONGER, NATIONAL GEOGRAPHIC PHOTOGRAPHER

DEAN CONGER, NATIONAL GEOGRAPHIC PHOTOGRAPHER

Heeling to a spanking breeze, a Sailfish skitters over the waves off Cape Cod

Skipper at the stern bends over backwards to steady this seagoing surfboard. Swimsuits anticipate a dunking in waters chilled by the Labrador Current.

Recreation facilities, expanding as the national seashore grows to full size, feature swimming and picnicking. A visitor center near Eastham explains the origin of the Cape and recalls its fascinating history. Nature trails meander through thickets of bearberry and azalea, dip into marshes, glacial kettles, and a cedar swamp; one leads to a spring where the Pilgrims are believed to have tasted their first fresh water on the Cape. Near an ocean overlook stand the remains of the first wireless station in the United States.

Campgrounds, privately owned, are crowded in summer. For information write the superintendent, South Wellfleet, Mass.

On we rolled along the Cape's curving forearm, enjoying moor and marsh, cliffs thrust out by continental glaciers and dunes washed up by the sea. The beach buggy halted by the gaunt timbers of a long-wrecked schooner. College youngsters sat amid the stark bones, singing and romancing. Moving on, we passed by a solitary fisherman casting for striped bass from a tide-bared island, skirted picnics carefully lest we sand the hot dogs, and finally pulled up for a dip.

And so we made friends with this new 27,000-acre addition to the nation's recreational treasury. Even behind low hills or in piney woods we felt the sea's nearness, in the cool, briny breeze, in the mewing of gulls above the inland lakes, in the smell of clam flats at low tide, in the sheen of tough meadow grass that must stand in sand and drink salt mist.

As it does the land, the sea marks the people of Cape Cod. "Down-Cape" in Provincetown, where a soaring monument recalls the arrival of the *Mayflower* in 1620, Portuguese-descended fishermen mended their nets and patiently answered our questions while their sons dived for coins in the clear water. And "up-Cape" in West Falmouth we ended our stay with a visit to Bertha Boyce, who had sailed with her captain-father to whaling waters 90 years before.

"Pshaw," she said when I spoke of nostalgia. "Life is so good here you never look astern, you're that busy waiting for tomorrow."

Surf casters ride a rattling rainbow to try for striped bass, king of saltwater sport fish at the Cape. Offshore waters abound in tuna, mackerel, herring, and the cod for which Capt. Bartholomew Gosnold named the peninsula in 1602. Owners of the ancient beach buggies drive with care over designated routes.

Evergreen islands spread beneath nature hikers on Cadillac Mountain, roof of Ac

ACADIA NATIONAL PARK

By EDWARDS PARK, National Geographic Staff

AT DAWN an outbound lobster boat pants through a muffling fog, "so thick ye cud stick yer knife in it to mark the passage back." Gray waves boom and suck on kelp-slick rocks. A breeze clears the air and morning's sun warms up the smells of fish scales, tar, pine needles, and 3,000 miles of ocean. Gulls scream above the lobstermen as they chug homeward in midafternoon to sell the catch to summer folk. Finally the lowering sun turns pointed spruces black against the crisp sky.

This is the coast of Maine.

And this is the essence of Acadia, mostly on Mount Desert Island, where mountains tumble to the Atlantic to end in battered cliffs, where breakers claw into twining coves and inlets, where a man can fish with one hand and strip a wind-stunted blueberry bush with the other.

Superlatives adorn this national park, oldest east of the Mississippi and first

MURRAY WEISS, DPI

and high point of Maine's tortuous coast. Local boatmen offer short cruises to park visitors.

to be donated to the Government. Nowhere else along the east coast of the United States does such high land overlook the ocean. The pink granite summit of Cadillac Mountain, 1,530 feet above the waves, is the first point on the Nation's coast to catch the sunrise. The road up it many engineers consider the best mountain road in the world, never exceeding a seven percent grade. Somes Sound, cutting the island nearly in two, is the only true fiord on the U. S. Atlantic coast. Mount Desert Island itself has been called the "world's most beautiful" so often that its State of Maine residents, by nature embarrassed by extravagant compliment, are afraid they may start believing it.

Like most Maine coast regions, Mount Desert bounced between French and English hands. Jesuits established a mission on it in 1613. Virginia colonists raided the island; pilgrims from Plymouth, paying off the *Mayflower* expenses with Maine furs, used it as a base. Louis XIV gave the island as a fief to Sieur de la Mothe Cadillac, the French explorer who founded Detroit.

In 1820, when Maine became a state, Mount Desert Island was still remote and obscure. It was not until 1844 that a visiting artist "discovered" the island's secluded beauty and began to talk it up so enthusiastically that a growing stream of summer people turned the little fishing village of Bar Harbor into one of the

Clawing surf and tranquil, glacier-carved lakes comprise Acadia's island treasures.

Surging seas rush into Thunder Hole (opposite), pounding its walls with a resounding boom. Relentless waves, combining with wind, rain, and frost still sculpt Maine's coast, continuing the work of ages. Mile-thick glacial ice overran Mount Desert Island less than 20,000 years ago, widening and deepening stream-cut valleys, and leaving pockets of water like Jordan Pond (right). Today travelers on the Park Loop pause at Jordan Pond House to sample its famous "tea and popovers."

Forest trails top steep hills and skirt fish-filled streams (fishing license required). Ranger-naturalists conduct walks, explaining wonders of mountain and sea (below). Sandy beaches await swimmers who can stand 50° water.

Acadia is accessible all year by highway; by bus or air via Bangor, Maine; campgrounds, park activities, air service to Bar Harbor in summer only.

MURRAY WEISS, DPI (ALSO OPPOSITE). BELOW: JACK BOUCHER, NATIONAL PARK SERVICE

Water turns to wine in Anemone Cave as tide ebbs, baring rock crusted with tiny red algae. A naturalist's delight, Acadia combines rich sea life with plants and animals of forest and lake.

LUIS MARDEN, NATIONAL GEOGRAPHIC STAFF

world's most fashionable resorts. By the turn of the century, huge mansions, each staffed by at least seven indoor servants yet invariably known as "cottages," looked down on gleaming yachts that crowded the anchorage. Everyone who was anyone arrived by water. One sporting pair of gentlemen made a practice of sculling all the way from the Union Boat Club at the foot of Boston's Beacon Hill—which must have taken a good bit of the summer.

Through the generosity of such "cottagers" Acadia National Park was born. A square rod of land, donated "for public use" in 1903, started it. Huge slices of private property followed. In 1916 these gifts were turned over to the Federal Government and became a national monument. The park, formed in 1919, now includes 50 square miles, partly on Schoodic Point on the mainland, and on Isle au Haut. Though ravaged by a forest fire in 1947, Mount Desert has thick woods marching down to the sea cliffs. Far from a desert (explorer Champlain's name meant "wild, uninhabited"), it abounds in lakes, ponds, and brooks. Beavers splash in hidden backwaters. Deer trot along the maze of paths that cut from one viewpoint to another. Bird song is everywhere.

Thronging people seem to vanish from sight along Acadia's roads and trails. Yet the human types that frequent the Maine coast are all here—carloads of sightseers, old-time summer residents tending their neat lawns; artists, tennis champions, yachtsmen, tanned children with sun-bleached hair. And among them all are the down-Easters who fill gas tanks and grocery orders, and answer questions with sober courtesy ("... daown the ro-ud past the Haskell bahn, then bear right ..."). With a sense of relief these year-rounders say goodbye to the "summer complaints" in September—yet with furtive pleasure welcome them again next June. For the summer folk are part of Maine, part of Mount Desert, and certainly part of the park that they conceived and brought to life.

PAUL G. FAVOUR, JR., NATIONAL PARK SERVICE

Summer's yachts sweep in like migrant gulls. Here at Northeast Harbor, Cadillac Mountain looms behind, flanked by lesser heights. On these waters children learn to sail, navies come to call, and visitors motorboat to the historical museum on Little Cranberry Island.

MAMMOTH CAVE

By PAUL JENSEN

W. RAY SCOTT

"Through caverns measureless to man, down to a sunless sea." Coleridge's lines strike a responsive chord in boaters on Mammoth's Crystal Lake, an emerald wrapped in rocky folds 270 feet below the central Kentucky woods. Higher water tables in times past scored the horizontal grooves; dripping water cut the fluting.

THE TOUR LEADER smiled wryly. "Somebody asked The Question again today. In twenty years I bet I've heard it 500 times: How many miles of *un*explored passages are there in the cave!"

We sat on the lawn in front of Mammoth Cave Hotel. Buses from the Frozen Niagara entrance were delivering tour groups nearby.

"Actually," he went on, "the answer is probably thousands of miles. Maybe you noticed, driving in this country you hardly ever cross a creek, but you see lots of sinkholes. Rainwater seeps into the ground, dissolves the limestone layers underneath, and the surface caves in. These sinkholes catch more water, and it eats out large chambers and long corridors. Mammoth Cave is mostly ancient stream bed. Take its 150-odd miles of explored passages and multiply by the size of this whole flat-bed area and you've got a right smart amount of cave."

I had just returned from the 7-mile All Day trip and that seemed like a right smart amount of cave to me. Four other tours explore shorter routes.

Tour Supervisor Ritter took me in the Historic Entrance, which a pioneer named Houchin is said to have stumbled on while chasing a bear in 1798. But long before, Indians penetrated its gloom with reed torches to gather gypsum, probably for use as a cathartic. One brave pinned under a six-ton rock was found in 1935. You can see Mummy John in a glass case near the entrance.

Ritter pointed to wooden pipes, once used to carry water. "During the War of 1812 our supplies of nitrates for making gunpowder were cut off. Fortunately, Mammoth Cave dirt contained saltpeter. The 'peter dirt' was put in wooden vats to leach out the nitrate, the solution was pumped to the surface, the water boiled off, and the salts shipped to the powder works in Philadelphia."

Soon people came to see the now-famous cave. No American could say he knew his country who had not seen Niagara Falls and Mammoth Cave, "the greatest cave there ever was." Tourists came first by stagecoach, then by steamer up the Green River, or by rail to Cave City. Dom Pedro, Emperor of Brazil, arrived, and Grand Duke Alexis of Russia. In 1851, the silent corridors awoke to the golden voice of Jenny Lind, and 25 years later Edwin Booth intoned Hamlet's soliloquy in a room now known as Booth's Amphitheater.

"Right up there he stood," said Parker Ritter. "Go on, give it a try."

Blind fish feel their way through pools of blackness

Thousands of generations of Echo River's minnow-size fish had no use for eyes. Darkness also robbed them of pigment; backlighting will reveal the skeleton. Eyeless crayfish scuttle through the Stygian waters, and cave crickets creep on the walls.

I mounted the rock. My imagination peopled the chamber below with men in silk hats and ladies in rustling crinoline. "To be, or not to be," I piped. The crowd vanished. Ritter alone grinned up at me. Blushing, I descended and followed him to see the Giant's Coffin and the huts where consumptives had vainly sought cure in the dry cave atmosphere. We skirted the Bottomless Pit, threaded the narrow channel of Fat Man's Misery, and descended to the River Styx.

Beyond, the cave was not lighted for a mile and a half. Padding along in silence through the puddles of light from our hand lanterns, I felt I really was in a cave. With darting shafts of light we fought back the pressing darkness until, at the Snowball Room cafeteria, we joined a party taking the Scenic Trip.

Off we trooped, through the now brightly lit cave. At Mammoth Gypsum Wall we examined the riot of flowers, needles, fluffy masses like cotton candy at a fair—all composed of fragile gypsum crystals. At Grand Central Station we met

DAVID S. BOYER AND ARLAN R. WIKER, NATIONAL GEOGRAPHIC STAFF

Man's lights gleam cheerfully through vaulted chambers where once in inky gloom a hidden river flowed

From this stone pulpit Shakespearean actor Edwin Booth delivered Hamlet's soliloquy in 1876. Now Booth's Amphitheater is a regular stop on trips through Mammoth Cave.

Water fashioned these underground halls and channels. For millions of years it seeped into the limestone and chewed it away. Later, dripping water formed strange and spectacular figures and also carved out the cave's distinctive features—vertical shafts called pits or domes. On one trip visitors peer down 105-foot Bottomless Pit, gaze up 192-foot Mammoth Dome, and descend with lanterns to Echo River. Here, 360 feet below the surface, they take a mystery ride in a flat-bottomed boat.

After exploring the cave many tourists linger to camp and hike in the park's 80 square miles of rolling woodland. The Green River, winding through the area, offers fine boating and fishing—no fishing license is necessary. In this hardwood country, oak, ash, hickory, poplar, and elm add their changing foliage to the transient blossoms of dogwood and other flowering shrubs. And 170 species of birds try to outshout each other.

Hotel, lodge, and cabins stay open all year. Campground closes from November to April.

another group. "Who are they?" a woman wanted to know. The tour leader told her they were taking the Frozen Niagara trip.

"Oh," she said abstractedly. "I thought they were left over from yesterday."

Most spectacular of Mammoth's onyx formations, Frozen Niagara is a mass of fluted stalactites spilling from a ledge, its motion frozen by nature's magic.

On the surface, the sun seemed brighter, the trees and grass greener, the rustling leaves had a crisper sound than before. I became freshly aware of the beauty of these rolling Kentucky lands.

Nearly a million visitors come each year to see the cave, 100 miles from Louisville or Nashville. The park and hotel are open the year round. One early visitor had different plans. At dusk he held up one of the Cave City-Mammoth stagecoaches, relieving its passengers of $831 and jewelry. Shot soon after, the bandit still had some of the loot. His name: Jesse James.

Excavating man's oldest known home in the Southeast reveals a continuous record of more than 9,000 years of Stone Age life

BROOKS HONEYCUTT

Cave men sharpened bone awls on stone.

RUSSELL CAVE

By CARL F. MILLER

Leader, National Geographic-Smithsonian Russell Cave Expeditions

HE WAS SHORT, naked, and desperately afraid. He ran, bending over to make himself smaller, for an enemy was close behind. Suddenly, a stone-tipped shaft plunged, with stabbing pain, into his back.

The warrior stumbled on, somehow dragged himself back to his dark cave home on an Alabama mountainside, and there he died. No grave was dug. His body, with the spear point still in his back, was simply laid on the cave floor and covered with earth. This Stone Age American lived and died about 1000 B.C., yet he was a comparative latecomer to the great limestone cavern. For at least 6,000 years before his lifetime it had sheltered primitive man.

The remarkable story of Russell Cave unfolded during three seasons of excavation, 1956-58, under auspices of the National Geographic Society and the Smithsonian Institution. To preserve the cave for scientific study, The Society purchased it and the surrounding 310-acre farm near Bridgeport, made liberal research grants to further the work, then presented the site to the people of the United States for preservation as a national archeological monument.

A few inches below the present cave floor we found relics of Indians who lived here during early colonial times. These people, of the so-called Mississippian culture, date from about A.D. 1500 to 1650. Through the next 4½ to 5 feet we read the floor-by-floor record of the preceding Woodland peoples. Bone needles and fishhooks, arrowheads, shell ornaments, all told their mute story.

Imagine with me for a moment Russell Cave as it was then.

Each morning the sun pours into the yawning mouth of the great cavern, 107 feet wide and 26 high, facing east. Just below flows Dry Creek, which turns and

Life in Russell Cave: a suitor of the Woodland era offers a finely wrought ax as price of a bride. Eavesdropping, the girl brings clay for her mother's pottery making. Hide canopy diverts dripping water.

PETER V. BIANCHI, NATIONAL GEOGRAPHIC STAFF ARTIST

disappears into the mountain through an even larger cavern next door. The men soon depart into the endless forest. With bows and arrows, stone-headed spears and axes, they hunt deer, bear, wild turkey, and smaller game. Or they scour the woods for berries and nuts. Farming, if known, is primitive. Why farm, when the forest holds food for the taking?

The women squat at work under hide canopies which keep off dripping water. They roll moist clay into ropes, then coil and shape these into wide-mouthed jars, some holding five gallons. They add decoration by pressing carved paddles or coarse mesh into the smooth surface, scratching a design, or painting it with a slurry of hematite. Then they place the pottery on glowing coals to harden. Other women weave sleeping mats from rushes, scrape bear hides with stone knives, or sew deerskin bags. They thread bone needles with animal sinew or

BATES LITTLEHALES, NATIONAL GEOGRAPHIC PHOTOGRAPHER

An ancient hunter took to his grave the missile that killed him

Like a detective sifting debris for clues, the author brushes earth from a skeleton buried about 3,000 years ago; he determines that the cause of death was the white-quartz spearhead near the spine. A later cave man dug into the grave and tossed away the skull and other bones. Spear and arrow points on notebook were found nearby.

Interestingly, a small dog found at a lower level had been given a far more careful burial than the man.

Russell Cave dwellers were abominable housekeepers. Instead of sweeping out their trash, they buried it under fresh dirt. In these layers archeologists read the story of the passing generations.

Russell Cave yawns above Dry Creek. Here primitive man found life was good—ready-made shelter, mild climate, clear water, a forest full of game. Members of the Tennessee Archeological Society first probed the site in 1953.

BROOKS HONEYCUTT

BROOKS HONEYCUTT

Floor levels in this cross section span 4,000 years. Dips mark fire pits. Ladder of time (left) keys layers to history. Charcoal from about 7060 B.C. was found 10 feet below lowest sign.

gut. Naked children dash about. As sunset nears, the men return. If the hunt was good, no one will go hungry.

Each family gathers around its fire to eat, laugh, and boast. The hubbub dies; only the glow of embers testifies that humans are here, asleep.

Generations pass. Whenever the stench of gnawed bones and rubbish grows too great for even these untidy people, women bring in baskets of earth and spread a new floor—thus preserving for archeologists a record of their way of life.

My wife Ruth, who works with me, found a stone axhead unlike any seen before at the cave—grooved to fit a notched handle and painstakingly sharpened to a

Giant's staircase into the past reached bedrock at 43 feet. Radiocarbon tests dated a hearth at 23 feet as 9,020 years old, plus or minus 350. Scattered artifacts still lower suggest earlier occupancy. At 35 feet the author found a hearth that warmed men possibly 12,000 years ago.

WILLIAM W. CAMPBELL, III, AND (LEFT) BATES LITTLEHALES, NATIONAL GEOGRAPHIC PHOTOGRAPHER

BATES LITTLEHALES, NATIONAL GEOGRAPHIC PHOTOGRAPHER (ALSO OPPOSITE)

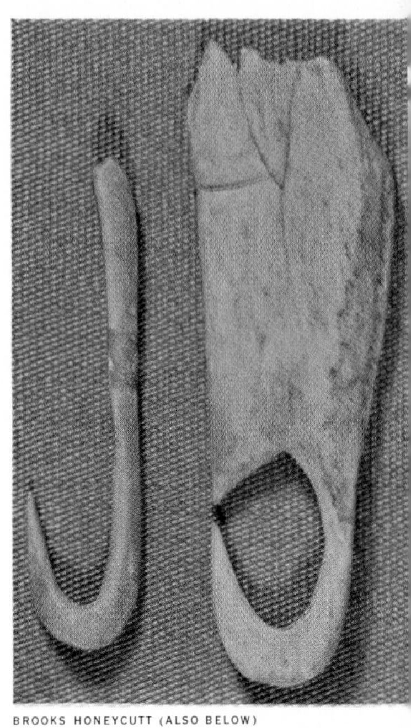

BROOKS HONEYCUTT (ALSO BELOW)

Local students, turned archeologists, sift the dirt of a hundred centuries for stone points and knives,

Deer antler chips flint to a deadly edge. Primitive men split flakes from large pieces of flint with hammerstones, then pressure-flaked the edges with bone tools. This Russell Cave spearhead, though later, shows less skill than the fluted points Folsom man left nearby 10,000 years ago.

Coal miners, who could have quickly emptied the entire cave, were stunned when asked to trowel out six inches at a time in five-foot squares.

Painstakingly they peeled off the layers, examined each trowelful, and passed the dirt along for screening. They squeezed each ounce of wet clay and dynamited stone slabs in their way. Three tons of finds went into sacks keyed to square and depth. One thing the crew didn't find: train robber's gold of local legend.

One culture's skills may be lost to the next. Woodland peoples knew only the one-piece deer-bone fishhook, shown above in two stages of carving. Earlier men hinged two pieces; this more efficient hook (right) resembles those of the Far North.

You can see relics like these and an exhibit of the excavation all year in the visitor center and the cave.

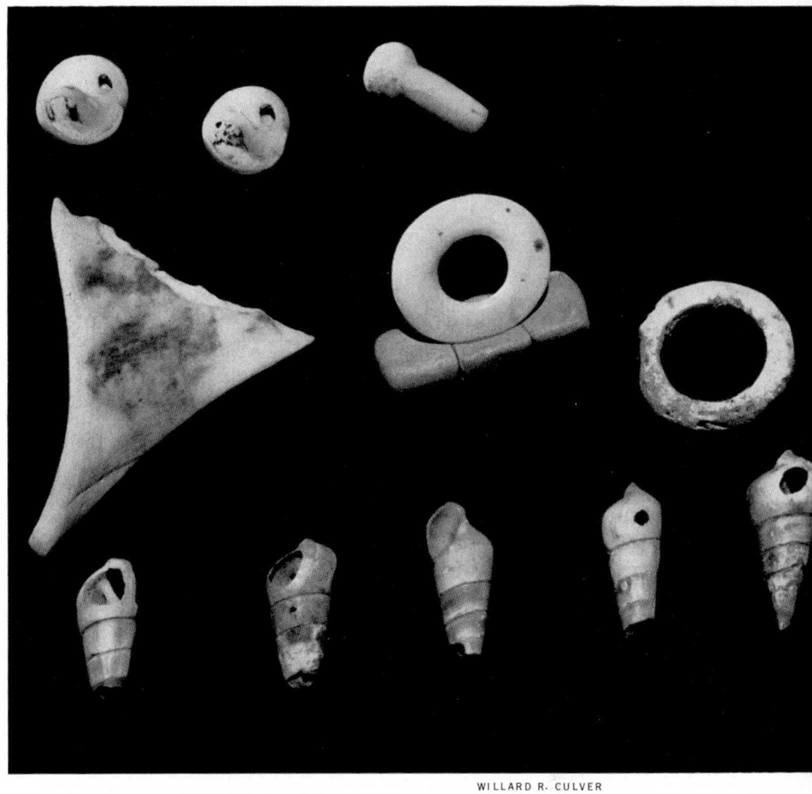

WILLARD R. CULVER

bone fishhooks and needles, shell rings and necklaces, and the plugs that adorned pierced ears.

keen edge. With such a valuable ax, a primitive man might buy a wife, as the artist depicts on page 494. We also discovered two hairpins of polished bone.

Four feet down, in the early Woodland period, we found the grave of a newborn baby. Twenty-five feet away, at the same level, Ruth came across the remains of an adult male. Very carefully we brushed the earth away.

"Carl," Ruth said suddenly, "this man was killed!"

Close beside the backbone lay a large quartz projectile point. The spear had been driven in from behind, probably in the way described. It had struck a major nerve, and must have left his legs paralyzed. Neither in these graves nor in a third at the nine-foot level was anything buried with the dead—no ornaments, weapons, or provisions for the journey to the hereafter. Perhaps possessions were too few, or were owned in common.

At the five-foot level we had entered the time of Archaic man, who knew neither pottery nor the bow and arrow. His chief weapon was a spear and throwing stick or atlatl. We found two atlatl parts of notched deer antler.

At six feet the soil changed to sticky clay, and we had to knead each handful, like dough, to find hidden objects. Here we began finding artifacts of a type never before discovered in the southeastern United States: hinged fishhooks, unlike the single-piece hook of the Woodland peoples; and polished foreleg bones of large bears, cut cleanly and scraped out so that bear fat and a wick could be

stuffed into the cavity. Cave man could carry this torch like a candle. How did such artifacts, heretofore found only much closer to the Arctic, come to be used so far south? During the last Ice Age, 10,000 years ago and more, there was apparently a slow movement eastward across the continent. Later, peoples of Archaic culture moved north and south along the Appalachians. Those coming south, perhaps bringing tools of the Far North, met people from the West and

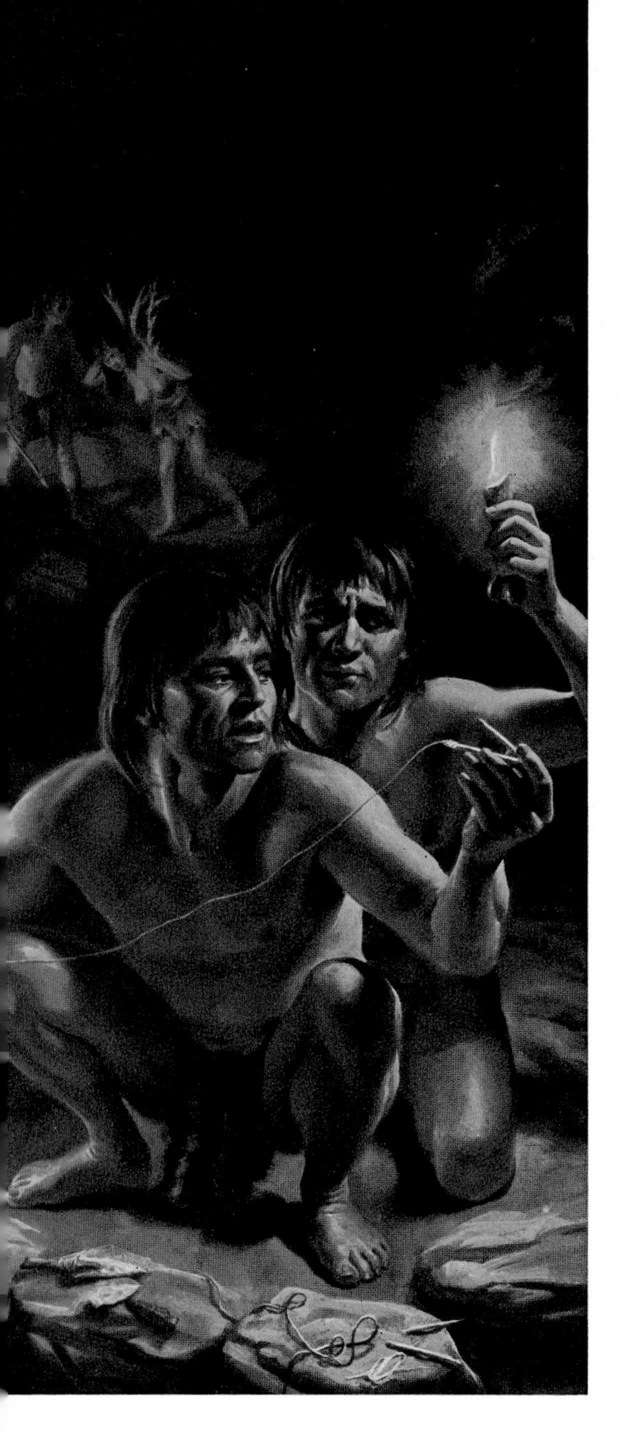

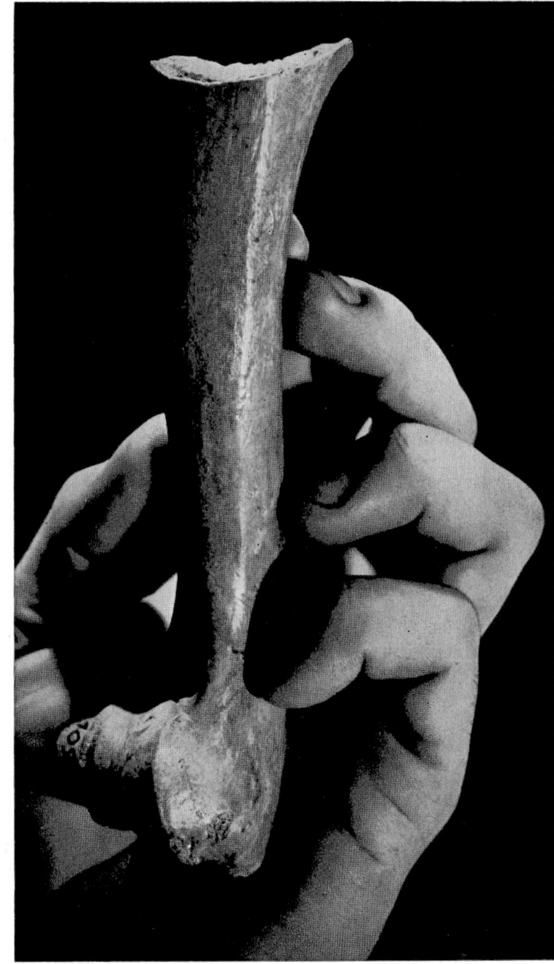

BATES LITTLEHALES, NATIONAL GEOGRAPHIC PHOTOGRAPHER

Alabamians of 8,000 years ago work by firelight. Artist Peter V. Bianchi reconstructed this scene from such clues as bear-bone lamp above and fishhook (page 501) found on the spot.

Archaic hunter skinning bear with stone knife downed it with a spear thrower, the atlatl, which preceded bow and arrow of Woodland times (page 494). These people are probably "overdressed." Author found no sign they wore even these scanty garments.

South at the southern end of the mountains—the region around Russell Cave.

Then, at 23 feet, we found a pocket of charcoal by the north wall. I sent a sample to the University of Michigan's radiocarbon laboratory. There Professor H. R. Crane determined that the fire had burned some 9,000 years ago—well within the era of Early man. No other site in the Southeast has yielded a layer-by-layer cross section of continuous human life over so long a period.

JACK E. BOUCHER

Painted braves chipped stone for ceremonial pipe bowls from the ledge at ranger's back.

PIPESTONE

IMAGINE you are in another century, visiting a Sioux chief in his great tepee. Plains Indians sit in solemn council, perhaps negotiating a tribal treaty or an agreement with white men. Whatever the occasion, etiquette decrees its climax. A coal from the fire kindles tobacco in a richly ornamented pipe. The pipe passes slowly around the circle. With each puff, smoke spirals from its carved stone bowl. This aromatic "handshake" binds the parties.

To Indians, the peace-pipe ceremony was sacred, a ritual with beginnings deep in tribal lore. Also sacred were the sources of soft red stone from which pipe bowls were shaped. Quarries were common ground, where hostile tribes met in peace. Pipestone National Monument in southwestern Minnesota preserves the most famous of these ancient sites—first described by artist George Catlin in 1836. You can see the vein of catlinite that Indians still work today; and in the museum, pipe bowls their ancestors laboriously carved and polished. Legend says the Great Spirit hovered over the quarry and set Indian maidens to guard it. Three huge boulders—the Three Maidens—stand vigil there today.

EFFIGY MOUNDS

A HAWK'S SPREADING WINGS, a bear's burly outline—these effigies, fashioned in dirt, covered the graves of Midwestern Indians a millennium ago. Thousands of these burial mounds, large and small, simple and elaborate, were scattered through the upper Mississippi Valley. Many have been leveled by the march of civilization. Others survive, notably at Effigy Mounds National Monument on the river bluffs near McGregor, Iowa. Beads, earthenware pots, copper ornaments, and other artifacts buried in the mounds help tell the story of their builders, who, never seen by white man, were ancestors of the Indians we know.

OCMULGEE NATIONAL MONUMENT

IN A COUNCIL CHAMBER domed with logs and covered with Georgia's red clay, 50 warriors sit in a circle planning an ambush. Before each seat a receptacle holds pipe, tobacco, magical charms. A raised platform represents a sacred eagle. Beside the central fire pit a squatting figure chants. The powwow follows strict ceremonial procedure, for rite makes might.

Here at Ocmulgee Monument, near Macon, visitors can see the 900-year-old earth lodge and flat-topped temple mounds where priest-chiefs worshiped the sun. Museum exhibits trace Indian cultures of the Southeast: first the primitive hunters, then the Shellfish Eaters of 5,000 years ago, the Early Farmers, the Master Farmers who raised the earthen mounds—finally the historic Creeks, who built a village here and ushered in their New Year with midsummer corn rituals.

MOUND CITY GROUP

American artists fashioned the copper headdress (above) and stone effigy pipe (right) when Rome was in its glory. Dug from hillocks at this national monument near Chillicothe, Ohio, they show the skill of the Hopewell people, whose Burial Mound culture reached its zenith 300 B.C.—A.D. 100.

Mound City, like other monuments on these pages, is open all year, has no camping or lodging facilities, but is near towns with accommodations.

OHIO HISTORICAL SOCIETY

ISLE ROYALE NATIONAL PARK

THIS WILDERNESS PARK lies in the western half of Lake Superior, a score of miles from the mainland shore where Canada meets Minnesota. True devotees spend chilly nights in sleeping bags beside wooded lakes teeming with pike, perch, and walleyes, or they putter among the archipelago's 200 rocky islets in outboard cruisers. The more faint at heart stay in the comfortable lodges at Windigo or Rock Harbor.

Dense forests mask the scars of Ice Age glaciers on the 210-square-mile island. Moose, wolves, minks, muskrats, and foxes have migrated from the mainland across Superior's ice, but bears, deer, and skunks have not. One of the boons of isolation: no poisonous snakes, ragweed, or poison ivy. Visitors embark at Houghton or Copper Harbor, Mich.,

Everybody hikes; they must, for there are no cars or horses. But hiking is a joy. Trails springy with pine needles and damp moss lead past flashing beaver ponds and glades purpled with wild iris. Pits deep in blueberry thickets mark where Isle Royale's Indians long ago mined native copper with fire and hammerstone—copper that found its way to Florida along the amazing trade trails of the red men. Orchids peep from the underbrush, and Indian pipes gleam by rotted logs. Here, as nowhere else, one can envision the Great Lakes region as it was when Champlain struggled up its rivers, or when Nicolet stepped ashore at Green Bay in clothes he donned to meet the Emperor of China.

NATHANIEL T. KENNEY, NATIONAL GEOGRAPHIC STAFF

or Grand Portage, Minn. Deck-load your boat, or rent one on Isle Royale. For lodgings (June 25–Labor Day) or information, write supt. at Houghton.

Colored pebbles, even semiprecious greenstones adorn the island's shores. Indians mined pure copper here nearly 4,000 years ago. In 1669 French trappers took possession of the Michigan island and named it in honor of Louis XIV.

DUFF JOHNSTON

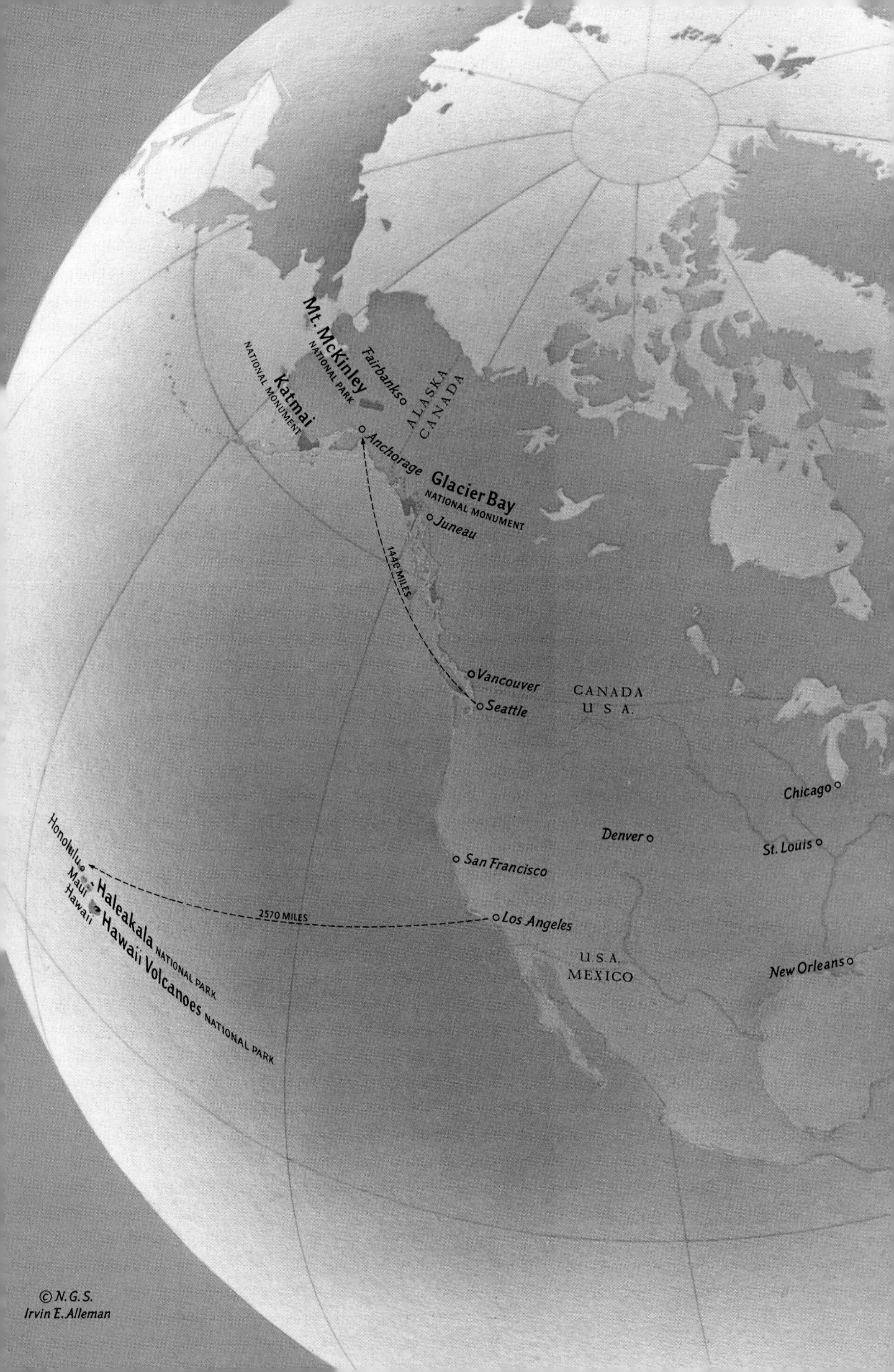

Mt. McKinley
NATIONAL PARK
Katmai
NATIONAL MONUMENT
Fairbanks
ALASKA
CANADA
Anchorage
Glacier Bay
NATIONAL MONUMENT
Juneau
1440 MILES
Vancouver
Seattle
CANADA
U.S.A.
Chicago
Denver
St. Louis
San Francisco
Honolulu
Maui
Hawaii
Haleakala NATIONAL PARK
Hawaii Volcanoes NATIONAL PARK
2570 MILES
Los Angeles
U.S.A.
MEXICO
New Orleans
© N.G.S.
Irvin E. Alleman

PART SEVEN

ALASKA, HAWAII, AND THE VIRGIN ISLANDS

AMERICA'S CROWN JEWELS are her national parklands. On her perimeter gleam three alluring gems.

Rough-cut Alaska weighs out big. It dazzles with McKinley's blue-white spire, the glistening ice of Glacier Bay, and Katmai's sparkling lakes. Here the sun shines at midnight; the aurora borealis explodes into a thousand rainbows. "If you are old, go by all means," counseled Dr. Henry Gannett, a founder of the National Geographic Society. "But if you are young, wait. The scenery of Alaska is much grander than anything else of the kind in the world, and it is not well to dull one's capacity for enjoyment by seeing the finest first."

A gentle climate enhances Hawaii and the Virgin Islands, lustrous pearls of the tropical seas.

Mauna Loa, its heart aglow, crowns the 50th of the United States. "When will it erupt again?" asks the Honolulu visitor on his way to see Pele's Pit, the black sand beach, and the rare silversword that blooms but once.

Six thousand miles to the east, in the Caribbean where pirates roistered and islanders still hint of buried treasure, vacationists find tiny St. John, unflawed gem of the Virgin Islands, one of our newest national parks.

Inching up West Buttress on slopes "slippery as greased glass," weary climbers hack a new trail to the continent's roof. Indians call 20,320-foot McKinley "Denali," the Great One; few other peaks in the world tower so far above the surrounding terrain. "Denali's Wife" (beyond) is 17,400-foot Mount Foraker, second highest in Mount McKinley National Park.

Landing by light plane on one of Alaska's biggest and roughest glaciers, climbers pioneer a new route to conquer the white-crowned monarch of North America

MOUNT McKINLEY

By BRADFORD WASHBURN
Photographs by the author

"BELT FASTENED TIGHT?" shouted Terry Moore above the idling engine. I nodded, my heart pounding, and our little plane bumped down the runway at Chelatna Lake. Ahead towered mighty Mount McKinley, loftiest peak in North America. We were going to try the "impossible": climb McKinley's rugged West Buttress—a third of the way by airplane.

Beneath stretched unexplored Kahiltna Glacier, snout buried under boulders, ice so broken nothing could land on it. Rock walls towered on both sides; above was a solid ceiling of fog. It was like flying through a gigantic tunnel.

At last a rift split the clouds. Far up the valley, where snow covered the glacial ice, we made a perfect landing. Supplies unloaded, Terry sang out, "So long, partner!" and roared away in a swirl of snow. I was alone, 7,700 feet up, close under McKinley's flanks. Lightly it began to snow.

When the weather cleared, Terry flew in my three companions. We then broke trail up to Kahiltna Pass at 10,300 feet—first to set foot on this lofty saddle. It took us till midnight; the sky was deep red as twilight merged into dawn.

Another day we scaled "Peak Z" and built an igloo. When a storm struck that afternoon, we retreated inside and at the height of the tempest enjoyed a cup of tea. For several days we surveyed for the first complete large-scale map of the region. Finally, joined by four other team members who had circled the mountain by pack train, we launched our assault on McKinley's western barriers.

Skirting crevasses, we made our way up snow-and-ice slopes that ended abruptly in a massive granite shoulder. Above towered the 16,000-foot crest of the West Buttress. Right under it, at "Windy Corner," we set up our first advanced camp. After a cozy night in our igloo, we dug out into a howling storm, gusts hitting 80 miles an hour. It was 14° above zero. For two days we carried supplies up; then Jim Gale and I started for the next campsite. Our snowshoes slid back at each step. Shedding them, I broke through crust up to my waist. So with shovels we carved flat steps. After an hour's work I looked back at where I had left my pack; it was only 100 feet behind us.

Regal McKinley's "impregnable" western face succumbed to a fly-and-hike assault

The author's 1951 expedition made climbing history: the Great One had been conquered only six times before—never from this side. A plane equipped with skis landed the explorers far up Kahiltna Glacier. Later, supplies were

airdropped. One object of the expedition, sponsored by Boston's Museum of Science, the University of Denver, and the University of Alaska, was to make the peak more accessible for scientific research. In July's 18-hour days the team also mapped and studied the granite mass, its upper reaches blackened by slate, once the bottom of a prehistoric sea. All eight men made it to the top. Plane landings and airdrops are no longer permitted on McKinley.

McKinley's front porch offers a spectacular view—but watch that first step. It's a lulu!

"Like looking out the very windows of Heaven," said Archdeacon Hudson Stuck, leader of the party that first scaled the true summit, South Peak, in 1913.

Standing 3,000 feet from the top, near the author's highest campsite, a climber here looks over the ridgepoled West Buttress. Kahiltna Glacier flows like a sluggish river toward the lowlands where haze hides Anchorage, Alaska's largest city. Mount Spurr, 130 miles away, shows plainly through the cold, dry air.

All is not ice and snow in Mount McKinley National Park. Beginning in early June, arctic plants, including Alaska's state flower, the forget-me-not, chase retreating snows off meadows and ridges.

Winding within sight of glaciers, a park road slips through the alpine tundra along valleys and lower slopes, leading motorists to Eielson Visitor Center and on to Wonder Lake. Linked to the famed Alaska Highway, the park road makes North America's highest peak accessible to any traveler. Climbers must get the superintendent's permission.

Wildlife thrives in the park—as the following pages show.

We reached our "Crow's Nest" campsite on a 15,400-foot shelf utterly exhausted and suffering from anoxia—lack of oxygen—which saps will power and impairs judgment. The last slope to the crest of West Buttress rose sharply 600 feet above our shelf. Jim and I took turns chopping steps in the most wretched snow imaginable. Roped together, we just chopped and chopped; neither of us spoke. Still a stone's throw from the ridge, we were forced down by rising wind which roared over camp all night. Next day, fresh and rested, we made it.

In gale winds that day and dense fog the next, Jim, Bill Hackett, and I packed

our loads over a granite knife edge studded with boulders and across a snow field to the foot of Denali Pass. At 17,300 feet we built an igloo.

July 10 dawned clear, and we started toward the pass. As the grade finally lessened I saw a shapeless bundle—a cache left by our 1947 expedition which had climbed the other side. I gave a shout of joy! We had conquered McKinley's western face. Four hours later we topped the summit and the panorama to the east burst upon us—100,000 square miles of Alaska in a single sweeping glance! Our new route had proved an ideal approach to the roof of North America.

Golden Eagle

Sharp talons clutch a hoary marmot; powerful wings spanning more than seven feet will carry it to the eagle's cliffside nest. Predators and prey live unmolested by man in this spectacular arctic refuge.

Wildlife of Mount McKinley National Park

By ADOLPH MURIE, former Biologist, National Park Service

Paintings by WALTER A. WEBER, National Geographic Staff Artist

IN THE CREEK AHEAD we saw a dark object that reached almost from shore to shore. We stopped for a better look. A grizzly bear was lying in the water enjoying the cool play of the current; a cub frolicked at her side. "It's probably Nokomis," I said as we scrambled from the rattletrap truck. "She's the only grizzly in the area with one cub."

Suddenly the old bear, 80 yards away, stood up and eyed us. I thought she was standing up to stretch, but my confidence vanished when she nervously chomped her jaws together. We could see her yellow teeth.

Squalls and barks erupted behind us! Another grizzly cub was pacing back and forth on the hillside directly above. This was not Nokomis at all. Our bathing bear must be Old Rosy, mother of *two* cubs. Now we found ourselves between an irate grizzly and her frightened cub—a classic example of the wrong place to be. We grabbed our cameras, sprinted down the road, jumped into the truck, and drove away. Seconds later the grizzly broke out onto the road. Stopping at a safe distance, we watched the family's reunion.

Walter Weber said that he wanted to see grizzlies. Here, on our second day in the field, we had found them. The National Geographic artist-naturalist had come to Mount McKinley National Park to study and paint Alaskan wildlife. It was my pleasant duty to act as his guide.

In a few days we drove to Wonder Lake, near the base of Mount McKinley, and set up headquarters. It was late August, and hill and tundra blazed with brilliant crimson, yellow, and gold. Forests of white spruce and cottonwood clung to semi-frozen soil; fireweed, aster, and larkspur huddled in bright patches. Against this vivid backdrop we set out afoot to stalk that handsome relative of the domesticated reindeer, the caribou.

I have counted as many as 4,500 in a single band when these restless migrants cross the park in spring and early July. Now we found scattered groups. We circled downwind on two fine bulls with sweeping antlers and slowly set up our cameras. The caribou's eyesight is poor; only sudden movement would betray us. The bulls looked our way as if suspicious, but finally lay down contentedly. Suddenly both jumped to their feet and dashed off. Our comments were sulphurous. Probably the animals had been set upon by nose botflies or warble flies.

Caribou are the chief source of food for the timber wolf. I told Walter how I had discovered a wolves' hideaway one May morning, and, crawling inside, found six dumpy, blunt-nosed puppies, eyes still closed. I wrapped one in my parka and carried it home. The little female grew rapidly on canned milk. She became a pet and my 5-year-old daughter Gail named her Wags.

For three years I watched Wags's family and made notes on their habits. Surprisingly, besides Wags's mother and father, two adult males and a female lived at the den, all friendly with one another and the pups. Before a night hunt they often ceremoniously wagged tails and rubbed shoulders, and sometimes romped. Several times the unattached female baby-sat with the puppies while their mother hunted!

Once I watched the five adults stage a memorable battle royal with a big grizzly. The bear was heading straight for some meat, cached by the wolves near their den, when the pack attacked. The grizzly ran, but was soon overtaken and encircled. The wolves nipped at him, easily avoiding his

Dall Sheep

Handsome targets for camera-toting climbers, these white-robed lords of Alaska's high country display slender, wrinkled horns. Rams' keen eyes watch for wolves.

Stone's Caribou

Majestic nomads of the North scent the wind for danger as they cross a ridge near Mount McKinley. Caribou's antlered kin, the moose, is the biggest animal in the park.

Timber Wolf

Wary of man, who has exterminated wolves in most other parts of the United States, these nimble, powerful-jawed night prowlers stalk caribou and other game.

lunges. The battle lasted ten minutes, but its outcome was never in doubt. The bear retreated slowly, and eventually the wolves permitted him to lumber off.

McKINLEY PARK holds many a treat for ornithologists. They invariably inquire about two of its most elusive residents, the wandering tattler and the surfbird, whose nests were unknown to science until the 1920's. Raising its family above timber line in Alaska's interior, the surfbird winters along rocky Pacific coast beaches as far south as Chile. The wandering tattler winters as far away as New Zealand.

Not so mysterious is the powerful golden eagle, to me one of nature's most splendid creatures. Some years ago the park eagles were suspected of preying upon the lambs of mountain sheep, so I turned detective. Visiting many cliffside nests, I gathered pellets of undigested bones, feathers, and fur which the eagle regurgitates after a meal. More than 90 percent of the bird's diet proved to consist of ground squirrels and hoary marmots.

The bird that perhaps best typifies the North is the willow ptarmigan. We met

Alaska Red Fox Foxes become fairly tame in the park. Some will even take food from visitors' hands. Lean winters, with rabbits and ptarmigan hard to catch, follow summer's feast of rodents, fledgling birds, and berries.

many of them prospecting for gravel along the road. Also present in the park are two other ptarmigan species: the rock and the white-tailed. All three change dress with the seasons, matching winter's snow with white outfits, donning brown-and-gray plumage in the spring, and displaying snowy underparts and brownish feathering in late summer and fall.

While camping in a spruce woods we studied the activities of a winsome little field mouse, the Toklat vole, named for Alaska's Toklat River. Each summer it harvests hay to feed on in winter. Near our cabin we found many miniature haystacks piled between branches of dwarf trees.

Too soon mid-September was upon us, and there was only time for one more camera hunt. We set out for the high, craggy ridges in search of Dall sheep. For 60 miles the park road passes through sheep range. Rattling along in our truck, we sighted 20 rams in the cliffs high above us. A dry river bed promised an approach. Afoot, we began a slow, laborious climb.

The park sheep, though they possess keen eyesight, can often be stalked in the open. They seem to feel at ease so long as they keep you in view. As we neared our ridgetop goal, the sunlight, which had been brilliant, began to grow dim. Soon the entire ridge was bathed in a curious half-glow. To add to our woes, a stray ram jumped from behind a rock and stampeded the band.

Willow Ptarmigan Fly south for the winter? Not this tundra dweller with the feathered snowshoes. Like the magpie, Canada jay, and chickadee, he's set for the cold. Soon he'll doff late summer plumage for wintry white.

MOUNT McKINLEY NATIONAL PARK

You can now drive here on Denali Highway via Alaska Highway, or come by rail or air via Fairbanks, Anchorage, Seward. Hotel at park entrance is open June to Labor Day. Bus service in park. Camp and trailer grounds, foot trails, good fishing await the vacationist. For further information write to Superintendent, Mount McKinley National Park, Alaska.

Goshawk

"Nevermore," quoth the goshawk, "will I attack ravens when a pigeon hawk is on my tail!" The words are fancied but not the scene. From a hilltop the author saw a scrappy pigeon hawk break up the aerial dogfight and chase his larger rival all over the sky.

Lynx

Snowshoe hares are this big cat's main food, though supply doesn't always meet demand. The hare is a cyclic animal, alternately plentiful and scarce; consequently, so is the lynx. Other rabbit fanciers: coyotes, foxes, owls. McKinley's chill climate excludes snakes and turtles, and all but one species of frogs.

"Four hours reaching these sheep," Walter grumbled. "Finally we get here, then no luck and no light. The sun is out, but what happened to the light?"

Returning to camp, we learned the answer: an 82-percent eclipse of the sun! But luck, and the sun, favored us a few days later. We maneuvered to within 40 yards of another band of rams and photographed them for several hours.

It was Walter's last day in the park. For a month we had roamed an unspoiled wilderness, enjoying the same majestic scenery that trail-blazing Charles Sheldon, the hunter-naturalist, had explored in the early 1900's. Largely because of Sheldon's accounts, part of the Alaska Range was set aside in 1917 as a national park. McKinley covers 3,030 square miles, and 130 species of birds and 36 species of mammals have been identified within its boundaries. A 100-mile road through the refuge provides ready access to wildlife areas. Sheep and caribou can often be seen from the road.

As we clambered down the mountainside, I noticed that Walter's gaze lingered on the magnificent sweep of horizon, the dark, tumbled ridges, the jagged crags, and the aloof, snowy hood of distant Mount McKinley. He seemed to be etching the scene in his memory.

WINFIELD PARKS, NATIONAL GEOGRAPHIC PHOTOGRAPHER

Mount Katmai cradles a jade lake, tranquil reminder of the volcanic cataclysm which decapitated the peak. Mount Griggs rises beyond; the Valley of Ten Thousand Smokes disappears into mist at left. This vast preserve covers an area more than twice the size of Delaware.

KATMAI

NATIONAL MONUMENT

By ERNEST GRUENING, United States Senator from Alaska

I STOOD IN ALASKA'S Valley of Ten Thousand Smokes, where few men have walked and no man has lived. As I gazed across this volcanic wonderland, half a century flashed backward before me. In June of 1912 one of the most tremendous eruptions in history rocked this remote corner of the earth where North America and Asia meet. Around the first of that month, earthquakes began to shake the northern Alaska Peninsula. Then, with a thunderous roar, the face of Falling Mountain let go. A hurricane caused by the avalanche roared down the 15-mile-long valley; a great cloud of dust from the mountain darkened the sky. The entire region rocked in the throes of titanic subterranean convulsions.

On June 6, at the southeastern end of the valley, a vent—later appropriately named Novarupta—suddenly opened. From it, and from a hundred new fissures

in the valley floor nearby, boiled up melted rock. Monstrous columns of incandescent pumice leaped hundreds of feet. New volcanoes formed, belching flame and rock and sand. Down the valley poured this seething stuff covering an area of 42 square miles to a depth in places of 700 feet or more. Some seven cubic miles of debris were ejected. And after 60 hours . . . silence.

In 1916, Dr. Robert F. Griggs, leader of a series of National Geographic expeditions to the scene, discovered and named the Valley of Ten Thousand Smokes. "The whole valley," he reported, "as far as the eye could reach was full of hundreds, no thousands—literally, tens of thousands—of smokes curling up from its fissured floor. . . . Some were sending up columns of steam which rose a thousand feet before dissolving. . . ."

By 1918, largely as a result of these expeditions, the steaming-hot, tortured geography of this part of Alaska had been set aside by President Woodrow Wilson as a national monument. It was later enlarged to protect the moose, bear, red fox, mink, Canada lynx, and other land animals outside the Valley of Ten Thousand Smokes, and the seals, sea lions, and other marine life along the coast of Shelikof Strait. Today—as befits our largest state—4,215-square-mile Katmai, with its still faintly smoking valley, outstrips all other United States national parks and monuments in size.

I had come to Katmai to learn more of the vigorous efforts being made to open its wonders to more people. Construction was underway on the trail which today enables visitors to ride from the nearest floatplane base at Brooks River Lodge to the foot of the valley. My companions, Winfield Parks and Robert Jordan of the National Geographic staff, and I flew all the way. For the last leg our plane was a two-seater, and bush pilot Ed Seiler took us in one by one. I went first. As the Piper Cub came in low for a landing, the sight was breath-taking.

Valley of Ten Thousand Smokes spreads before discoverer's camp

"It was as though all the steam engines in the world, assembled together, had popped their safety valves at once and were letting off surplus steam in concert," reported Dr. Robert F. Griggs of his 1916 discovery. A year later, he camped among the vapors.

Lacking wood, the party cooked over natural steam; once the acid fumes ate holes in the pans. Today most of the fumaroles have vanished; visitors (right) warm their hands over one of the few left.

Scheduled air service links Anchorage, Alaska, to Kulik Lodge and King Salmon; nonscheduled floatplane flights continue to Grosvenor Camp and Brooks River Lodge in the monument. Both facilities offer summer lodgings; write Northern Consolidated Airlines, Anchorage, for reservations. From the lodge, a rugged 22½-mile trail leads to a shelter overlooking the becalmed valley. Camping is allowed anywhere in the park with a fire permit from the ranger in charge or the superintendent at Mount McKinley National Park.

WINFIELD PARKS, NATIONAL GEOGRAPHIC PHOTOGRAPHER, AND (UPPER) ROBERT F. GRIGGS

Steam from buried rivers and springs in the baking substrata once had risen through vents in the valley floor as far as the eye could see. Now there were perhaps a dozen fumaroles.

Seiler set the tiny plane down, its oversize balloon tires bounding up the slope of Baked Mountain. I squeezed out, and he taxied around to fly back to pick up Win and then Bob. Just above me a lonely fumarole slanted its plumes skyward. I peered down its gaping throat and warmed my hands in its moist heat.

Beyond Baked Mountain lay Novarupta. When Win and Bob arrived, we set off afoot. Hiking in the debris of the valley is strenuous—like trudging through desert sand, only worse. Scramble down the bank of a watercourse and your feet slip out from under you. Haul yourself up the other side and the sharp sand skins your hands. Walk where valley floor meets mountain slope and you don't see the snow lying there—well insulated and camouflaged by wind-blown ash and pumice. Down you go again. Struggle up Novarupta's still-steaming side and you leave tracks as deep as a bear's on the puttylike incline. Suddenly one foot breaks through; you sink to your knee. Does a smoldering cavern lie below? You don't stay to find out.

We made our way to Novarupta's edge. Before us lay what had been one of the region's many beautiful valleys. Its lower reaches had been covered with balsam poplar, birch, and white spruce, interspersed with bog. Wild-

River Lethe, warmed by volcanic fires, easily cuts a canyon through pumice and ash in the Valley of Ten Thousand Smokes.

life had been plentiful: caribou, bears, wolves, wolverines, many kinds of land and water birds.

We could see the beachline left by the flow of white-hot melted rock on the mountainsides 900 feet above the valley floor. At Novarupta itself, as volcanic activity subsided, a plug of viscous rhyolite 1,300 feet in diameter had welled up to seal off that great vent. I marveled at the titanic force required to thrust this bung—weighing millions of tons—up from the depths.

WINFIELD PARKS, NATIONAL GEOGRAPHIC PHOTOGRAPHER

Puffs of featherweight pumice formed when blobs of molten lava shot out of volcanic vents and cooled. The soft stones can be cut with a knife; they float on the lakes like corks.

Summer comes fast to the 49th state and wildflowers like the rice lily (left), the wild rose (lower left), and Alaska's *Iris* (below) burst into bloom across the land.

VIRGINIA L. WELLS AND (OPPOSITE) SETSUWO TSUNODA

WINFIELD PARKS, NATIONAL GEOGRAPHIC PHOTOGRAPHER (ALSO OPPOSITE)

Bald eagle brakes for a landing on its bulky treetop nest. Emblem of the Nation, the species remains abundant only in Alaska.

In the Valley of Ten Thousand Smokes below us to the west, I saw no roads, no buildings, no bushes, no trees: There would be no wood for cooking or for comfort. My eyes at last came to rest on our distant airplane, perched like a red fly on a huge sandpile. Reluctantly we headed for it.

We flew to the valley's foot and then, banking right, coursed north nine miles to land on the Ukak River Delta. Here we stood well out of the valley but still within its shadow of death. A mile's walk brought us to a stark forest. Pumice carried by the Ukak from the valley had choked these spruce trees to death. They were bleached skeletons in a shimmering desert. A few held hawk nests. Beside me, etched in the pumice, were a moose's hoofprints.

That night at Brooks River Lodge we dined on salmon. Our cooks, Ken and Lydia McLennan, spread a bounteous table. "A couple of days here," I said, "will undo a month's dieting." And the McLennans beamed.

Some of the world's finest fishing lies but seconds from

Alaska brown bear guards his salmon snack against intruders. Sated, he may take just a couple of bites and leave the rest for wolves, foxes, coyotes, otters, eagles, and ravens. The largest flesh eater walking the earth, the mighty brown bear towers up to nine feet standing on its hind legs and weighs as much as 1,500 pounds.

CECIL E. RHODE

Struggling sockeye, bearing a biologist's red tag, vaults a six-foot-high cascade on the Brooks River. Most salmon return unerringly from the open sea to their home streams to breed. Soon after spawning, they die, completing a four- to five-year life span.

Floatplane revs up for take-off, roiling serene Lake Grosvenor; anglers casting for trout came all the way from Switzerland. At Brooks River Lodge (below), guests preview a sumptuous dinner as the cook hefts two fat salmon.

WINFIELD PARKS, NATIONAL GEOGRAPHIC PHOTOGRAPHER

one's cabin—whether at Brooks River or Lake Grosvenor, named for Dr. Gilbert H. Grosvenor, longtime President and Editor of the National Geographic Society. Next morning I visited the lake. Here rainbow, Dolly Varden, and lake trout, and grayling abound. One angler was casting in water rushing through the narrows between Lakes Grosvenor and Coville. A deft flick of his rod arched the fly out.

"I'm usually a three-cast man," he said. "Three casts, no fish, I quit." On his second cast he hooked a 3½-pound trout.

Back at Brooks River Lodge that afternoon, I chatted with fishermen who were so busy landing salmon that they complained of being arm-weary. That night a dozen or so of us sat around the fire talking of the superlative fishing that we had all to ourselves. I doubt if there were at that moment a hundred persons in the length and breadth of Katmai.

In addition to the Valley of Ten Thousand Smokes, Katmai National Monument encompasses a mountain and lake country of unsurpassed beauty. It has more than 125 miles of ocean bays, fiords, harbors, lagoons, and sharp peaks rising sheer from the water. I mused over something one of the park rangers had said: "Most of our national parks and monuments are known for one feature or another. In Katmai we have them all—and space to boot. Man doesn't dominate here."

GLACIER BAY

NATURALIST JOHN MUIR believed that the Creator taught His children with every sublime expression of nature. Glacier Bay was one of Scotsman John's greatest teachers; and, since his discovery of the 50-mile fiord in 1889, this scenic wilderness on Alaska's southeastern coast has taught the world much about glacier behavior.

Within the 3,554-square-mile national monument, created in 1925, visitors can see at work the same glacial forces that sculptured California's Yosemite and scoured Maine's Acadia and Michigan's Isle Royale.

Alaska's frozen cataracts, some of them thousands of feet deep and several miles wide, grind irresistibly down the towering Fairweather and St. Elias Ranges like giant plowshares, carving their own valleys, wedging into, even splitting apart, whole mountains, carrying within their icy bowels the composites of crushed landscapes. Many flow into the Pacific Ocean or into Glacier Bay, terminating in ice cliffs, such as Muir Glacier's 265-foot face.

Here in Muir Inlet, from a cautious half-mile out, the mariner might see the

W. ROBERT MOORE, NATIONAL GEOGRAPHIC STAFF

Stranded berg awaits the tide; adrift, it can roll over and swamp a near boat.

shore line change before his eyes. Great chunks of ice crack off and crash into the water, sending out huge waves and crowding the inlet with bergs. Thus a glacier retreats, exposing new shore. John Muir built his cabin near the foot of the flow; today the receding snout is more than 17 miles away.

Not all glaciers in the monument reach the sea. Many melt in warm lowlands, depositing vast rock-strewn moraines as they recede. Mosses and lichens attack these barren ridges to help make soil for fireweed and alpine flowers. Dwarf willow thickets follow, and clumps of alders. Giant spruce and hemlock forests complete the camouflage. But tree stumps, standing like grotesque tombstones on the bay's western shore, bear witness that glaciers recede but to return, to crush relentlessly those bold growths again and again as the pendulum of climate swings in the ponderous rhythm of the ages.

From Juneau it's less than 100 miles by boat or plane to park headquarters and a lodge and boat dock at Bartlett Cove, near the mouth of Glacier Bay. Ashore, the visitor invades virgin forest, haven for bear, mink, and deer. Afloat, he shares the bay with spouting whales, nesting waterfowl, and seals basking on ice cakes. He marvels at the glaciers, especially that named for Muir.

Here in its cavernous crevasses God-fearing John Muir became lost one day. Stumbling back to camp in the middle of the night, he exclaimed to his partner: "Such purity, such color, such delicate beauty! I was tempted to stay there and feast my soul, and softly freeze, until I would become part of the glacier."

Reid Glacier's snout gets a close look by seagoing rangers. In 1700 the entire bay was under 3,000 feet of ice. Today glaciers crawl to open water an inch or two a day—a foot is fast. Muir Glacier's speed: 20 to 30 feet!

J. P. EATON, U. S. GEOLOGICAL SURVEY

Volcanic fires of the 50th state draw 600,000 visitors a year to . . .

HAWAII VOLCANOES AND HALEAKALA

NATIONAL PARKS

By PAUL A. ZAHL
National Geographic Staff

LURCHING and bucking, our jeep climbed through a world of blue sky and black lava.

"When is Mauna Loa's next eruption due?" I asked geophysicist Jerry Eaton.

Jerry explained that Mauna Loa was way off its average of one eruption every three years—the most recent had occurred in 1950. "Let's hope she can hold off a little longer," he quipped.

We attacked the 13,680-foot volcano on foot, camping on the top, where July's night temperature drops below freezing. Next day we crossed the crater floor, past fantastic crevasses and red-lipped spatter cones glowing as if hot.

This scorched land is part of Hawaii Volcanoes National Park—344 square miles of lava-built scenery on the island of Hawaii. Mauna Loa's eruptions have made news since Captain Cook's days. More sporadic is Kilauea, joined to

Roaring fountain of rock blasts 400 feet into the air during 1955's eruption of Kilauea on the island of Hawaii. A shift in wind could fry the watching scientist—lava often reaches 2000° F. The park's volcanoes are the most accessible, best studied in the world.

Spellbound sightseers stare at the spectacular eruption of Kilauea Iki (Little Kilauea) in 1959. Its glow bathes motorcade headed for the "drive-in" crater.

A fiery juggernaut rolls down a green-banked roadway, turning it to black desolation

From a vent on Kilauea's lower slope, this remorseless tide of molten rock oozed through a forest in 1955, toppling 100-foot ohia trees like matchsticks. Here it moved slowly—but Hawaiian lava can flow a frightening 35 miles an hour. Its fluidity explains the comparatively gentle nature of the island's eruptions.

Traditionally, Hawaiians attribute their volcanoes to the erratic goddess Pele, depicted as either a ravishing beauty or an ugly hag.

When Kilauea's long inactivity slackened the tourist trade in 1934, the innkeeper of Volcano House on the crater rim implored Pele to manifest herself. He tossed a lei of ohelo berries into the lifeless fire pit, adding a bottle of gin since the goddess is said to hanker for strong drink. That did the trick. Smoke mushroomed, lava flooded the crater, and visitors filled the inn!

ROBERT B. GOODMAN, BLACK STAR. ABOVE: J. P. EATON, U. S. GEOLOGICAL SURVEY

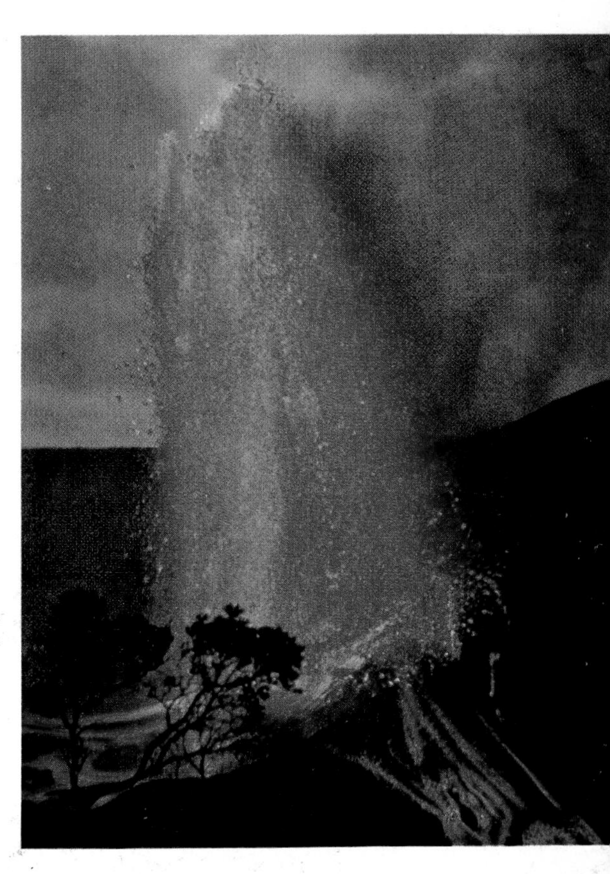

Kilauea Iki's fountain of flame spurts 700 feet (right); later the jet roared to a record 1,900 feet. The show went on for weeks. Veteran watchers called it "our volcano"; when the torch died down, one man wept.

Haleakala, one of earth's largest craters, could almost swallow Manhattan. Cinder cones pock the

Mauna Loa by a tract of park land. I looked down into its 2,600-acre caldera, wreathed in steam caused by water seeping onto hot rock hundreds of feet below the surface. Lava slopes changed from gray to blue to pink. Kilauea's awesome fire pit, Halemaumau, held a lake of cold stone. How different it must have looked on May 31, 1954, when a long fissure opened and lava spurted up more than 500 feet. But nearby Kilauea Iki outdid even this: in December, 1959, it shot a fountain of fiery rock to a record-breaking height of 1,900 feet!

I was spellbound by the fern forest on Kilauea's eastern slopes. Hawaiians say

PAUL A. ZAHL, NATIONAL GEOGRAPHIC STAFF

half-mile-deep bowl on the island of Maui. Mauna Kea (left) and Mauna Loa jut 80 miles away.

"little folk," menehunes, peek from behind each lacy frond. The flutters I saw came from birds, reminding me that Hawaii's official bird, the nene or Hawaiian goose, struggles to return from near extinction on these lava slopes.

Airhopping 30 miles of Pacific to Maui, where Haleakala National Park was established in 1961, my family and I plodded down Sliding Sands Trail on horseback into 19-square-mile Haleakala Crater. Here we discovered another rarity—glittering spheres of slim, curved leaves. These strange plants were silverswords, found nowhere on earth except here on Maui and on Hawaii.

Tropical incongruity: waving palms, creamy surf—and a black beach! Lava from Kilauea met cool seas at Kaimu on Hawaii and exploded into obsidian fragments. Waves smoothed them to sand. Tree ferns on Kilauea's windward slopes (opposite) are fed by up to 180 inches of rain a year; on leeward slope, in rain shadow, Kau Desert exposes naked lava. Snow at times whitens nearby Mauna Loa.

PAUL A. ZAHL, NATIONAL GEOGRAPHIC STAFF

ROBERT WENKAM. OPPOSITE AND BELOW: PAUL A. ZAHL, NATIONAL GEOGRAPHIC STAFF

Its fires banked, Haleakala slumbers under tropical snow

Flower-decked, ukulele-strumming snowman delights his creators on the lofty crater. Visitors approach the 10,023-foot summit on the highest paved road in the state. On a clear day, the spectacular vista includes the neighboring islands of Hawaii, Lanai, Molokai, and Oahu.

For a close look at the slumbering volcano, hikers and horse riders descend to the crater floor where cabins await. Write the superintendent for reservations. Once part of Hawaii National Park, Haleakala achieved separate status in 1961.

HAWAII VOLCANOES and HALEAKALA NATIONAL PARKS *Area 385 sq. mi.*

Features: Volcanic wonderlands on islands of Hawaii and Maui. Craters, lava tubes, colorful cinder cones, fern jungles, bird park, Kau Desert.
Activities: Visitor centers at Kilauea (Hawaii) and Haleakala Observatory (Maui). Scenic roads; rim, crater, and self-guiding nature trails; horses at Haleakala. Talks, exhibits.
Weather: Pleasant days, frequent showers, cool nights at lodges. Parks open all year.
What to bring: Thick-soled hiking boots, rough-it clothing; woolens for high-altitude camping. Rain gear, hat, canteen, camera.
How to get there: By air (several flights daily) or unscheduled ship from Honolulu. Taxis, tour cars to parks; car rentals at Hilo and Kailua-Kona (Hawaii), Kahului Airport (Maui). Write Hawaii Visitors Bureau at Honolulu, Hilo, Wailuku, or 3440 Wilshire Blvd., Los Angeles, Calif.
Accommodations: Volcano House, Kilauea (c/o park); for Haleakala, write visitors bureau. Hikers' cabins, campgrounds at both parks.

For information write superintendents, Hawaii Volcanoes National Park, Hawaii, and Haleakala National Park, Box 456, Kahului, Maui, Hawaii

Glittering silverswords enliven cinder slopes. The sphere of saberlike leaves raises a golden flowering stalk, then dies. Near extinction in the 1920's, the plant thrives today under Park Service protection.

Pasty red lava belched from Mauna Loa's cone in 1949; then pahoehoe swirled down like blackstrap molasses. Actually it's as brittle as thin glass.

VIRGIN ISLANDS NATIONAL PARK

PEARL-WHITE SANDS mark a jagged border round the island of St. John, one of the Johnnys-come-lately of U. S. national parks. In 1956, two-thirds of its 19 square miles was dedicated. In 1962, seven square miles of offshore lands around the island were added, preserving multicolored marine "gardens" of corals, sponges, sea fans, and fishes for exploration by snorkel-geared swimmers. This jewel of the Caribbean greeted its first tourist in

Trunk Bay, graced by one of the world's most beautiful beaches, invites the St. John visitor to a new experience—a swim along a submerged self-guiding nature trail (left). Small floats on the surface, in center below, mark the route. Underwater photography of the marine life is a fast-growing sport. Camping facilities are available at nearby Cinnamon Bay.

1493. Christopher Columbus, struck by the myriad islands of its setting, named the archipelago "Las Virgenes," honoring Cologne's martyred St. Ursula and the 11,000 virgins. Earlier, peaceful Arawak Indians inhabited St. John. Their stone picture writings, believed to mark a sacred shrine, can be seen today at Reef Bay.

Following Columbus came Dutch, English, Spanish, and French adventurers. Then in 1717 Danes moved in, bringing slaves to work the sugar plantations. When the slaves revolted in 1733, some of the planters took refuge at Peter Durlieu's estate, now Caneel Bay Plantation. In the mid-1800's, after slavery was abolished, planters abandoned their fields to the creeping forest. In 1917, Denmark sold the islands to the United States for $25,000,000.

Not influenced by Miami's glitter 1,000 miles away, and unlike domesticated neighbors St. Thomas and St. Croix, St. John retains its primitive charm. Philanthropist Laurance S. Rockefeller, a National Geographic Trustee, worked to keep it that way. On behalf of Jackson Hole Preserve, of which he is president, he donated 5,000 acres to the Federal Government, and the park was assured. Here

MELVILLE BELL GROSVENOR AND (OPPOSITE) WINFIELD PARKS, NATIONAL GEOGRAPHIC STAFF

Modern explorers delight in Virgin Islands' diversions

Vine-tangled ruins of a sugar mill at Caneel Bay (right) recall earlier days when sugar and cotton plantations covered St. John. Abolition of slavery in 1848 spelled the end of the estates. Caneel Bay now welcomes vacationists (opposite) who set sail to explore coves and the tiny cays offshore.

At Buck Island Reef National Monument (below), 35 miles from St. John, swimmers don masks and snorkels—best way to view the underwater trail's rainbow realm of grottoes, corals, gorgonians, and reef fishes. Pelicans and frigatebirds frequent the 850-acre site, and giant turtles lay eggs on the beach. Buck Island is reached by boat from nearby St. Croix.

FRITZ HENLE, PHOTO RESEARCHERS, AND (OPPOSITE) JIM HANSEN, JACKSON HOLE PRESERVE, INC.

coconut-laden palms, cinnamon, guava, and wild lime trees grow eagerly in a tropical climate that averages 79° and varies only a few degrees between summer and winter. Ferns, orchids, flamboyant trees, hibiscus shrubs, and cactus 20 feet tall flourish. Bird life abounds, and game fish thrive in the coastal waters. There are no poisonous snakes, few flies and mosquitoes.

U. S. and Canadian citizens need neither passport, visa, nor health certificate to visit the islands. For accommodations write Caneel Bay Plantation, Box 1091, St. Thomas; for information on housekeeping cottages write Cinnamon Bay Camp, St. John, or Superintendent, Virgin Islands National Park, Box 1707, Charlotte Amalie, St. Thomas, V.I. Awaiting you are crescent coves with gleaming beaches, forested ravines, and trails leading to bush-covered ruins. This is where civilization takes a year-round holiday. This is where the living is easy.

HOW TO MAKE THE MOST OF YOUR NATIONAL PARKS VACATION

PHILEAS FOGG, *the imperturbable hero of* Around the World in Eighty Days, *embarked on his journey with a valet and a valise full of money.*

The average vacationing American, however, is not so nobly equipped. In place of Passepartout he has a wife and headstrong children. Instead of a bag bulging with money, he has a budget stretched thin, and his holiday is all too short.

In his shoes? You'll find tips here to enhance your trip.

PLANNING IS VITAL

First, decide what you want to see. Geysers? Caverns? Cliff dwellings? Wildlife? This book will help you make up your mind. Do you want to boat, fish, climb, camp in the wilderness, or just absorb the view from your car? The choice is yours.

BUDGET YOUR TIME. How many days in the park, how many to and from? Use maps in this book to rough out your itinerary.

Pick a theme (Indian ruins) or concentrate on a region (the northern Rockies). Better still, plan an extended stay in one or two parks. You can spend all summer in Yosemite, Yellowstone, or Glacier and never run out of things to see and do. (Park Service has a pamphlet on each area; write Supt. of Documents, Wash., D. C. for Price List 35.)

BUDGET YOUR MONEY. How much for transportation, how much for lodging, food, tours, horses, incidentals? Will it be a luxury hotel or lodge, a modest cabin, a campground? (For listing, *Visitor Accommodations,* write National Park Service, Wash., D. C. For out-of-park spots, write chambers of commerce.) *Make reservations early to avoid disappointment.* Remember, more than 100,000,000 others are planning park vacations too!

HOW TO TRAVEL

Before loading the car, investigate other transportation. Fly-and-drive plans save travel time; trains, buses save driving; group tours (see travel agent) take planning details off your mind.

AUTO TOURING. Get road maps and travel data from your auto club or oil company (get request card at gas station).

Purchase of annual Recreation/Conservation Permit lets driver and passengers enter 2,000 Federal areas as often as they wish.

Have car checked thoroughly. Take jack, tool kit, flashlight, gasoline can, extra fan belt. Attach a bug screen to radiator grill.

Don't plan more than 400 miles a day on long trips (exhaustion invites accidents); snack rather than feast (big meals make drowsy drivers); don't dawdle along the way.

About wee travelers: For a long trip think twice about taking tiny tots (perhaps grandmother would be so kind . . . !) or pets (they grow restless in car and in parks must be kept on leash).

Coloring books, simple toys, car games (counting cows, identifying state auto tags), cookies hold children's interest, cut down rest stops and backseat brawls.

DID YOU REMEMBER TO . . .

- Buy traveler's checks (allow extra for emergencies)?
- Get oil-company credit cards (don't carry too much cash)?
- Make overnight reservations?
- Tell milkman, postman, paper boy, police (to spot prowlers)?
- Arrange to board pets?
- Leave extra key with neighbor?

WHAT TO TAKE

CLOTHING. Take comfortable, drip-dry apparel that looks neat without ironing. Don't overload. Include denims, khakis, if planning to rough it; long underwear to prevent chafing on horseback. Be sure to take sweater and warm jacket (park nights can be surprisingly cool), comfortable walking shoes, swim suit, raincoat. In most parks informal sportswear is all you'll need.

OTHER ITEMS. First-aid kit is a family must; include Red Cross text, motion-sickness pills, salt tablets, suntan lotion, insect repellent. Take laundry bag, litter bags, knife, bottle opener, stationery, tissues, extra flashlight batteries. Also thermos jug or water bag (porous, cools when hung on branch or outside car). For baby: a bottle warmer (plugs into dashboard lighter), disposable diapers.

Wear glasses? Play safe—take an extra pair, also prescription. And don't forget sunglasses, binoculars, camera, portable radio.

TIPS ON PACKING. Keep overnight essentials in separate, easy-to-reach bag (don't unpack car to find toothbrush!). Put wet washcloths, swim suits in plastic bags. Carry hangers, clothesline. *Pack light,* especially if going by plane, train, or bus. *Don't be a slave to your luggage.*

CANADA'S MAGNIFICENT NATIONAL PARKS DELIGHT U. S. VISITORS

For information on parks in this 29,000-square-mile system, write Canadian Government Travel Bureau, Ottawa. Here is a sampling:

ROCKY MOUNTAINS. *Mount Revelstoke,* B. C. Alpine plateau; skiing. *Glacier,* B. C. Climber's paradise. *Yoho,* B. C. Peaks, falls, lakes; climbing. *Kootenay,* B. C. Canyons, hot springs. *Jasper,* Alta. Ice fields; resort; climbing. *Banff,* Alta. Famed resorts Banff and Lake Louise. *Waterton Lakes,* Alta. (pages 130-36). Glacier-carved scenery.

PRAIRIES. *Elk Island,* Alta. Buffaloes. *Prince Albert,* Sask. Lakes. *Riding Mountain,* Man. Wildlife.

GREAT LAKES. *Point Pelee,* Ont. Lake Erie beaches, bird refuge. *St. Lawrence Islands,* Ont. Among the Thousand Islands.

ATLANTIC COAST. *Fundy,* N. B. Rugged bay shore. *Prince Edward Island.* Coastal strip, beaches on Gulf of St. Lawrence. *Cape Breton Highlands,* N. S. Mountains meet wild Atlantic coast; beaches, golf. *Terra Nova,* Newf. Scenic coast, forest, lakes.

AUTO CAMPING

Camping in the parks can be a rewarding, inexpensive family vacation. For success take proper equipment (but not too much), get to your campsite before 5 p.m. ("full up" signs greet late arrivals), assign specific tasks to each member of family. Many park campgrounds are free, or nominal in fee, and provide tables, benches, rest rooms, water. Some even have showers and electrical outlets. Most parks offer trailer sites (check access road conditions in back areas).

BASIC CAMP SUPPLIES. Tent, travel trailer, or camper; sleeping bags, air mattresses (don't overinflate), wool blankets. Veteran campers also suggest:

tarpaulin	folding table
flashlight	plastic plates, cups, utensils
lantern	can opener
folding shovel	spatula
hatchet or saw	pot holder
sheath knife	dishpan
water jug	soap
insect repellent	scouring pads
folding toilet	aluminum foil
camp stove	paper towels
aluminum nesting pots	toilet tissue
skillet	matches
coffee pot	whisk broom

Optional: ice chest. (Canned, packaged, instant foods allow variety, need no refrigeration. Fresh foods, anchored in plastic bags, can be cooled in brooks.) Forget about bulky cots (chill air freezes you from below) and gadgets (keep things simple).

Some auto campers tow a rental utility trailer; most find everything (including packsacks, canteens) fits into car and waterproof case on roof rack. Collapsible boat, life preservers ride on top. You can rent camp and sports gear in some parks.

Caution: Bears will rip open tent to get food. Keep it covered so odors won't attract them; hang it from a line high between trees or put in closed car. Burn or bury scraps. *Don't feed wild animals.* Drinking water impure? Boil it.

WHERE TO CAMP. Most parks in this book have campgrounds. En route you can camp in hundreds of state-park and national-forest campgrounds. For listings:

Camping, National Park Service, Wash., D. C.

National-Forest Vacations, U. S. Forest Service, Wash., D. C.

Campground Guide ($1), Campgrounds Unltd., Blue Rapids, Kans.

Handbook of Auto Camping ($4.95), Harper & Row, N.Y.C.

Campground Directory, American Automobile Assn. (members).

Director of State Parks at the various state capitals.

Nat'l Campers & Hikers Assn., 7172 Transit Rd., Buffalo, N.Y.

PHOTO TIPS

Park scenery begs to be photographed. Heed the plea and you can relive summer's pleasures on many a winter evening. Follow these hints for better pictures:

Include people in the scene; have the camera look beyond them and record what they see. A picture of a giant tree alone is static—a child at its base with a chipmunk gives scale and interest. Hikers heading toward a mountain focus attention on it.

Avoid self-conscious posing and staring at lens. Have subjects walk, talk, examine something, do as they would if no camera were near. Close-ups are more dramatic than full-figure shots.

Always frame your picture; don't just point and shoot. Take a broad general view, an "establishing shot," then move in on details. Don't overlook signs; they can take place of copious notes.

Use telephoto lens for distant peaks, birds, animals; portrait lens for flower close-ups. *Obey your light meter,* but make different exposures to be sure: mountain, desert, seashore light is deceptive.

FOR REFERENCE

The more than 870 issues of the *National Geographic Magazine* contain a wealth of information on American travel, exploration, geology, plants, animals, Indian life. Check the Index.

These stimulating National Geographic books will make your trip more meaningful:

America's Historylands
Indians of the Americas
Wild Animals of North America
Song and Garden Birds of North America
Water, Prey, and Game Birds of North America
Wondrous World of Fishes

Catalog on request from National Geographic Society, Wash., D. C.

INDEX TO PARK AREAS

Acadia 484
Arches 217
Assateague Island 476
Aztec Ruins 313
Badlands 156
Bandelier 314
Big Bend 261
Black Canyon of the Gunnison 230
Blue Ridge Parkway 462
Bryce Canyon 199
Buck Island Reef 548
Canyon de Chelly 320
Canyonlands 221
Cape Cod 479
Cape Hatteras 471
Capitol Reef 208
Capulin Mountain 285
Carlsbad Caverns 245
Casa Grande Ruins 334
Cedar Breaks 208
Chaco Canyon 288
Chiricahua 275
Colorado 230
Crater Lake 408
Craters of the Moon 241
Death Valley 370
Devils Postpile 356
Devils Tower 148
Dinosaur 233
Effigy Mounds 505
El Morro 282
Everglades 420
Fire Island 476
Gila Cliff Dwellings 335
Glacier 111
Glacier Bay 534
Grand Canyon 161
Grand Teton 93
Great Sand Dunes 284
Great Smoky Mountains 450
Haleakala 537
Hawaii Volcanoes 537
Hovenweep 312
Isle Royale 506
Jewel Cave 155
Joshua Tree 375
Katmai 524
Kings Canyon 359
Lake Mead 182
Lassen Volcanic 415
Lava Beds 414
Lehman Caves 241
Mammoth Cave 490
Mesa Verde 297
Montezuma Castle 333
Mound City Group 505
Mount McKinley 511
Mount Rainier 396
Mount Rushmore 151
Muir Woods 355
Natural Bridges 217
Navajo 316
Ocmulgee 505
Olympic 379
Oregon Caves 414
Organ Pipe Cactus 275
Padre Island 476
Petrified Forest 277
Pinnacles 356
Pipestone 504
Point Reyes 352
Pueblo Bonito 288
Rainbow Bridge 211
Rocky Mountain 139
Russell Cave 495
Saguaro 275
Sequoia 359
Shenandoah 466
Sunset Crater 327
Theodore Roosevelt 148
Timpanogos Cave 241
Tonto 335
Tuzigoot 333
Valley of 10,000 Smokes 524
Virgin Islands 546
Walnut Canyon 329
Waterton Lakes 130
Wetherill Mesa 307
White Sands 265
Wind Cave 154
Wupatki 330
Yellowstone 67
Yosemite 339
Zion 185